To
darling

THE CHEEKY GUIDE TO BRIGHTON

from

felicity

X X X X X
X X X
X

happy birthday
blondie !

WANT TO GET YOUR OWN BACK ON AN UNCARING WORLD THAT PUSHES YOU AROUND AND TRAMPLES ON YOUR NAUGHTY BITS?

THEN ENROL TODAY AS A...

BRIGHTON TRAFFIC WARDEN!

FEEL POWERFUL IN A UNIFORM!!

BRING MISERY TO THE LIVES OF OTHERS... EVERY DAY!!

VICTIMISE PILLARS OF THE LOCAL COMMUNITY AS YOU SLAP TICKETS WILLY-NILLY ON BUILDERS' VANS, HEARSES, AMBULANCES, FIRE-ENGINES, AND EVEN THE VEHICLES OF THE POOR FOOLS WHO PAY £1,000 A YEAR FOR A RESIDENT PARKING PERMIT BUT **STILL CAN'T FIND ANYWHERE TO PARK!!!!!!**

LAUGH MANIACALLY AT THE INJUSTICE OF IT ALL AS THE SCUMBAG COUNCILLORS WHO DREAMT UP THE SCHEME, DRIVE BACK TO THEIR £500,000 HOMES AND PRIVATE GARAGES!!!!

SCREAM DEMONICALLY AS YOU DRINK THE BLOOD OF A FRESHLY CULLED NAKED VIRGIN AND INVOKE BEELZEBUB TO TAKE YOUR SOUL AND TRANSFORM YOU INTO *A CREATURE OF THE NIGHT!*

APPLICANTS WITH A CONSCIENCE NEED NOT APPLY

THE CHEEKY GUIDE TO BRIGHTON

FOURTH EDITION

Written and researched by
David Bramwell
with Tim Bick

The Cheeky Guide to Brighton 4th edition

Created by David Bramwell and Tim Bick

Comments, suggestions or flirty emails: david@cheekyguides.com
Business enquiries/angry rants: tim@cheekyguides.com

ISBN 953611078
Published in 2006 by Cheekyguides Ltd
PO Box 243, Brighton BN1 3XT
www.cheekyguides.com

Thanks to the following contributors:

Fred Pipes for *Weird Cycle Lanes* (p21) and *Open Houses* (p49); **Sadie Mayne** for *The Year that Killed the Pier* (p53); **Dave Mounfield** for *Things To Do in Hove* (p68) and innumerable restaurant reviews including Brighton Pagoda, Sapporo and Sukhothai Palace; **Marcus O'Dair** for braving those cold Brighton waves which can tower over 100cm high in *Surfing in Brighton* (p76); **Andy Roseman** for the majority of the record shop reviews (pp79-81); **Brian Mitchell** for *Greasy Spoons* (p120); **Cath Quinn** for putting on 300lbs whilst reviewing Bona Foodie, the Real Eating Company, Taj Mahal and Yum Yums (pp122-124); **Joseph Nixon** for his expert advice and exemplary veggie lifestyle in *Vegetarian Brighton* (pp126-127); **Andrew Bird** for reviews of Gingerman and Moshi Moshi (p144) that I should have thanked him properly for aeons ago; **Dave Robinson** for Indian Summer (p145); **Dave Morrison** for casting a critical eye over the whole *Music* chapter and whipping it into shape with his encyclopaedic knowledge of all things sonically crafted; **Eric Paige** for pulling out all the stops and giving the *Gay Scene* a once-over (ahem!) in the name of research and literary finesse; **Letitcia** for her expert knowledge of all the carnal goings-on in this naughty town with her *Brighton Sex Tour;* **Pearl Bates** for her mini *Guide to Lewes* (p311) and some lovely dinner parties during the making of this book; everyone at **ABC Magazine** for helping with the *Kids' Brighton* chapter (your jelly is in the post); **Stella**, **Dave**, **Mait**, and **Carole** for *My Brighton*; and **Alistair Strachan** and **Carl Vincent** for you know what.

Special thanks to Jeremy for seven years' dedication to Cheeky – I know you've gone on to bigger and glitzier things but you won't be forgotten! Gratitude is also due to Andy Bass, the layout guru, for sage advice. And thanks to Kirsty and Amber for patience, support and the odd bit of grub.

Photo credits
Gordon Ayres: Stella and the gang pp189, 196, 255 ; **Alexis Maryon**: naked boys p27; **Barry McFarlane**: Volks Railway p50; **Brighton Swimming Club**: pp73 and 74; **Greg Neate**: the Pavilion p15, Wax Factor p82, Fishbowl p168, Jump the Gun p94, the Albert p205, Clearlake p287; **Eliza Skelton**: spoof Tesco ad p107; **Chris Teasdale**: sexbed centre and naughty sticks of rock pp113 and 266; **Cathy Teasdale** (vividphotography.co.uk): Spymonkey p198, disco kids p178, DJ man p186, angels p187, Letitcia p268; **Mark Bennett:** various Voodoo Vaudeville images p199; **Toby Amies** (tobyamies.com): Drako p223, Fairy p243; **Clive Andrews**: birdlady p225; **Eric Paige**: naughty gay men pp245, 249, 252, 254; **Pimple.tv**: p267; **Jo Lidbetter**: stone skimmers p287.

Illustrations
Huge thank yous as always to **Lisa Holdcroft** for the cover, maps, games and innumerable cartoons that appear in this book. She is Brighton's answer to Rolf Harris (but not quite as hairy) and should you wish to employ her talents or send her a saucy email she can be contacted at *lj.holdcroft@ntlworld.com/(01273) 705658…*

…and thanks also to the inimitable **Antony Hodgson** for the surreal *Sealife Centre* p71 and **Myfanwy Nixon** for the cuddly loveable traffic wardens on p22.

Editing
Thank you eagle-eyes **Eve Poland** for showing us the error of our ways with erroneous commas, apostrophes and occasionally whole paragraphs.

Cheeky Profile #1: MR TIM BICK

Since winnning a Zoe Ball lookalike contest at the Zap in 2002, Tim has commanded nothing but love and respect from this celebrity-obsessed town. And with the real Zoe still tied up in his loft, he continues to make a handsome living out of guest appearances at local clubs, though he nearly got rumbled at The Church recently when, as guest dancer with Brighton Can Can troupe *Les Ooh La Las*, he did a high leg kick and realised he'd forgotten to wear any undies. A typical Piscean, Tim collects tinned meat products and is excellent at identifying wild mushrooms.

Lives in: Brighton's fashionable 'Muesli Belt' better-known as Hanover

Best feature: inner ear

Favourite metal: tungsten

Cheeky fact: for this edition of the book, Tim single-handedly reviewed over thirty Brighton clubs in less than two weeks and has only recently started to 'come down'.

Not many people know that: Tim's tongue is *so* long, he could wear it as a large scarf in winter, though he chooses not to.

Most likely to say: 'I'm sorry, I'll clean it up.'

Cheeky Profile #2: DR DAVID BRAMWELL

A medical man and drunkard by profession, Dr Bramwell turned to guide book writing when – owing to his notoriously shaky hands – a routine operation left a patient with the design for a novelty tank-top sewn into his chest. Having lived in Brighton for over sixteen years now David still recalls those halcyon days when the beach was sandy, traffic wardens helped you double park and Chris Eubank hadn't been invented. A typical Aries he enjoys shouting, wrestling woodland creatures and going 'brrrr'.

Lives in: Brighton's unfashionable district of failed artists and disgruntled teachers; better-known as Hanover.

Best feature: coccyx

Favourite metal: zinc

Cheeky fact: David is so dedicated to the guide that he took part in a four-hour naked cycle ride this year just to get a good photo, and has only recently started to sit down again.

Not many people know that: David collects stuffed animals and has two bum holes.

Most likely to say: 'I do apologise, I had cabbage for lunch.'

The making of this book

Back in the good old days, Cheeky Guides were cobbled together in an afternoon using whatever resources were at hand, which was often little more than an old photocopier, a pencil, some flour, water and warm towels. Nowadays, creating a Cheeky Guide requires a crack team of experts labouring day and night to bring you the jocular reviews, aesthetically pleasing photographs, pithy captions and exotic spellings that our devoted fans have come to know and love.

We have of course toiled day and night to be accurate with prices, times of opening etc, but we're only human (except Tim, who's from Tunbridge Wells) and things change quickly in Brighton; a library today could be luxury flats tomorrow. If you spot any changes or mistakes, please do drop us a line. Gushing adoration in the form of gifts and money will also be warmly received. Alternatively, if you would like to contribute to a future edition, have an area of Brighton-related expertise that you think would benefit this book, or simply wish to hang out with stylish people who have made something of their lives, then do drop us a line.

How is it that Cheeky Guides attain such honesty in their reviews?

Well, I'm glad you asked. Rather than bully places into paying for a review (ie. advertorial), we at Cheeky hold lofty ideals about integrity and wish it to be known that *nobody* paid to be reviewed in this book. And, with the exception of a DVD, half a Guinness and the odd meal, we still haven't had any freebies. May I also add that we *never* discuss the fact that *all* the Cheeky team sacrifice their valuable free time helping out in a local orphanage.

David and Tim are currently available for village fetes, gala lunches and children's tea parties, though not to host them, just to join in.

CONTENTS

In the beginning there was only Herring...

1500s Brighton starts life as a prosperous fishing village, paying the government 400 herring a year in taxes.

1783 The town becomes a fashionable health resort when noted quack Doctor Russell declares that drinking the seawater will get rid of boils and put hair on your chest. This is not advisable today unless you want to get rid of your hair and have boils on your chest instead.

1790s Brighton's first massage parlour is opened by 'Brighton Shampooing Surgeon' Sake Deen Mohammed. It is in actual fact, a *genuine* massage parlour, unlike the ones advertised in the back of *The Argus*.

1823 The Prince Regent has the Royal Pavilion built as somewhere he can bring back a few mates after the pubs have closed.

1930s Torsos start turning up in boxes around the town, heralding the reign of the infamous trunk murderer. The king's elephant was suspected but nothing was ever proved.

1939 Movie star Johnny Weismuller opens the brand-new lido at Saltdean with the immortal line – *"Me Tarzan, you Saltdean Lido"*.

1940 The West Pier is chopped in half by the War Office to prevent (and I quote) *"a German invasion via the ice-cream kiosk"*.

1960s Brighton is host to the 1964 *It's a Knockout*, featuring Mods and Rockers battling it out on the seafront. The town remains a popular choice for deckchair rage for the next twenty years.

1972 Sir Laurence Olivier campaigns fiercely for kippers to be returned to the menu on the Brighton Belle railway line. He succeeds (for a while).

1973 Singer David Lee Roth relocates to Brighton after quitting his band The Red Ball Jets, and opens an unsuccessful sandwich shop called Roth and Rolls. A year later he returns to LA and forms the legendary Van Halen.

1974 The Eurovision Song Contest is held at the Dome Theatre. Swedish supergroup Abba scoop this prestigious award with *Waterloo*, while neighbouring Norway again score *"nul points"* with *Yes, We Have No Roll-Mop Herring*.

1979 Quadrophenia is released and Sting has his equity card revoked. Scuffles start up again on the beaches for a while as all the Mods completely miss the point of the movie.

1984 Lady Thatcher visits the bathroom and survives the IRA bombing of the Grand Hotel. Others are not so lucky.

1989 Hundreds of packets of cocaine are found washed up on the beach at Peacehaven. Police cordon off the area when Julie Burchill arrives for a closer look.

1992 Local cult The Temple of Psychic Youth join hands around the Pavilion and attempt to levitate it, but are stopped at the last minute by police. Apparently their founder, Genesis P.Orridge, had dropped 20p and just wanted to check that it hadn't rolled under there.

1995 The West Pier is declared an independent state by a bunch of squatters but after two weeks they run out of Rizlas and abandon their plans.

1998 A chip-pan fire causes the famous Albion Hotel on the seafront to burn down. *"Meester Fawlty, is fire! Is fire!"*

1999 The city's first independent guidebook, *The Cheeky Guide to Brighton* becomes the town's best-selling book, spawning a host of copycat rivals, including the *Saucy, Scratchy, Funky, Groovy, Kooky, Licky* and *Cheery* Guides to Brighton.

2001 Brighton achieves city status after 1,000 cyclists ride all the way to Downing Street to present Mr Blair with several compromising photographs taken during the Labour Conference here in 1992. The photos are said to feature the Prime Minister, a horse, an egg whisk and three blonde Swedish students at a well-known Waterloo Street bordello.

Revellers at the now legendary Fatboy Slim beach party

July '01 The citizens of Brighton awake one morning to discover an army of uniformed thugs patrolling the streets and victimising nurses, doctors, builders, OAPs, teachers and local residents alike. The council claim the group to be traffic wardens, put here to 'improve' parking conditions in the city, though many are unconvinced and there is much anger at the controversial decision to supply them with firearms.

July '02 A quarter of a million people turn up for a mass piss-up on the beach. The Fatboy Slim gig isn't bad either.

Dec '02 The West Pier continues to fall into the sea. Many blame it on storms, but the actual cause is discovered to have been the excess weight of over two tonnes of starling shit in the Concert Pavilion.

Jan '03 The Palace Pier catches fire. Nothing is damaged except the ghost train, which needed repairing anyway. Convenient that.

May '03 The West Pier burns down and, overnight, 20,000 starlings are made homeless.

Dec '05 Carbon monoxide emissions in Brighton go down a staggering 60% after Chris Eubank is declared bankrupt and forced to sell his monster truck.

Feb '06 Surprisingly, Brighton is judged to be Britain's healthiest city, with more fruit and veg sold here than anywhere else in England. Even more surprising, it all seems to be thanks to the record sales of cucumbers and courgettes at the little grocers next to the lube shop on St James Street.

June '09 Taking its inspiration from Dubai's Palm Island, a two-million-space park'n'ride is built offshore in the shape of a giant handlebar moustache. The lack of Wi-Fi facilities causes an outcry, as does the council's "*no rust, no refund*" policy.

Sept '10 Brighton's last remaining public buildings, The Pavilion, Sussex County Hospital, the newly built West Pier and the Library complex are finally converted into luxury flats.

BRIGHTON MYTHS

Hippy Stuff

New Age legend has it that a stone circle once stood in the Old Steine, but was smashed up by the Victorians and used to form the base of the big fountain there. This feature is actually claimed by some as being the source of all Brighton's energy and weirdness. It is interesting to note that Old Steine means 'old stone'. Give Julian Cope a ring: he'll put you straight.

Grave Tales

Brighton seems particularly rich in tales of underground tunnels and burial chambers. One story tells of a house in Orange Row which is said to be built over the original entrance to the old Brighton catacombs. Although blocked off with railway girders now, the room is rumoured to be littered with dead bodies from an ancient flu epidemic.

Also, keep your eyes peeled for the pyramid-shaped grave of a guy called Mad Jack, who insisted on being buried sat upright at an iron table, wearing top hat and tails, a bottle of claret at arm's length, with his dinner in front of him*.

And where else would the world's most infamous occultist, Aleister Crowley, be cremated, than our very own Woodvale Cemetery?

Phoebe Hessel

Phoebe Hessel, a local trader of fish, pincushions, gingerbread and apples, was a local celebrity in Brighton during the late eighteenth and early nineteenth century, and lived through six different monarchies to the glorious old age of 107. She was a celebrity, however, not for her longevity and comestibles but thanks to her heroism and love. The story goes that when her lover, Samuel Golding, prepared to leave Brighton and join the army, Phoebe was unwilling to desert his side and so accompanied him disguised as a man. The two continued to serve in the army for 17 years and even fought and were wounded at the Battle of Fontenoy!

OK, so the fact that Phoebe lived to a ripe old age certainly gave her plenty of time to embellish her tale, and I am inclined to wonder how she hid her boobs for all those years, but the story does have a happy ending, as the two did finally return and get married.

Her grave can still be found in the churchyard of St Nicholas halfway up Dyke Road, where it is surrounded by a small metal fence for keeping out dwarves.

*Last year I discovered this to be true. The pyramid is in Brightling (well, it's nearly Brighton) and his real name was John Fuller.

Murder Mystery

Take one of the tours during the festival and you will learn about some of the gruesome murders that happened in the 20s and 30s here. There are many accounts of body parts being left around town in trunks, and a bagged, severed head is said to have been left once in the Horse and Groom bar in Hanover (which, if you've visited the place, isn't all that surprising).

One year, Jason, a friend of mine, decided to do the murder tour, and left his house to walk down to Bartholomew Square where it was starting. The guide introduced the tour by saying:

"We'll commence by visiting the location of probably the most gruesome murder Brighton has ever known," and proceeded to walk the group back to Margaret Street, where Jason lived.

"Hey this is the street where I live!" he thought, with growing alarm.

"And it was in this house that the body was dismembered and stored in a cupboard for two weeks..." said the guide, pointing at Jason's bedroom window.

Jason now lives in America.

The Ubiquitous Eubank Tale

This short and simple tale comes in many forms but the basis of it is that Chris (*wherever* he is) is making a big public display of the fact that he's got a mobile telephone and is making a real show of taking important calls from important people, when, to his utter embarrassment, the phone starts ringing in his hand. Now several people I've met lay claim to this one and seem to get a bit annoyed when I suggest it's an urban myth, even though I've heard countless versions, ranging from Chris shopping in the Old Lanes and Chris jogging along the seafront, to Chris sitting in a bath of baked beans in the Condom Store. For visitors to Brighton, this story can be adapted and applied to any C-list celebrity from your hometown. Take it away, play with it, make it your own.

The Hand of Glory

A charm believed to cure lumps on the throat once carried the name of the Hand of Glory. This involved a number of gruesome things including the severed hand of a recently hung man, which was rubbed on the offending article or made into a candle (!). The last hanging to take place in Brighton was at the Steine in 1834, where a woman with a gammy neck is said to have run from the crowd, taken the dangling hand of the dead man and joyously rubbed it all over her affliction.

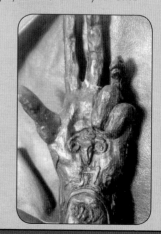

Subterranea

Perhaps it's down to childhoods filled with Blyton-esque stories of bookcases that swivel round when you pull on the curtain rope, to reveal secret staircases disappearing darkly down, but virtually every long-term Brighton resident has a tale of some underground tunnel or other. Some of the most popular concepts are those under Queens Road, whose purpose is lost to the mists, and a vast network of tunnels emanating from the Pavilion, used by Prinny for everything from visiting Mrs Fitzherbert's pad on the Old Steine, to puffing on a pipe in a Western Road opium den, to riding his horse back and forth from the stables across the road. There really is a tunnel across to the stables, built during the Prince's latter-day publicity-shy era (Regency paparazzi were of course notoriously slow off the mark with their easels, but very good at drawing from memory), although I'd recommend a Shetland pony as your mount if you don't want to bash your bonce on the doorframes.

Those Pebbles

Possibly one of the most curious (and certainly most persistent) Brighton myths centres around the origin of the pebbles on our beaches. Some of the most sensible Clark's-shoes-wearing-friends still swear blind that the stones were deposited here in the 20s to prevent beach erosion and that Brighton actually once had sandy beaches. Where this story originated from is a mystery but it does throw up a few interesting questions to the plethora of believers of this myth, such as: where are the photos and newspaper stories about such a mammoth undertaking? Where were the stones from? And don't the stones run for more than 100 miles of coast? What kind of loony would pebbledash 100 miles of glorious sandy beaches? And besides, what's a groyne for anyway? Saying all that, I have this horrible feeling some bugger is going to email me and prove me wrong…

How
To Get
Here

BY RAIL

National Rail Enquiries
08457 484950
www.thetrainline.com
www.ticketmaster.co.uk

Trains from London leave Victoria and Kings Cross Thameslink about twice an hour. The Victoria link is usually quicker – about 50 minutes for the fast train. Be careful when returning to London late at night however, the last train usually leaves before 12am, even at weekends. There are also direct train services along the coast if you are not coming via London. Rumours abound about a 30-minute service to London starting sometime in the very near future, but I'm beginning to believe this is an urban myth as it's been circulating for about ten years now.

At the Station
You'll find cash machines, a bureau de change, a hotel reservation kiosk and buses and taxis waiting outside. If all that seems too formal just head straight out, keep walking and you'll be at the beach in less than ten minutes.

SUNDAY TRAINS

Irritatingly, Railtrack (or whoever) have been 'repairing' the line between Brighton and London now for over 16 years. Why it is taking them so long to fix 40-odd miles of track is a mystery but it does mean that if you catch the London-to-Brighton train on a Sunday your journey could take several hours, as you find yourself rerouted via Littlehampton, Eastbourne and Barnsley, shoved onto a bus for half your journey and then fined £50 on arrival for your ticket being an awaydaysupersaver instead of a superdayawaysaver. I kid you not, I have spent some miserable Sunday evenings dreaming of being at home by the fire sipping fine wines, when instead I'm standing in the rain in the middle of sodding nowhere, waiting for some surly driver who turns up an hour late and doesn't seem to know where he's taking you. And to top it all, after five minutes the bloody bus breaks down. And you don't have a seat. And yes, this has happened more times than I care to mention. Now that's off my chest I feel much better. Ignore this at your peril.

BY PLANE

From Gatwick

A train will get you to Brighton in 20 minutes. If there are four of you a taxi will probably cost less because the trains are so damned expensive here. The cheapest option is to get a coach or walk.

From Heathrow

What a drag, you must really enjoy doing things the hard way. Get a tube to Victoria then a train from there. It'll take two hours at the most.

BY COACH

Mega Bus
0900 1600900
www.megabus.com

Why bother with National Express when you can take a ludicrously cheap double-decker sporting a bow tie from London to Brighton for a quid *and* get the chance to sit upstairs at the front and pretend to be the driver? Brmm brmm.

BY ROAD

Once you've packed your sandwiches, toothbrush, bucket and spade, make your way to the London orbital then take the M23/A23 all the way to Brighton. It shouldn't take more than 45 minutes once you've left the M25. It's as simple as that. To avoid the London rush hour it's best to stay away from the M25 between 4am and 11pm. If you're lucky enough not to be coming via London you'll probably be taking the coastal route along the A27.

BY SEA

Catch the two-hour hoverspeed from Dieppe to Newhaven and it's only a 25-minute drive from there.

BY HELICOPTER

You'll get as far as Shoreham airport and then it's a two-hour walk to Brighton along the seafront. What do you mean you haven't got a helicopter?

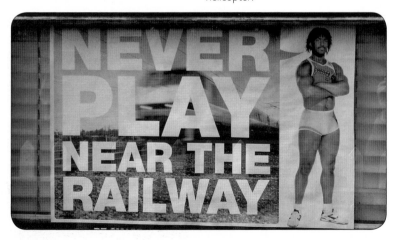

Getting Around

BUSES

Brighton & Hove Bus Company

(01273) 886200

Buses in Brighton are frequent and plentiful. So plentiful in fact that Western Road is chockablock with them, with the rather unfortunate result of making it almost as polluted as when cars were allowed here but with the added bonus of an endless barrage of buses blocking out sunlight and creating more noise.

For the six people who travel from Newhaven to Worthing every day, Brighton buses are great value for money; for the overwhelming majority who travel a few stops in the centre of town because they've got kids, heavy shopping etc, the flat-fare system is a rip-off and works out even more expensive than London buses. In some instances it's actually cheaper for four people to go home in a taxi than take a bus, which is ironic as the taxis here are also overpriced. Now, don't get me wrong, I think buses are great and the system here **is** really efficient, but if Brighton followed Amsterdam's example of electric trams and proper bike lanes we'd have a genuine reason to call ourselves a green city. Anyway, must dash, the four-wheel drive needs refuelling, I'm out of fags and those bears won't bait themselves, will they?

Open-topped Bus Tour

Runs April-November, tours daily
from 10am
www.city-sightseeing.com

Brighton for lazybones. Do the lot in one hour for £6.50. Meet opposite the Pool Valley coach station on Brighton seafront.

TAXIS

(01273) 202020 • 204060 •
747474 • 205205

There are plenty to choose from and all the services are pretty much the same. Only two types of Brighton taxi drivers seem to exist: the friendly cabby who chats amiably all the way to your destination and the silent, morose type whose only words are "*fucking idiot*", which he shouts at every other driver on the road. Typically, taxi fares in Brighton are among the highest in the country and more expensive per mile than flying Concorde (RIP). Taxi drivers in Brighton are required by law to carry inflatable life jackets under their seats so check when you get in. If there isn't one you should be able to blag a free ride.

BRIGHTON SUBWAY

Closed due to subsidence and water-logging, Brighton's once-famous Metro used to stretch as far as Eastbourne, Worthing and London. Nowadays it is home to Brighton's expanding subterranean community, several fight clubs and the Brunswick Yeti.

PARKING

Devilishly tricky **and** expensive. Parking meters have been phased in for most streets close to the city centre (and many that aren't). There are, however, several multi-storey carparks in the town, which are all signposted. One of the cheapest places to leave your car is the carpark near the bottom of Trafalgar Street, just down from Brighton Station. If you want my advice though, park out of town and walk/get a bus: it's never that far to anywhere in Brighton and should you park illegally and leave the car for more than ten minutes you **will** get a thirty quid fine. There are more traffic wardens in Brighton than zits on a coachload of teenagers.

WALKING

Visitors from LA might be interested to learn that this mode of transport is still immensely popular in Brighton.

BIKES

Along with *The Simpsons*, cheese on toast, socks with separate toes and subservientchicken.com, bikes are one of man's greatest achievements. Despite this (oh god, here he goes) cycling in Brighton can, at times, be more dangerous that sticking your arse in a hornets' nest and farting the national anthem. You'll be taking your life in your hands cycling along Western Road and North Street, where there aren't any cycle lanes and the constant cavalcade of buses squeezes you off the road onto the busy pavement. Elsewhere – such as parts of North Laine where cyclists can go the wrong way down one-way

streets – things are equally hazardous. While contraflows work in a cyclist's favour in theory, in practice drivers do not seem to respect or realise cyclists have the right of way here and will often just drive at you, forcing you off the road or worse. And don't get me started on the Seven Dials roundabout...

To end on a more positive note, I've been cycling round Brighton for fifteen years and lived to tell the tale, and the seafront really is great for bikes – it's long and flat and you can go all the way from Hove to the Marina and Rottingdean via the undercliff pass. In summer though, invest in a horn, as you'll be spending half your time dodging the dozy gits who walk in the seafront cycle lanes. Damn, and I promised I'd end on a positive note.

Suicycle!!

WEIRD CYCLE LANES

*by freewheelin' cyclin' spokes-man
Alan (Fred) Pipes*

Flabike-asting!!

Brighton & Hove, which in October 2005 received £3 million of government money as a Cycling Demonstration Town, has lots and lots of cycle lanes. However, they don't all join up. In fact, few do, and there are many strange short ones here and there to mystify urban cyclists, who are forever told to dismount, walk a couple of feet along wide pavements, and then remount.

These have been documented in www.weirdcyclelanes.co.uk, a website started in 2000 that grew out of an article in *The Guardian* claiming that some cycle lane up north was the shortest in Britain. The shortest in Brighton at the time was by the Gloucester nightclub and led into North Laine, but stopped after about a car's length. As time went by, even shorter and weirder ones began appearing!

This town (er, city) has a love/hate relationship with cyclists and the letters page of *The Argus* is filled with apoplectic correspondents from Hove banging on about demon cyclists jumping red lights, going down St James's Street the wrong way, cycling on pavements and not paying 'road tax'. Hove Esplanade, in particular, although about a mile wide, is festooned with No Cycling signs and guarded by impenetrable barriers each end.

The problem is that the land for cycle lanes is either stolen from the roads, thus annoying motorists who need to park on them, or from the pavements, thus incurring the wrath of pedestrians who like nothing better than to stroll nonchalantly along the seafront cycle lanes between the piers. Should you swerve to avoid them, you could be subject to an instant 30 quid fine for cycling on the pavement from one of our growing number of cycle bobbies!

A RANT ABOUT TRAFFIC WARDENS

The council's answer to the SS, Brighton traffic wardens – noted for their green Nazi-style uniforms, halitosis and lack of social skills – are the largest patrol working in the UK for a town this size, and a constant source of irritation to anyone who owns a vehicle. While understanding the need for traffic-calming schemes in Brighton, I know I'm not alone in finding that the system here not only dissuades visitors from parking willy-nilly all over the city centre (as it should), but also cynically victimises local residents whose only crime was to move to Brighton and buy a car.

A FEW HARD FACTS:

• Parking tickets are issued at a rate of one every two minutes in Brighton and generate more than £1 million profit for the council.

• The council has fitted solar-powered pay-and-display meters across most of the town. Stop anywhere for more than three seconds and you'll be expected to cough up. It is interesting to note, however, that if a black piece of card is placed over the solar panel on the top of the meter, the meter ceases to function after three days. Erm, allegedly.

• Brighton & Hove traffic wardens once issued a ticket to a hearse when the undertakers were moving the body.

• Brighton has no park and ride scheme.

• Drivers with severe medical conditions face a fine if they park illegally while making a dash for a public toilet.

• Traffic wardens should receive our pity and *not* our contempt, being, as they are, victims of a loveless childhood.

AREAS FOR DEBATE:

Can a driver be issued with a fine if double-parked?
Does a traffic warden need to be wearing a cap to issue a fine?
Is a driver exempt from a fine (for a couple of hours anyway) if they display a sign in the car saying *"Broken down, AA called"*?
Is it better to use a chisel or a sledgehammer when attacking a meter?

Here, There & Everywhere

NORTH LAINE

As Brighton's most bohemian quarter, North Laine has some of the best shops, pubs and cafés in town. Glamorous, young, posey, vibrant and pretentious it may be, but Cleethorpes High Street it is not: this colourful area does its best to be Haight Ashbury, Carnaby Street and Greenwich Village, all squeezed into just a handful of streets.

Many of the independent shops here are kitsch, retro or shamelessly glitzy. From Borderline and Cissy-Mo to Harlequin, Revamp and Blackout, if it's CDs by the Chocolate Watch Band, silver thigh-high platforms, a kimono or a Ganesh ashtray you're after, you'll be spoilt for choice. And while some of the shops' merchandise seems perfectly normal to long-term Brightonians it can appear a tad bizarre to new visitors – see Wildcat's urethral vibrators, Cyber Candy's scorpion lollies, Pussy's range of offensive greetings cards (including one with the caption "*Jesus loves everyone except for you, you cunt*") and pretty much anything in the Guarana Bar.

Unsurprisingly, North Laine is also a posers' paradise. From 60s kitsch to nu-goth, every fashion gets a look-in. Walk down Kensington Gardens in full KISS make-up with cream crackers stuck to you and few heads will turn.

The shops in North Laine are also a good starting point for checking out what's going on in the clubs and venues, as the streets visibly sag under the weight of posters and flyers in every window. In fact it can feel like you're in a ticker-tape parade as they are handed to you on street corners and thrown from the tops of buildings. Stand around in the same spot for too long in Kensington Gardens and someone will bill-poster you.

Priding itself on its café culture, North Laine really blossoms during the summer months when balconies heave with milkshakes and suntanned legs, and tables and chairs start to sprawl across the roads. It's a pleasure then just to hang out in some of the cafés here and watch the world and its dog go by. The Dorset, Kensington's and Pavilion Café are good haunts for this (though if pornographic displays of food are more your thing, Bill's is not to be missed).

Of course it would be churlish of me not to mention the gentrification that has been happening here in the past few years, resulting in more

---

THREE THINGS TO LOOK OUT FOR IN NORTH LAINE

1) Big Ian standing outside Immediate Clothing on Sydney Street having a fag.
2) The bloke with the big hair and outré military garb, who looks like he stepped out of *Yellow Submarine* (you'll know him when you see him, trust me).
3) Simeon the cat lolling around in Brighton Books on Kensington Gardens.

---

than 3,000 new juice bars. And while the recent arrival of Tesco Express, another bloody Starbucks and a posh bathroom shop don't bode well, at least we've finally got a library, Brighton's first in over 200 years.

Truth is, it'd take more than a few trendy restaurants and chains to spoil things. The old adage "*In North Laine anything goes*" is as pertinent as ever. Fashions and sub-cultures fight for space along these busy streets, so don't be surprised if after an afternoon's visit you end up going home with an exotic tattoo, a leopard-skin suit, a bag of herbal ketamine and pierced genitals.

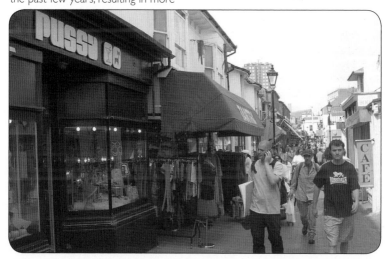

KEMP TOWN

Cross over the Old Steine from the bottom of North Street and you'll find yourself in Kemp Town, a haven of B&Bs, cafés, restaurants, some good shops and home to much of Brighton's flourishing gay and lesbian community, not to mention its eccentrics. Buy your strawberries next to a drag queen in Safeway, stumble across the guy who sports a sparkly top hat and decorates himself with posters of his guru, Maitreya, or witness (as I have) two guys rolling around on the street half-naked at three in the morning singing at the top of their voices, *"the hills are alive with the sound of music"*.

Kemp Town may not be a part of Brighton that has been dressed up for visitors, but it is the rough edges that actually provide much of the appeal. Perhaps in truth this is the part of Brighton that genuinely deserves the label 'bohemian'. I mean, where else in the United Kingdom would a local charity shop (the Sussex Beacon) have an annual sale of second-hand

rubberwear and bondage gear?

To explore Kemp Town simply take a walk up St James' Street and keep going: you'll discover restaurants, cafés, second-hand shops, health food stores, barbers, pubs, gay-lifestyle boutiques and innumerable bars. There's even Doggy Fashion, should you be caught short needing a T-shirt and bow-tie for your pooch. Venture down the side streets that run to the sea from St James' Street and you'll soon discover where the bulk of Brighton's B&Bs and hotels are to be found

Follow St James' Street far enough and it eventually becomes St George's Road. Here Kemp Town begins to feel more like a village (and *is* actually known as Kemp Town Village) and is really taking shape as a colourful new shopping area.

Continue further and, after a mini-pub crawl at such classic boozers as the Hand in Hand, Hanbury Ballroom, Barley Mow and the Rock, you'll reach Sussex Square and Lewes Crescent. These stunning white flats are occupied by some of Brighton's most affluent bohemians, and have had their fair share

A couple of happy poofs

A shopper peruses the available wares in Kemp Town's red light district

of celebrities – Lewis Carroll, Gaz Coombs, Kevin Rowland and Howard Marks, to name just a few. If you want to head back into Brighton you can simply turn on your heels and go back the way you came. Alternatively, you could take a stroll along the seafront, though (depending on your tastes) you may have to turn a blind eye to the crowds of men enjoying a bit of rough and tumble in the bushes at Duke's Mound.

KEMP TOWN VILLAGE

Nowhere in Brighton will you find a more pleasant, active and friendly community than the stretch of shops, pubs and food outlets on St George's Road in Kemp Town. Not only do these places have a convivial, supportive and easy-going spirit, but they even try and outdo each other every year with an over-the-top window-display competition. Even the local charity shops join in the fun. Marie Curie won one year with its Barbara Cartland theme, despite the kitchen utensil shop Egg and Spoon's enticing display of nearly-naked men in its window. In recent years the Kemp Town Village community has also organised an annual June carnival and winter festival when St George's Road gets pedestrianised for the day and the street is filled with stalls, food, live music and entertainment.

With such fabulous shops and pubs as Wallis MacFarlane, Kemp Town Books, Cupcake, Pardon my French, the Barley Mow and the Hanbury Ballroom, Kemp Town Village harks back to the good old days when pub landlords left a bowl of water by the door for your dog, shopkeepers were friendly and only sailors had tattoos.

Well worth the trek.

THE OLD LANES

A series of wonderfully confusing narrow passages and cobbled streets make up this antiquated corner of Brighton, steeped in history and stories of smugglers, ghosts and randy nuns.

The passages are known locally as twittens (an old smugglers' term for 'thin street with over-priced shops') and are enclosed by West Street, East Street and the seafront.

You should enjoy wandering around here and perusing the shops but don't worry if you get lost, even long-term residents like myself still do from time to time.

The Old Lanes is renowned for its abundance of jewellers, antiques shops, cafés, restaurants and expensive clothes boutiques and, though relatively conservative compared with the fashionable North Laine, at night the busy restaurants and pubs such as the Cricketers, the Hop Poles and the Victory give it a new lease of life.

At the centre of the maze lies the dolphin sculpture in the fountain at Brighton Square. It is an old Brighton custom to run around it twice, throw your trousers in and make a wish, though for the more prudish a coin will suffice. If you head past Rounder Records, have a look at their back

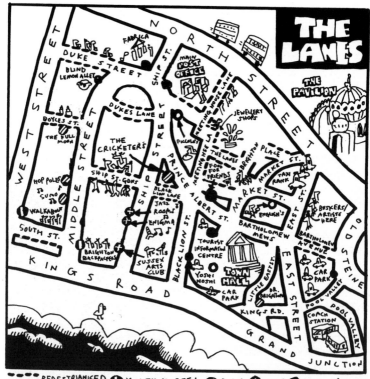

ᴵᴵᴵᴵ PEDESTRIANISED WALKWAY ❶ YOUTH HOSTEL ❷ BAR ✚ CLUB ⬤ RESTAURANT

wall to see which album they have spray-painted on it this month. As a reference point, you'll be on your way to East Street.

If you haven't got long in Brighton, you should definitely make a stroll round here a priority; choose from any number of enticing restaurants such as Food for Friends, Moshi Moshi, English's or the Mint Leaf and make sure you poke your head in at Fabrica Gallery (opposite the old post office market on Ship Street) to see what dazzling art installation they have in this beautiful building.

The best time to visit the Old Lanes is at dawn, when the noise of the seagulls and the light of early morning pierce the empty alleyways. At times like this, eerie folklore tales about ghosts and ghoulish fishermen no longer seem like a load of old cobblers.

In summer this is a popular area for street entertainment. On East Street you'll find jazz bands, performance artists and tarot readers. Once I even saw a girl busking with a rat here. She kept it on her shoulder whilst playing her guitar, and now and again she let it drink from her mouth. Eurrrgghh!

WEST STREET

With its amusement arcades, nightclubs for the under-twelves, theme pubs and burger bars this is Brighton's answer to Las Vegas. But without the glamour. And more violent. Hang around here of an evening and, chances are, you'll get into a fight with a seventeen year old. Stick around too long and her boyfriend will have a go as well. If you do venture into this wasteland of the human soul, look for the giant translucent cones in the middle of the road, originally intended as sealed performance spaces for mime artists.

THE SEAFRONT

"The beach washes away the ills of mankind." Dr Richard Russell

Stretching from the nudist beach by the Marina across to Hove and beyond, this is one of the key inspirations behind all that is Brighton. In summer the seafront is *always* swarming with life – you'll find families with kids, groups of foreign visitors, young couples indulging in a spot of heavy petting and the obligatory loony with a metal detector.

Hey, I found another ring-pull

When the sun is out you'll most likely want to join the crowds down here and brave the sea for a swim, hang around the cafés or indulge in a spot of sunbathing.

The most popular stretch lies between Brighton Pier and the remains of the West Pier. Here you'll find café-bars, clubs, amusement arcades, the Fishing Museum, Jack and Linda's (for a fine drop of fish soup), the Carousel, the Artists' Quarters, palmists and an assortment of outdoor entertainment during summer. If you want a good walk,

follow the seafront path all the way to the multi-coloured beach huts in Hove and stop for some grub at the Meeting Place Café on your way back. This is also a hotspot for many of Brighton's best-known clubs – the Zap, the Honeyclub, Funky Buddha Lounge and the Beach are all here – and on summer evenings you can expect the clubbing crowd to be out in force, particularly around the Fortune of War and other seafront bars.

East of Brighton Pier is a stretch of seafront known as Madeira Drive. While this whole area of the seafront is in need of rejuvenation it does come alive when there are car and motorbike rallies which, in summer, seems to be every other weekend. The loopiest of these is the coach rally, where identically dressed white-shirted drivers in black tie, replete with 'steering bellies', demonstrate their skills at parking and slaloming their lurching behemoths between sets of cones.

Apart from two crazy-golf courses and the Concorde 2, there isn't much in the way of entertainment here, though the very lack of development does mean that in summer the stretches of beach here are mercifully quieter than between the two piers. And for kids, of course, running along this stretch of the seafront all the way to the Marina is the miniature Volks Railway – a reminder of how much smaller people were in the old days.

The Nautical Gardens on Brighton seafront

If you do take a wander down here, look out for the strange old house set into the promenade just beyond the Concorde 2. The story goes that before the promenade was built, all the houses along the front were sold and demolished, apart from one belonging to some stubborn old guy who refused to sell. The council couldn't move him, so in desperation they built the promenade over his house and it's still there today.

Get orf my larnd!

Beyond this point is the once controversial Nudist Beach, now mainly populated by the gay community and a character known as Windmill Man. I'll leave you to figure out how he got his nickname.

Whichever part of the beach you prefer, sometimes, when it's a warm night and you're in the mood, it's good to bypass the busy bars and clubs. Just find a quiet spot, get some beers and food, and bring some friends to watch the sun going down.

If you're still around after all the clubs have cleared, the beach does *eventually* get pretty empty, although there's always the odd clubber who's crashed out after too many pills, and a guy still looking for his contact lens. In fact, even in the cruellest winters you will find little pockets of life here, like lone penguins on an iceberg.

And, finally, it's time to come clean. Yes it's true, I'm afraid, there is no sand, only pebbles. According to Dr Malcolm Cornwall at Brighton University, around 100 billion to be precise (he also reckons it'd take 2,500 years to count them all at the rate of one per second!) and not a decent one for skimming but, as a small compensation, when you take your picnic down the beach and the wind whips up, at least you won't be crunching your way through a tuna-and-sand ciabatta…

PARKS AND GARDENS

Let's face it, Brighton is not renowned for its greenery. Down on the seafront the council seems to have done everything in its power to remove all traces of the stuff, while the town centre boasts little more than a bit of grass and a few flowers outside the Pavilion. But all is not lost. Head inland and Brighton has a modest selection of parks and open spaces to keep even the most ardent picnickers, tree-huggers and Ultimate Frisbee teams happy.

The Level
By St Peter's Church

Come and walk the dog whilst watching teenage boys imperil their gonads doing BMX tricks in the skateboarding park. There's a nice bit by the paddling-pool area with its trellises, little kiosks and surreal bridges but don't get too excited, this open space between London Road and Hanover officially belongs to the skateboarders, frisbee-throwers, fire-jugglers, football teams and the London Road Drinkers Club

Famously tricky Tai Chi move "The Caesar Salad With Croutons"

(membership available on presentation of half-empty can of White Lightning). Don't miss the fair though; it comes here for two weeks at the end of April and August.

Dyke Road Cemetery
Dyke Road, opposite St Nicholas' Church,

From the Clock Tower go up Dyke Road and you'll find the cemetery on your left, just after the traffic lights. Part cemetery, part park and relatively unknown, this is a perfect spot to flop about, read a book, bring a picnic or do some meditation. I love it here. It's always quiet, though there's usually a lone soul doing tai chi or chi kung if you need some excitement. Keep your eyes peeled for Gandhi's grave.

The Pavilion Gardens and Café

After a morning's shopping in North Laine, these gardens behind the Pavilion make an ideal spot for a bit of lolling around in the sun. Sure, it gets busy here in summer, with groups of foreign students, picnickers, snogging couples, pigeons and that bloke who's always there playing the sax, but it's a pleasant alternative to the concreted seafront and the closest Brighton gets to the cosmopolitan atmosphere of a city centre square like those in Amsterdam or Rome. It's also one of the rare spots in Brighton with a bit of decent greenery and has a commanding view of the Pavilion to boot.

If you're in need of refreshments the café here offers drinks, hot snacks and those famous rock cakes. Look for the photos on the café history noticeboard on the side of the hut. They sure had big ears in those days.

Queen's Park
Between Kemp Town and Hanover

Queen's Park may be a bit of a hike if approached from the town centre or seafront, but you'll soon forget those aching corns and bunions once you arrive at this beautifully sculpted park with its sloping hills, large green areas, lake and tennis courts.

Approach from the sea up Rock Gardens and Egremont Place and you'll find it. If you've got kids, hunger pangs or a dicky belly you'll find an excellent kids' play area, café and

toilets on the western side of the park as you enter. If you've come to escape kids/crowds etc, head around the lake (formerly a rollerskating rink in the 60s) and up the hill to discover such curiosities as the tiny waterfall, the scented garden by the eastern entrance, and the 'Wildlife Area' full of butterflies, birds and wild fennel in the summer. Such features as this small overgrown wilderness demonstrate that Brighton council can be surprisingly inspired sometimes (though equally it could just be a ploy to save on pruning expenses). Other features to look out for in the park are its carved wooden benches and strange old monuments.

When you've had enough of the chaos and trendiness of the beach and city centre, it's good to know there's somewhere you can have a picnic, climb a tree, feed the ducks, play hide and seek in the bushes or simply curl up under an old oak for the afternoon with a good book and a treacle sandwich.

Preston Park
London Road

Brighton's largest park is located a little way down Preston Road about half an hour's walk from the seafront. It's a great spot for cycling – you can use the professional track at the top of the park and then race back down over the bumpy road or simply cycle around the park's perimeter. There's also a café in the middle and loads of space for big sports games.

Whilst it's a good place for a picnic, the ever-present noise of cars from the main road can sometimes spoil a tranquil afternoon here so it's best to plonk yourselves further up the hill if it's peace and quiet you're after. And if you do visit, look out for the Steve Ovett statue at the bottom of the park, facing the road. Remember the *Alan Partridge* sketch where he 'pops out' of his skimpy satin shorts? You're seconds away, Steve…

St Ann's Well Gardens
Somerhill Road, Hove

This small, pretty park in Hove has a scent garden, a newly refurbished family-friendly café, a few picnic areas and tennis courts. It's a popular spot for mums out with the young-uns and has a resident old lady called Madge, who'll engage you in conversations about boxing given half the chance. Tennis fans might like to know that if you want a free game, they don't charge here before 10am.

The park's most curious feature has to be the strange clock on a pole that overlooks the tennis courts and bowling green. It's straight out of the 60s cult TV show *The Prisoner* and, in keeping with the spirit of the programme, never, ever, ever tells the right time.

Woodvale Crematorium
Lewes Road/Bear Road

Hidden away down the Lewes Road, Woodvale Cemetery is one of Brighton's best-kept secrets. The largest expanse of greenery in the whole of the city centre, it is in turn mysterious, spooky and beautiful, particularly in spring when everything is in bloom.

Wander round its spacious and hilly terrain and you'll stumble across the columbarium, the memorial gardens, strange mausoleums (there's even one where you can peek through a crack in the door and see the dead bodies inside) and the little paths that disappear off into the undergrowth. If you want a quest you can look for the graves of Lance Schumacher (one of Custer's men) or the original Mr Hannington, though they might take a good couple of days to find.

Come on a cold overcast February and it can feel a little sinister, particularly with the hospital high up on Elm Grove towering over like some dark satanic mill. If *Buffy the Vampire Slayer* lived in Brighton, she'd doubtless spend most of her evenings here, as in the gloom it can't help but inspire thoughts of the supernatural. Not surprising then that it's also the favoured haunt of local shaven-headed eccentric Adrian Shepherd, who can occasionally be spotted wandering among the graves recording the disembodied voices of the dead.

When it's warm, however, the crematorium is the perfect place to clear the cobwebs, draw inspiration, picnic, meditate or simply enjoy a bit of nature and peace and quiet in a town that never stops.

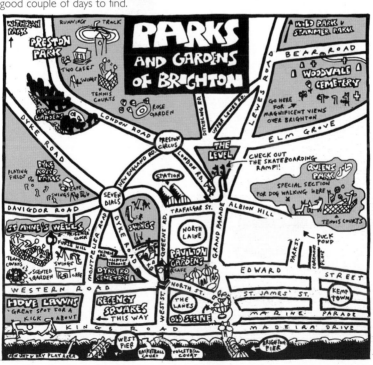

HOVE... AN APOLOGY?

Dear Readers,

Over the years I have continually offended tens of people
by not including Hove in the title of this book, as
officially Brighton & Hove come as a package these days. Of
course, unless you're a hardcore Hoveite, you're probably
wondering what all the fuss is about. I mean after all, you
say, isn't it just a poor man's Brighton offering sheltered
accommodation for right-wing old ladies (who spend their
time making jam and writing angry letters to The Argus)
and Nick Cave? In fact, you shout, rising to your feet in
indignation, come on, there're hardly any decent pubs and
the only sources of entertainment are the goth night at
Babylon Lounge, colonic chanting classes at Planet Janet
and a rather incongruous lapdancing club!
And while you'd be right in such matters, Hove **has** got a
few tricks up its sleeves, hence I'm devoting the rest of
this page to no fewer than ten amazing Hove facts!

Hove fact number one: Hove begins at Boundary Passage (the
longest alleyway in Brighton) and continues most of the way
to Dorset.
Hove fact number three: Hove is home to some of the city's
most dazzling architecture, including Brunswick Square,
Adelaide Crescent and Blatchington Road.
Hove fact number seven: Hove is the birthplace of cinema,
hip hop, croissants and Jackie Chan.
Hove fact number eight: Hove rhymes with cove.
Hove fact number ten: Hove is very close to the magnificent
city of Brighton.

Curiously, there is an age-old joke that Hove should be
renamed Hove Actually owing to the countless times its
residents, when asked if they live in Brighton, reply with
snooty indignation – "No, Hove actually". As a catchphrase
it has, however, become as naff and tiresome as "Ooh, I
could crush a grape", "Shut that door" and "Turned out nice
again". Oh god, now I'm really showing my age. Perhaps I
should move to Hove…

Your humble servant

Dr Bramwell
Brighton, obviously

BRIGHTON EMBARRASSMENT

THE MARINA

Mercifully hidden away in the outer reaches of Brighton seafront lies the Marina – a concrete jungle of factory shops, casinos, an Asda, a drive-through McDonalds, the world's largest multi-storey carpark and a really tacky Walk

of Fame for such Brighton celebrities as er… Leo Sayer and er…*The Argus*. The antithesis of Brighton's saucy, seedy, devil-may-care spirit, the Marina resembles some god-awful nautical theme park crossed with Moss Side. The best solution for this place would be for the council to throw its hands in the air, say *"Ooops"* and send in the bulldozers. But, like a sore tooth you can't resist poking, the buggers can't seem to leave the place alone. The latest £50 million investment to be thrown at it will fund the construction of two enormous Legoland tower blocks in day-glo colours, right in the centre. Just what the place needs -- more concrete.

THE LONDON ROAD

Dirty, smelly and unsightly, London Road is the home of the discount-meat store, boarded-up shops, Brighton's grimmest pubs and the occasional dead body. The visual equivalent of waking up after a heavy party to discover that someone's emptied an ashtray into your mouth.

THE AQUARIUM TERRACE

When the old Concorde and go-kart track opposite Brighton Pier were demolished a few years ago, did the council use the opportunity to add a bit of much-needed greenery to the seafront, or install something fun like an open-air pool? No, of course not! Instead it opted for the Aquarium Terrace – a monstrous, neon-lit white blob that has bizarrely remained empty for more than five years. Currently home to one café, a Burger King, an amusement arcade and 300 For Rent signs.

THE BANDSTAND

Naturally, since this rather beautiful iron sculpture is a council-owned listed building, it has been left to rot for the best part of 30 years, the top half serving as a depository for seagull guano and the bottom half for the human version. There used to be a small bridge connecting it to the promenade but this was pointlessly removed, leaving the bandstand stranded on the seafront like a beached Victorian wedding cake left out in the rain. Like the West Pier before it, its future is currently mired in Heritage Lottery grant applications, so it shouldn't be too long until it's ravaged by fire, carelessly-discarded gelignite and poorly-aimed intercontinental ballistic missiles, before a giant tidal wave carries the remains out to sea.

WESTERN ROAD AND THE CHURCHILL SQUARE SHOPPING CENTRE

Let's be honest, Western Road could be the high street for pretty much any grotty UK town from Reading, Scunthorpe and Wolverhampton to Doncaster. While no worse than any other city-centre high street for its bland selection of chain stores and coffee franchises, it is the *endless* stream of buses that make Western Road particularly unpleasant on the eye, ear and nose, not to mention the huge crowds at weekends that fill the narrow streets.

What is especially tragic about *Churchill Square* is that this area was once home to row upon row of beautiful flint fishermen's cottages and cobbled streets, until they were flattened to make way for a 70s shopping arcade. If Prince Charles had ever set eyes on the *original* Churchill Square Shopping Centre he'd have thrown himself off Beachy Head as the one we have today was rebuilt in the 90s and, though a remarkable improvement, that's still like saying drinking wee shandy is preferable to drinking it neat.

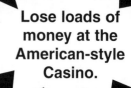

HARBOUR TOWN AT THE
MARINA
Brighton's architectural masterpiece
See all the latest American movies at our multiplex cinema. Over 300 screens and no subtitled foreign shit.
Enjoy our factory-outlet shops offering overpriced tat, Dynasty style blouses for the modern lady and knitwear for rugged men.
BRIGHTON MARINA
Concrete galore!!!
Coming soon! The Brighton Marina American Baseball Stadium!!!

Wonderful Things To Do

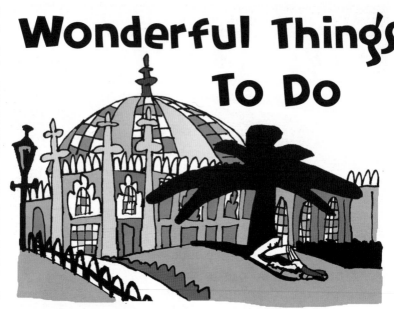

MUSEUMS

The Pavilion

Old Steine (01273) 290900
Open 10am-5.15pm Oct-March,
9.30am-5.45pm April-September
Adults £6.10, children £3.60

If you have a pathological hatred of dreary stately homes full of rooms that all look the same, with weird shiny-faced waxwork dummies like Des O'Connor in awkward poses and hordes of people gawping at a four-poster bed where King Steve IV died of consumption, then you are not alone, my friend.

Not only is the Pavilion the city's most famous landmark but the very emblem of the place. Could you really visit Paris and not go up the Eiffel Tower? Or come to Brighton and not visit the Marina? OK, bad example.

And while, yes, it's true that the Pavilion does have that crushingly familiar set-up with those awful little rope chains and hordes of American tourists giving "*oohs*" and "*aaahs*" in every room, you cannot escape the simple fact that the whole thing is utterly bonkers. An Indian palace in a small English seaside town with an interior modelled on a top-of-the-range oriental brothel, surely that's got to be worth a look? And it is.

Step inside and enter a labyrinth of bamboo, sculptures, fire-breathing dragons and the most outrageous chandelier in the universe. And where do I begin with the Music Room? There are some good tales about the building too. It is well documented that the Prince Regent was renowned for his love of women and food. He had two secret doors installed in the bedroom for his midnight rendezvous with Mrs Fitzherbert and the bloke selling seafood in a basket. The door for food is in one corner, the other right next to the bed. Legend has it that some nights Mrs F and the seafood guy would

accidentally enter through the wrong doors and if it was dark and the Prince was tipsy… well, you can guess the rest, but this is Brighton after all.

Dreamed up and partly designed by Prinnie in 1823 as a weekend retreat, this stately pleasure dome helped establish Brighton as a fashionable place to be seen. One hundred and eighty years later, the Prince's devotion to art, music, extravagance and philandering seems to have left an indelible impression on the town. Holiday cottages do not come more exotic than this.

Brighton Toy Museum
52/55 Trafalgar Street (01273) 749494
Open Tues-Fri 10am-5pm, Sat 11am-5pm
Adults £3.50, children/oldies £2.50

While not in the most glamorous of locations (housed under a damp railway bridge below Brighton Station), what this museum lacks in setting it makes up for with its pristine collection. There are over 25,000 exhibits, beautifully displayed and all clearly the pride and joy of founder Chris Littledale. Model railways make up the bulk of the collection and – unlike their full-scale counterparts upstairs – actually run. In fact, once a year in October they go mad and set off *everything* for the day – it's like a scene from *Toy Story 2*. Curios to look out for include the old Punch and Judy stand (with the baker hanging in the gallows), the pantomime horse underneath the model railway in the far right-hand corner, the Dribbler Train (also known as the Piddler), Edwina the wicked witch in the theatre and puppet section and – my favourite – the old Drunkards Dream machine (a drunk lies inebriated in a liquor basement, and if you stick in 10p you get to see his hallucinations, which range from scurrying rats to the devil, who pops out of a beer barrel!).

Children, trainspotter types and anyone with an interest in old toys and models will love this place. Weekend revellers will not. Watch out during schooldays, though: like the Booth Museum you may be surrounded by gangs of schoolkids trying their best to knock over all the little figurines in the cabinets.

Brighton Museum and Art Gallery

Church Street/Royal Pavilion Gardens
(01273) 290900
Open Tues 10am-5pm, Wed-Sat 10am-5pm
Admission free
www.virtualmuseum.info

Re-opened in 2002 after a much-publicised refurbishment, Brighton Museum is now modernised, spacious, and packed with imaginative displays. And after a local campaign, beloved Gallet cat Brunel (a giant model of one of the ornamental pair in the cabinet by Art and Design) is back by the entrance, awaiting a good stroke and your donations.

Much of the ground floor of the museum is now given over to the town itself, covering its social history from sport, work and religion to pub and club culture. Whoever designed this section went overboard with inventive layout and interactive facilities and in places it's a little confusing, with **way too much** emphasis on contemporary Brighton culture. Do

you really need to go to a museum to see club flyers, posters, BMX bikes and prostitute cards when you can walk down Sydney Street, where this culture lives and breathes? But we'll say no more on the matter. Wander round and you can watch old videos of Brighton, listen to recorded voices, feel the mystery objects (a dead seagull and a 'Prince Albert'), peruse the paintings of Sake Deen Mohammed and Dr Russell, play on the old What the Butler Saw seaside machines (if it weren't for the fact that they've been permanently out of order since re-opening), and learn all about the Mods and Rockers. You're not meant to sit on the scooter in the far-left corner, but it makes for a terrific photo so, go on, be a devil.

Elsewhere on the ground floor there's a Discovery Room for kids, which is an Alice in Wonderland style activity area with enormous wax crayons (sporting wigs!), House of Fun mirrors and a giant Daliesque shirt. The World Art Gallery is also on this floor and has a curious selection of costumes, carvings of old favourites such as Ganesh and two very phallic totems over the doorway. Nearby there's a room full of pottery and stuff for people who – unlike myself – get a kick out of perusing old plates in glass cabinets.

Upstairs are the gallery, café (unchanged since 1856), exhibition space, Human Body section (look for presidential candidate Barbie) and the History of Fashion, which isn't a patch on what it used to be but does at least still contain the Prince Regent's enormous breeches, handmade by High and Mighty.

Consistently excellent, however, is the museum's exhibition space.

taxidermy for the public. Should you stumble across any fresh road kill, just *"scoop it up and bring it in"*.

On entering the museum the first thing you'll notice is the smell of mothballs and the wonderfully gloomy atmosphere. Towers of stuffed birds line the walls, while in the centre lie two incongruous but beautiful stained-glass windows.

At this point, if you're in a group, I recommend splitting up and going it alone for maximum effect. Walk down the aisles at the side and enter Hitchcock's terrifying world of *The Birds*. Down the centre you'll find the discovery lab – a hands-on science area for kids – and, at the back, an impressive array of skeletons.

Look out for: the sheep that looks like Daisy in the Woody Allen movie, the charred remnants of a (half-eaten) dodo, the remains of a dog from Stanmer Park, the *Harry Potter* owls and the famous 'toad in the hole'. I bet you won't find the warthog's head though.

Previous highlights have included Fetishism, paintings by Captain Beefheart, some wonderfully bawdy images, stories and costumes on the Carnivalesque theme, and the History of Cinema in Brighton and Hove.

Come, enjoy a cake or two, see the latest exhibition and marvel at the finest contemporary display of contemporary display cabinets in Europe.

The Booth Museum of Natural History

194 Dyke Road (01273) 292777
Open Mon-Sat 10am-5pm, Sun 2pm-5pm, closed Thurs
Admission free

Originally opened as a private museum in 1874 by bird-stuffing enthusiast Mr Booth, this building has blossomed into one of the focal points and main archives of natural history for the Brighton area. As well as providing a home to thousands of creatures, skeletons and strange things in specimen jars, it is a resource centre for local schools, while on special days they even do live

What you see in the museum is, however, only a small percentage of what's been collected over the years as, owing to lack of space, they're unable to display everything. With special permission though, you can get a behind-the-scenes tour. I have been lucky enough to experience this and thoroughly enjoyed wandering through dusty old badger-lined corridors where they've got everything from the reindeer that defunct department store Hanningtons used to borrow every Christmas, to a scorpion found by a guest in the Grand Hotel. *"If you find odd things in your sandwiches they'll end up here,"* declared Keeper of Biology Gerald Legg. Later he took me into a room with a large metal worktop and muttered: *"I've had a tiger on that table".*

To find the museum, follow Dyke Road from the Clock Tower and you'll find it opposite the tennis courts after about a fifteen-minute walk.

Warning – check first for kids' visits, if you're childphobic they could spoil your experience. Could you spend the night here on your own, though? I swear they all come to life then.

Hove Museum

19 New Church Road, Hove (01273) 290200
Open Tues-Sat 10am-5pm, Sun 2pm-5pm
Admission free www.virtualmuseum.info

This beautiful old museum, situated way down Church Road in deepest darkest Hove, has had a makeover in recent years. Gone are the psychedelic carpets and cardboard cutout of Ringo Starr, but the 1970s teashop, thankfully, still remains. They've done a great job with the refurbishment here though: the rooms are brighter and the displays more interactive and imaginatively presented. And while the History of Hove section still does nothing to dissuade one from the opinion that Hove is quite dull, the Wizard's Attic and History of Cinema make the trek here very worthwhile.

The Wizard's Attic is a room that children (and adults) will thoroughly enjoy. The low-level lighting creates a wonderfully spooky atmosphere (to go with the attic theme); there are toys hanging from the ceiling, little cubbyholes with fairground mirrors, a tin bath full of soldiers, and even a painting where the eyes follow you around the room. And dare you put your hand in the hole below the box full of creepy-crawlies?

Elsewhere on the first floor, the History of Cinema section tells the fascinating history of Hove's role as the birthplace of the British film industry. The exhibits in this section range from old zoetropes and magic lanterns to a six-seater cinema, which shows three short films every half-hour. I can thoroughly recommend waiting around to see *Professor Heard's Magic Lantern Show*, where a talking skull guides you through a magical journey in which ghosts and goblins rise from a witch's cauldron and the cautionary tale of the Miller and Sweep is explained. Look out also for the seven or eight old films that are constantly running in the room next door – the footage of people cycling off the pier into the sea is wonderfully silly. And when you're through with horsing around in the Attic, watching films, perusing the latest exhibition downstairs and spending your pennies in the gift shop, make sure to pay your respects to Hove's loveable grannies and Mrs Doyle types by popping into the tea rooms for a big wedge of cake and a nice, hot cuppa.

The Artists' Quarter
King's Road Arches

Hidden away down on the seafront between the two piers and below the kissing statue, this small stretch of the beach has been home for nearly fifteen years now to a collection of local artists whose colourful workshops and galleries are permanently on display to the public.

Originally owned by fishermen, these little rooms would once have been used for descaling fish (to be sold where the carousel now stands), which still accounts for the occasional odd whiff. Far more in keeping with Brighton's bohemian nature than the plethora of café-bars found down here, the Artists' Quarter capture the creative and communal spirit of the town.

Open all year round, even in the most improbable gales, this is London gallery art at half the price, with work ranging from cards and paintings

The latest defacing by art terrorists of "that 'orrible green thing on the seafront" suggesting that the sculpture, in effect, be banned

to exotic furniture and puppets. Recommended.

The Big Green Bagel
Brighton seafront

This sculpture arrived about fifteen years ago and was a gift from the Mayor of Naples (we gave his city a large bronze herring). Officially entitled Il Grande Bagel Verde, but known locally as the Seasick Doughnut, it has survived five storms and several demolition attempts by local art puritans.

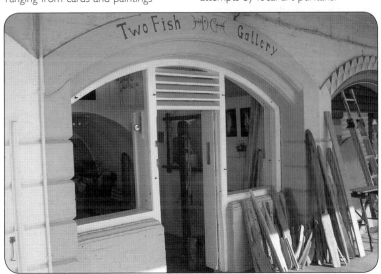

Who will buy my luvverly drift wood?

Fabrica

40 Duke Street (01273) 778646
Open Wed-Sat 11.30am-5pm, Sun 2-5pm,
closed Dec-April due to lack of heating
Admission free

Opposite the old post office on Ship Street (now a market), this converted church is a gallery space for installations and contemporary art, and is an essential drop-in spot when visiting the Old Lanes in summer; often the exhibitions are stunning for their size alone.

Groundbreaking wicker wig-wam thing at Fabrica

Permanent Gallery

20 Bedford Place (01273) 710771
Open Wed-Fri,Sun 1-6pm, Sat 11am-6pm
www.permanentgallery.com

If it hadn't been for regular weekly trips to the old Taj Mahal on Bedford Place for coriander and ghee (my favourite sandwich fillings) I'd never have known about this place and hope its obscurity won't result in a swift demise as it really is a genuine one-of-a-kind. This is first and foremost

an exhibition space for original and challenging artists and art – it's always worth the trip here just to see what the latest exhibition is. One year the guys at the gallery created a huge Brighton Memory Map, removed all the place and street names and encouraged people to write their experiences onto it instead. It was hugely popular and by the end had lines like: *"where mother's ashes were scattered"*, *"lost my virginity"*, and, *"I went for a job as a receptionist in a brothel here. What was I thinking?"* Get on their mailing list and you'll also find out about live drawing opportunities in the gallery, discussion forums and regular talks from artists.

The unsung hero of the gallery though is the bookshop, run by a Mafia-attired collective known as Borbonesa. It's an outlet for people making exceptional publications and sells hundreds of unique zines, illustrated books and CDs. It's mainly local work on sale but there is some stuff from farther climes. The zines from American artist Sophie Mol are particular favourites, as are the beautifully packaged CDs from local bands like Hamilton Yarns. Recommended.

The Phoenix Gallery

10-14 Waterloo Place (01273) 603700
Open Mon-Sat 11am-6pm, Sun 12noon-4pm
Admission free
www.phoenixarts.org

Over the past twenty years the Phoenix Gallery place has transformed from a grotty squat to a thriving art gallery with exhibitions changing on a monthly basis. Look out for more unusual events taking place here from time to time (maverick songwriter Daniel Johnson played here many years ago). They also organise a wide range of workshops, ranging from tapestry and ceramics to Super-8 moviemaking.

B righton (and Hove) has probably more artists per square metre than anywhere else in the known universe. Every May and December you can go and nose around their houses and gardens when they hold free weekend

www.openhouseonline.co.uk

mini-exhibitions, known collectively as the Artists' Open Houses. In 2005, there were more than 170 houses and studios, containing the work of over 750 artists and craftspeople. Most houses are grouped geographically into Trails, which originally had their own brochures. They are now all gathered together into one handy brochure, with maps. As well as the visual arts (paintings, drawings, prints and sculpture) you'll also find ceramics, furniture, jewellery, stained glass, clothing, cards and more on sale direct from the artist or designer at cheaper-than-gallery prices.

The oldest Trail is Fiveways, named after the road junction, which started in 1982 when Ned Hoskins (109 Stanford Avenue) opened his house to the public during the Brighton Festival. This Trail also has the distinction of its own pub, the Open House, on Springfield Road. Over the railway tracks, south of London Road station, is Beyond the Level, founded in 1996. Trails further afield include Rottingdean, Prestonville, Hove, Portslade and Shoreham, while in the middle of the city are Central Brighton Artists, The Hartington Trail, Hanover Art Trail, and Seven Dials Artists.

One outstanding feature of the Open Houses is the cake. Many houses offer home-made refreshments of a high standard, often in their gardens. Best house for cake is Kate Osborne's house at 32 Stanford Avenue, part of Fiveways, and the best place for Open House virgins (but no cake) is The Dragonfly House, 48 Ditchling Rise (Beyond the Level). The houses

do change from year to year, so check the brochure or www.openhouseonline.co.uk before setting out.

Make sure you add your address to their guest books when you visit: that way you'll be invited to next year's private view and be given lots of wine. Or try your chances on the Friday night before the first weekend on May.

Alan (Fred) Pipes

SEAFRONT ATTRACTIONS

The Sealife Centre

Marine Parade, opposite Brighton Pier
(01273) 604234
Open Mon-Sun 10am-6pm
Adults £9.95, children £7.50
www.sealifeeurope.com

This place has improved dramatically since I first reviewed it over eight years ago. Housed inside a beautiful Victorian building, it really is a fun place to take children now, as I discovered after coming here with my nephew Alex. Highlights for kids include the *Captain Pugwash* trail, a chance to see the fish being fed, a Jules Verne Nautilus room (which is impressive, if a little pointless) and, of course, the underwater tunnels where you get to see the sharks and other creatures swimming overhead. *"Look it's waving,"* said Alex, as a stingray flapped by.

Keep a sharp lookout for the seahorse tank, which is also home

COD. PLAICE. HUSS. ROCK

You've seen the show, now eat the stars

to an utterly ridiculous creature with a long snout; the horse-shoe crab (resembling a genuinely scary *Doctor Who* monster); the plastic shark; and the camera right at the end of the tunnel, which you can control and have fun with if one of you goes back into the tunnel and stands around pulling faces.

They've even done a good job with the décor here (it's all shadowy corners and endless loops of the *X-Files* music). Don't you love a happy ending?

THE VOLKS RAILWAY

The Volks opened on August 4th 1883, making it the oldest electric railway in the world (you'll find it in the *Guinness Book of Records*, sandwiched between the world's biggest pair of shoes and a photo of a man with four-metre long fingernails).

On its official opening day the railway's creator, Magnus Volks, invited a number of civic dignitaries for the first ride but, owing to their combined weight (civic dignitaries were notoriously portly in those days), they managed to break one of the planked pedestrian crossings that ran across the track. The train's first ever journey came to an undignified halt and the dignitaries were unloaded, to the jeers of a group of hostile cabbies, who believed it would take away their custom. They really needn't have worried.

Brighton Pier

The epitome of cheesy seaside fun. Not only Brighton's most popular attraction but the UK's top tourist spot to boot. Experience life on the ocean waves with the famous Dolphin Derby, see the Isle of Wight from the top of the Helter Skelter (on a clear day), sing Elvis at Horatio's Karaoke Bar, wolf down some fish and chips, scream your head off on the big dipper, have your palm read by an Australian backpacker called Gypsy Kevin, get absolutely soaking wet on the log flume, lose your car keys down the gaps in the floorboards, ride the world's crappiest ghost train, and be driven half crazy by the all-pervasive and relentless bloody noise.

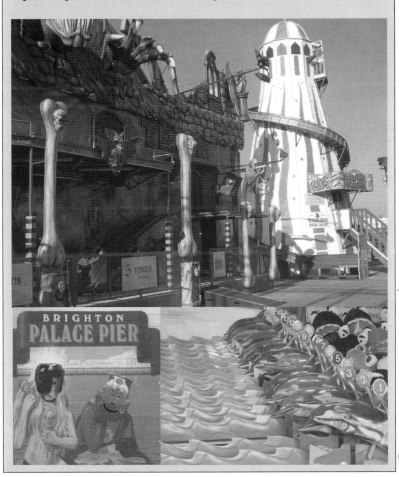

THE WEST PIER

A tragedy of epic proportions, the West Pier was cock of the town until it was marooned by a storm in the 70s and left to rot like Miss Haversham's wedding cake. Then in late 2002, over the space of a few months it endured a further storm and two suspected arson attacks which pretty much destroyed everything. And yet, there, like a small beacon of hope, much to everyone's surprise and delight, the little fortune-telling kiosk bravely hung on. Against all odds it had survived. Oh how it cheered our hearts with its courage and stoicism when all around was desolation and despair.

Then, at the end of 2005, it fell off too.

2003: THE YEAR THAT KILLED THE WEST PIER

By pierless scribe
Sadie Mayne

By the turn of the 20th century there were almost 100 piers in Britain, offering the first truly mass-market entertainment since the industrial revolution. It's easy to forget that before the invention of the family motor and bargain-basement airlines everyone holidayed at the British seaside. Wealthy holidaymakers would dip a toe in the water after changing into voluminous swimming costumes in wooden bathing machines, but most Victorians couldn't swim. Instead, they flocked to the coast to promenade along Britain's piers in their Sunday best. Now only 55 remain (piers, not Victorians), and some of those are sinking.

Brighton's original Chain Pier offered exotic attractions like a bazaar and a camera obscura. Destroyed in a storm in 1896, there's nothing left of it except a plaque in the sea-wall, but its kiosks were saved and added to the Palace Pier in 1901, where they flanked the amusement arcade.

While the Noble Organisation claims to attract more than 3,500,000 tourists a year to Brighton Pier, the fortunes of the West Pier have been in steady decline. One of only two British piers ever to be granted Grade 1 status, the pier was completed in 1916 and included a bandstand, weather screens, a concert hall and gas-lamp columns decorated with entwined serpents. Its attractions ranged from female high-diving acts to recitals by the resident orchestra, but after years of neglect the pier was shut in 1975. There followed a long period of public-funding applications while it struggled against the elements and opposition from the owners of the rival Brighton(neé Palace) Pier. Then it was nuked in a mysterious arson attack and in May 2003 the concert hall went up in flames. *"We finally had everything going our way,"* says Rachel Clark, general manager of the West Pier Trust. *"The attacks completely destroyed the pier."* Later disconnected from the shore by a freak summer storm which took the hall out to sea, the pier was abandoned by the Heritage Lottery Fund in 2004.

Brightonians are used to its twisted, burnt-out hull, once home to thousands of starlings, and some feel it is best left as a sea sculpture. After the remaining kiosk was swept away by a freak wave in December 2005, the National Pier Society's Chair commented, *"I may not be popular for saying this, but surely the time has now come to close the door on the whole sad saga, put up the money for demolition and move on".*

WHERE TO TAKE A GOOD STROLL

The Marina Breakwater

Down near the Marina is a breakwater that extends for about a quarter of a mile out to sea. Go when the sea's a bit rough and it can be a delightfully hairy experience. It'll take you about twenty minutes to walk there from Brighton Pier and, ideally, you should try and time it for sunset. Then you could stick around in the Marina for a drink (bad idea) or walk back into town and flop around at the Basketmakers (good idea).

The Undercliff Walk to Rottingdean

From Brighton Pier head to the Marina, find the undercliff path behind Asda, keep going and you'll reach Rottingdean in about an hour. Most of the path from the Marina onwards has been carved out of the imposing chalky cliffs which, together with the magnificent views of the sea, make this walk fairly spectacular. And it's good by bike too as it's completely flat. As you approach Rottingdean you'll start to chance upon rockpools and little coves where people go winkle picking and crab fishing.

Rottingdean is, in contrast to Brighton, one of those classic seaside villages with old-fashioned shops and boutiques. One particular shop, The Cabin (sadly long-gone), is even said to have been the inspiration behind the Local Shop in the *League of Gentlemen*. In fact years ago one person emailed to tell me, *"I went in to buy a copy of* The Guardian *and the woman said defensively,* 'Oh no. We only stock local papers in here…'"

Watch our for cracks in the Undercliff Walk

Once you've had a good nose around the village you'll need to head back to Brighton, though if you can't face doing the walk again buses do run regularly back to town from here.

This really is one of the best and most accessible local walks, whatever the season. In summer there's a café halfway (usually serving Coke and a piece of shortbread wrapped in clingfilm), while in winter you may have your head blown off but if you wrap up warm you can finish it all off with mulled wine and a cigar in the White Horse.

Glynde to Lewes

Although I've never done this walk, several friends have recommended it and one year I even got a nice email from a bloke called Adam urging me to include it. Directions are simple: take the train to Glynde and follow the "*stunning but straightforward walk back over Mount Caborn to Lewes*". You won't see a soul, the scenery is said to be spectacular and when you drop down the hill into Lewes, you are only a short walk from the Lewes Arms.

The Chattri - quite nice

The Indian Chattri on the Downs

High up on a hill overlooking Brighton is one the town's most curious but least-known memorials, built to commemorate the thousands of Indians who died in Brighton during the First World War. They were brought here because the Royal Pavilion was at that time used as a hospital for the wounded – on the grounds that the soldiers would feel more at home there. Despite these rather misplaced good intentions, the wounded were more than a little bemused at having been stationed in what looked like an oriental brothel and, of course, bringing Sikhs and Hindus from every cast together under one roof meant the atmosphere was not exactly convivial.

The 4,000 who died here had their ashes scattered into the sea; the Chattri was built as a memorial to them in 1921 and there is still an annual pilgrimage organised by the Royal British Legion and the High Commissioner for India.

Directions

Take the A23 out of Brighton, follow the A273 to Hassocks and go through Pyecombe. Take a right down Mill Lane and follow until you reach the windmill carpark. From the carpark go past the Old Barn Farm and golf course, and keep following the path until you reach a signpost. Go through the gate, keep the large clump of trees on your right and follow the South Downs way. (It's probably best to take an OS map, however, as these directions come from some illegible notes I scribbled years ago and it's easy to miss the Chattri, hidden by trees until the last minute. The reference is TQ304111.)

Glenda gets the willies

GUIDED WALKS

Brighton Walks

(01273) 888596
www.brightonwalks.com
info@brightonwalks.com
Ghost Walk runs first Saturday of every
month plus Halloween, depart 8pm from
Brighton Town Hall, one-and-a-half hours,
no booking. Adults £6, children £3.50

The Bard of Brighton, Glenda Clarke,
has been running her guided walks
for many years now, taking her wide-
eyed posses around Brighton's famous
landmarks and down secret alleyways
to regale them with menacing tales
and scare the willies out of them.

While there are plenty of tours
to choose from during the Brighton
Festival, it's the little touches that
make Glenda's extra special. As well as
having photos and newspaper articles
to hand for the Ghost Tour, she dons
a spooky pair of earrings and even
hands round a bag of Monster Mix,
leaving the group happily munching
on jelly bats and toads as she weaves
such hair-raising yarns as *The Grey
Lady of Meeting House Lane.*

This is an offbeat way to see the
city as the route takes in the oldest
part of town, The Lanes, two ancient
graveyards, the Royal Pavilion and the
Theatre Royal. It finishes outside a
haunted inn for those who like spirits of
a different kind.

SWIMMING

Saltdean Lido

Saltdean Park Road, Saltdean
(01273) 888308
Open 10am-6pm every day, end of May to
end of September
Adults £3, children £2

This original open-air Art Deco
swimming pool (and cover star of the
first Clearlake album, Lido) is only a
fifteen-minute drive from Brighton and
since being restored, repainted and
returned to its former glory ten years
ago, is well worth a visit.

Prince Regent

Church Street (01273) 685692
Adults £3.10, children £1.75,
OAPs £1.75
Open 7am-9.30pm most days

Across the road from the Pavilion, this
large pool has plenty of space, some
good diving boards, a big slide, a gym, a
sauna and sunbeds.

At weekends splashing-around
time for kids is between 9.30am and
4.45pm on Saturday, while on Sundays
adults can do lane-swimming 10.30am-
9.30pm. The boards are also in use for
most of the day during weekends and
early weekday evenings. Throughout
the week there is an adults-only early
swimming session from 7-9am. For
more details it's best to phone, as
timetables change quarterly.

My only gripe with the place is their
insistence on playing local radio all the
hours god sends. I like a swim to get

away from it all, not to listen to Robbie Williams and adverts for double-glazing, though they seem to have calmed down with this of late. Maybe my nagging has finally paid off.

King Alfred Centre

Kingsway, Hove (01273) 290290
Open 7.30am-9.45pm
Adults £3.10, children £1.75, OAPs £1.75
Phone for details of adult swimming times
www.kingalfredleisure.co.uk

Preferable to the Prince Regent as it's usually less busy, the water is warmer, it feels cleaner and they don't have local radio blaring at you. And, if you're driving, they've got a cheap carpark just round the back.

It's also due to be bulldozed and rebuilt as some high-rise metaphor for the tortured soul some time soon so it's best to phone ahead to check it's not a building site.

Pells Pool at Lewes

North Street, Lewes (01273) 472334
Open 12pm-6pm term-time, 12pm-7.30pm weekends and school holidays, end of May to beginning of September
www.pellspool.org.uk

Medium-sized open-air swimming pool with a claim to being the oldest of its kind in the country. Plenty of space for lounging if you don't mind being surrounded by snogging teenagers.

The sea

It's free, there's lots of it, and a visit to Brighton really is not complete without at least getting your feet wet. It's traditional to swim twice around the West Pier before breakfast here, but for newcomers a bit of splashing around will suffice. Be careful when the currents are strong: every year someone gets swept away by a surprising freak tide. For more information see the chapter on the sea.

The spotter's guide to

When in 2000 the Brighton and Hove Bus Company had the idea of daubing the names of more than 50 famous people with local connections on their buses, it gave celebrity spotting in this town a whole new twist.

No longer are you obliged to spend two hours in the rain outside the Brighton Centre just to catch a glimpse of Robbie Williams' flabby arse. All you need now is a pencil, a copy of this guide and a rudimentary knowledge of public transport. Just five minutes on Western Road and you could see Norman Cook, Winston Churchill or even Leo Sayer streak by and nearly knock you over.

We've only included our favourite fifteen here, but serious spotters can find the rest listed at www.buses.co.uk/name that bus.

When you've spotted all fifteen tear out this page, send it to us with all the boxes neatly filled in, and the first five we receive will each win a special Cheeky cagoule and a year's subscription to match.com.

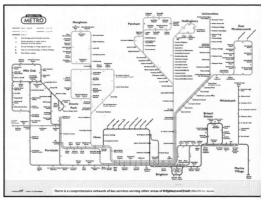

The territory of the Brighton & Hove bus

Brighton & Hove buses

- **John Wisden** (Bus number 863) – single-handedly kept the word almanac in use
- **Lord Olivier** (817) – grumpy kipper-obsessed luvvie
- **Jimmy Edwards** (648) – dead comedian with a moustache big enough to hide loaves of bread in
- **Sir George Everest** (848) – had a mountain named after him
- **Adam Faith** (649) – hiccuppy singer responsible for discovering Leo Sayer (down the back of his sofa)
- **Sir Winston Churchill** (825) – The Greatest Briton Ever (as voted by you the great British public) whose policies included "experimenting with chemical weapons on Arabs" and "the sterilisation of the feeble-minded"
- **Dusty Springfield** (865) – perma-beehived singer with a liking for the ladies
- **Ivy Compton-Burnett** (621) – racy novelist with a hatred of Hove
- **Rudyard Kipling** (869) – you've eaten the cakes, now read the book
- **Prince Regent** (803) – a swimming pool in town*
- **Charles Busby** (824) – small yellow man who spent much of his time hanging precariously from telegraph wires
- **John Nash** (811) – celebrated country-and-western singer, whose hit *A Cowboy from Whitehawk Buggered up my Patio* made him a superstar. I think.
- **Stanley Deason** (827) – one-time maverick mayor who, in the early 70s, famously elected Frank Zappa as the King of Hove
- **Carl Vincent** (845) – notorious birdwatching nut who spent a year living as a herring gull on Telscombe Cliffs
- **Charles Dickens** (828) – had a mate who knew someone in Brighton

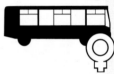

The male and female of the species

*not sure why this one is here.

Weird Things To Do

THE GREAT OUTDOORS

The Rabbit Roundabout

Follow the London Road out of Brighton, past Preston Park, and eventually you'll get to a big roundabout with a petrol station on your left. Look carefully, any time day or night, and you'll see the roundabout is home to hundreds of rabbits. Occasionally you might spot a huge pile of carrots in the middle that some kind soul has either expertly flung from their car or – risking life and limb – deposited there by running across the busy road and back. Marooned indefinitely, it'll only be a matter of time before in-breeding gets the better of these loveable floppy-eared creatures and we'll be seeing misshapen, idiot rabbits living there instead. The question is – how the hell did they get there in the first place?

Country and Western weekends

Info (01273) 701152
Running sometime mid-May admission free

Spend a day at Wild Park, where you'll meet Red Indians in tepees, gamblers, cowgirls and cowboys. Also expect rodeo, live bands, frantic shootouts, birds of prey and err… owls.

Why spend time in a sweaty club drinking your money away when you could wear a raccoon on your head and be a Wild West hero? Contact Colin on the number above for more details.

Whenever you're getting demoralised with your job, just think of this guy

The Dolphin Derby
End of Brighton Pier

Complete with its own catchy theme tune, the Dolphin Derby is probably the greatest game ever invented and, more importantly, a chance for those of you on the bread line to earn some beer money. Spend a week on your hands and knees practising rolling golf balls into paper cups and reap the rewards.

Adventure Unlimited
64 Edward Street (01273) 681058
info@aultd.org, www.aultd.org

I once spent a brilliant Saturday with a load of friends, clambering over assault courses and playing British bulldog, hide and seek and lateral thinking games, thanks to these guys. Not only was it fun and fairly cheap, but we were also entertained by some shameless flirting between my friend and the organiser.

They also offer other outdoor-pursuit days including canoeing, raftbuilding, pony trekking and abseiling, as well as a climbing wall at Stanley Deason Leisure Centre. And for the 8-18 market they run the 818 Club, which offers a mixture of outdoor pursuits and leisure activities. All outdoor events take place outside Brighton and transport is provided, should you need it. Book well in advance for summer events. Thoroughly recommended.

Spider-Cat

Scaling the wall on the corner of a building on the Old Steine, close to the entrance of Pool Valley, there's a small black cat that's been there almost as long as forever. Rumour has it that it's a witch who had a heart attack midway through her animal transmogrification process and became as the stone she clung to. Local wiccans frequently gather here in homage, though as it's very close to a bus stop they may simply be off on a trip to the country to gather enchanted moss or something.

WHERE TO CONTACT THE DEAD

Brighton National Spiritualist Church

Edward Street, opposite Devonshire Place
(01273) 683088
Sunday services 11am and 6.30pm

It starts off surprisingly similar to a Christian service (not least because the hymns are the typical tuneless mumbling affairs) except, instead of God, one gives praise to "*the greater vibration*". Expect a bit more chat and another hymn, then it all picks up when the guest clairvoyant comes on.

Most of these guys are commanding American-preacher-style speakers. There's a pep talk, some fabulous shaky-hands business then, through the preacher, the dead will start to communicate with a few members of the congregation.

Don't always expect to be chosen but, if you are fortunate enough, they'll ask you to speak so that the spirits pick up on your vibrations. What follows are nuggets of advice and information from the spirit world, channelled through the clairvoyant's voice, and all to the accompaniment of the shaky hands (whether it works without these I don't know).

The time I was picked I met my Grandad (apparently), and his message was –

"Stop worrying about your ears sticking out".

Having never given much thought to the orientation of my ears, I did wonder what that was all about, particularly as I had never met either of my grandfathers.

Afterwards it's cheese, biscuits and a chat, a flick through *Psychic News*, and then a well-earned lunch at the Barley Mow.

SÉANCES

If you are serious about wanting to be involved with a séance group e-mail me at the address at the front of the book and I'll pass your name and phone number on to the group. Unless you are staying in Brighton for some time though, this will not be possible.

If invited you will be expected to take the evening seriously, but I can guarantee you will have plenty of fun. It all takes place in pitch blackness and begins with singing a few old music-hall numbers such as *Roll Out The Barrel* and *Daisy, Daisy* to "*get the energy going*".

Then, once the spirits have manifested through the medium, watch out for stuff moving around the room and hope that you don't spend the night with a chair on your head as one lady did.

Expect also to get covered in ectoplasm and have some questions ready for when you meet some of the fantastic characters, such as James the Victorian transvestite comedian. And, if you ask, the ghosts will tell you who your spirit guide is. Do I get a Buddhist monk or a Native American Indian chief like everyone else? No, I get a chicken called Cyril.

At the end of the night not everyone will necessarily believe what they have seen but it is, of course, something to tell the grandchildren.

Pets get their paws read for free every other Saturday at Margaret's

PALMISTS AND CLAIRVOYANTS

Margaret

64 Elm Grove (01273) 683623
Open Tues-Thurs, Sat 10am-11.45pm
and 1pm-3.45pm

Step in here and be ready to enter
a time warp back 30 years or more.
The walls are littered with fading
newspaper articles and curling black-
and-white photos showing Margaret
on old TV shows. It'll feel like you're
in a Rita Tushingham movie, with
Margaret looking and playing the part
magnificently.

The readings take around twenty
minutes in a tiny room at the back of
the shop, where Margaret will read
your palm or tell your fortune from
a pack of cards. Along with the usual
stuff like *"you know someone who reads
the Daily Mail"*, Margaret also said
some pretty accurate and insightful
things on my first visit. Readings range
from £12 to £16. Go on, treat yourself
to a seaside speciality from a true
professional.

Paul Hughes-Barlow

Under Brighton Pier (01273) 677206
Open Mon-Sun 12noon-6pm
www.supertarot.co.uk

Said to be the number-one expert
on Thoth tarot, Paul lectures around
the world and is the author of *The
Magus – Opening the Key of Tarot
and Magic*, a book which presents
new methods of invoking spirits
using divination techniques. He can
also be found under Brighton Pier.
No, not sleeping off a night on the
tiles, it's actually where he operates
as a tarot consultant. He is the only
palmist/tarot reader in Brighton I
know whose room is full of interesting
books, rather than gypsy tat and the
usual mystical paraphernalia. Friendly
and honest about his profession and
possessing a good knowledge of the
occult sciences, Paul is easy to warm
to, and has a reassuringly boyish laugh.
Probably a good choice if you're
looking for something beyond the
usual nonsense. First sittings are a
standard £15.

STUFF THAT LEGENDS ARE MADE OF

Kappa

Bottom of Trafalgar Street
Opening times defy logic

Run by Peter Grant, Kappa is not only home to the world's largest collection of valves, but is also a graveyard to all of Brighton's dead TVs and radios. Despite looking derelict inside, if you peer through the closed door like I did, you may well find a desk lamp shone interrogation-style into your eyes; if the door's open it means the shop's open and, hidden away behind all the TV carcasses, you'll find Peter, a man who can bring a 1950s Ukrainian radio to life with just a wave of his magic wand. When not fiddling with old bits of electronic equipment, Peter is invariably out and about setting up pirate-radio stations or saving another Russian nuclear-power station from going under. If it's old, electronic and knackered, bring it here and Pete will endeavour to fix it. And return it to you in the next ten years or so.

Tony Young Autographs

138 Edward Street
(01273) 732418
Opening times akin to
MajorMajorMajorMajor's office in Catch 22.
In theory they're Mon-Fri 10am-12noon
and 1pm-3pm, Sat 10am-12.30pm

This tumbledown shop rescued from the 1950s has a surreal and curling collection of autographed photos and bizarre oddities. Where else could you get a copy of the homicide report of the JFK assassination *and* a broken banjo? Worth a visit for curiosity alone but treat the owner with respect, he's an old man and dislikes rowdy people in the shop. Come to think of it, he doesn't like people in the shop at all... which might just be for safety's sake owing to the fact that the only thing keeping the ceiling up appears to be a knackered old trombone.

A Spotter's Guide To
BRIGHTON
CELEBRITIES

What better way to spend your afternoon than going all gooey-eyed and weak-kneed at having stumbled across the bass player from local legend Anal Beard? Brighton is home to an eclectic bunch of celebrities, and I wish you every success with your sleuthing.

STEPHEN BERKOFF

The bald-headed champagne-socialist playwright and actor can be spotted rollerblading outside his apartment in Hove, merrily effing and blinding as he glides along.

Worth 20 points

NICK BERRY

The shiny-nosed superstar can sometimes be seen walking his four scottie dogs on the beach in the morning. Don't start singing *Every Loser Wins* as he is a sensitive soul and recently hurled one of his dogs at an *Argus* journalist just for saying, "*Hello, hello, hello, what's all this then?*"

Worth 15 points

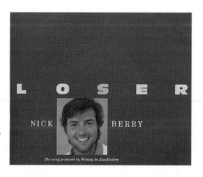

L O S E R

NICK   BERRY

The song featured by Wicksy in EastEnders

JULIE BURCHILL

Irritating squeaky-voiced journalist, renowned for her opinionated codswallop and having a chip on her shoulder about not going to university. Did you know she has a swimming pool and that Tony Parsons was crap in bed? You **didn't**?? Pop down Hotel Du Vin and she'll fill you in with the details.

Worth 4 points

NICK CAVE

The brooding Australian singer lives in deepest, darkest Hove (naturally), and can be spotted hanging around outside the King Alfred in a crumpled suit, dark glasses and smoking a fag or two. Either that or he'll be in HMV buying *Mr Bean* videos for his kids.

Worth 50 points
(60 if seen in Mothercare)

STEVE COOGAN

A rare spot now his film career has taken off but still most likely to be seen in a boozer. If you're an attractive female it's best to keep your distance or wear heavy protective armour, although he **has** recently started carrying a tin-opener.

Worth 30 points
(45 if he doesn't try and mate with you)

CHRIS EUBANK

Once an easy spot owing to the fact that Chris spent most of his waking hours driving his juggernaut, motorbike or tractor around the Old Lanes and waving at bemused strangers. Since the bankruptcy he's been keeping his head down. Give him time; he'll be back. Probably as the latest face for the *"I'm on the bus"* campaign.

Worth 2 points

HERBIE FLOWERS

He's played with every rock god from Bowie and T-Rex to Lou Reed, and got paid a measly £12 for writing the bassline to *Walk On The Wild Side*. Herbie's probably best-loved, however, for writing the classic pop ballad *Grandad*. See him down the Komedia doing his double-bass thing from time to time. If you want a good rock'n'roll story, ask him about the time he was in the Wombles on *Top Of The Pops*.

Worth 25 points

KEVIN ROWLAND

Dexy's Midnight Runners main man, famous for his costume-change-every-album approach and general lack of patience with music journos who didn't understand his 'vision'. Occasionally found in Infinity Foods squeezing an organic avocado with a look of grim satisfaction.

Worth 20 points
(25 if wearing a dress)

FATBOY SLIM

From Tarquin to Norman to Freakpower to Fatboy Slim (and a host of other pseudonyms along the way), local hero Norman Cook is still releasing albums, performing the occasional DJ spot at the Concorde 2, and doing his best to support Brighton & Hove Albion. God bless him. And someone buy his records, please, or he'll end up running a burger bar on Western Road…

Worth 30 points

DAVID THOMAS FROM PERE UBU

Strictly for the music lovers, this one. Look for him striding around Hove like some crazy Ignatious Reilly from *A Confederacy of Dunces*… Hmmm, I feel I've lost a few of you here. Never mind, read on.

Worth 35 points
(50 if wearing his red plastic bib)

DAVID VAN DAY

At one time the ex-singer from Dollar could be found running his burger stall by Churchill Square. Now he's vainly trying to kickstart his flagging career so you'll find him at the opening of an envelope and in every society page of the 3,000 free Brighton magazines currently in circulation. Tragic.

Worth 1 point

MARK WILLIAMS FROM THE FAST SHOW

To be found at Kambi's grabbing a takeaway kebab or hanging around pubs like the Lion and Lobster. Remember the *Father Ted* episode with Victor Meldrew before you go up to him and say *"Suit you, Sir!"*

Worth 22 points

If you've been missed out of our *Spotter's Guide* and feel that you ought to be included, please write to us finishing the following sentence:

I think I'm famous enough to be in your guide because.....................................

....

Please enclose £10 and a signed photo. If you are Simon Fanshawe or have just been in *The Bill* a few times, this will not be sufficient.

Things to do in Hove when you're (not) dead

By Dave 'BN1' Mounfield

While Hove is now officially part of Brighton – and we're all meant to be one big happy family – it unfortunately remains the straightlaced and disapproving maiden aunt who tries to ignore sleazy old Uncle Brighton being sick under the sideboard at family get-togethers.

Nevertheless, this "small piece of Rhodesia on the South Coast", as Pete McCarthy once described it, does have some saving graces, so indulge us, if you will, as we endeavour to pick out a selection of interesting activities and places to visit in this civic equivalent of the afterlife. But beware, gentle reader. In Hove, no-one can hear you scream.

Canhams
48 Church Road, Hove (01273) 731021

In a world where supermarkets are ruining quality meat production, good independent butchers are to be celebrated; none more so than this fine establishment, which offers heartbreakingly good meat pies, quality meat, smashing sausages and even haggis.

One Hove Place
First Avenue, Hove (01273) 738266

While Brighton has over one million bars and pubs, Hove has relatively few, and still fewer you'd want to go to. One exception in this pub desert, however, is One Hove Place, boasting lots of designer oak panelling, a lovely large Italian sunken beer garden and a clientele of shifty-looking geezers with lots of gold jewellery.

Marrocco's
8 Kings Esplanade, Hove (01273) 203764

Situated next to the soon-to-be-demolished-and-rebuilt-as-the-Empire-State-Building-once-King-Kong-finished-mauling-it King Alfred Centre, this family-run seaside café is endearingly chaotic and resolutely un-designer, with some very fine homemade Italian-style ice cream, a job lot of pine fittings and some pretty good basic Italian dishes gracing its otherwise fairly standard café fare.

To have a late-afternoon perambulation along this stretch of the front, ending it here with a knickerbocker glory and coffee while watching the staff run around in a permanent frenzy of Italian disorganisation, is a real pleasure.

Gwydyr Salon
Top end of Palmeira Square,
by the Floral Clock, Hove (01273) 732923

Remarkably, this establishment is the oldest barbers in town, having kept it short and neat for 125 years non-stop. It is also the only barbers in the city with no vowels in its name (well, the first bit anyway), and the only place I know where gentlemen can come for a 50s-style close shave. Situated in the basement of Gwydyr Mansions, there are some nice steps down to a spiffingly old-fashioned window display for pomade-type products. Enter its portals and you will be delighted by the original 30s decor, with black-and-white tiles and green vitriolite. A very pleasant and humorous gentleman gave me a good cut on my visit, made all the more pleasurable by his heavily ironic use of the word "sir". As in "does **sir** think that?"

They've even had a book of poetry written about them by a poet in residence, which you can buy while you're there. It's not bad either.

Kings Lawn and Brunswick Lawn

The only bit of grass left on the seafront that the council hasn't dug up and ruined. And lovely it is too. This long stretch of lawn is ideal for picnicking, frisbee throwing or just lolling around. And when you get a bit peckish, the Meeting Place Café is nearby for a hot cuppa and a slice of cake.

The Pussycat Club
(See *Sex and Fetish* for details)
Where else can you see sweating IT workers stuffing ten-pound notes into the g-strings of slightly bored but almost naked ladies? My trip here was dignified by an excited Arab saying *"So beautiful! So beautiful! I already go to toilet and masturbate five times!"* Sophisticated. Opposite the old gasworks on Church Road.

Hove Floral Clock

This civic wonder at the top of Palmeira Square is a clock, made of flowers!! How crazy is that?! For many Brightonians it stands as a gateway marker, beyond which lies the cold, blasted wasteland of Hove proper or Darkest Hove, as it is known. Even in the spring, when it's cheery, the hands point to (usually) the wrong time, as a kind of mute memento mori, insinuating *"It's only a matter of time, Brightonian, before you grow old and must perforce cross the shadow line, into Hove, and the arms of Death"*. It's very pretty though.

Hove Museum
(See *Wonderful Things to Do*)

HAVE A SURREAL AFTERNOON IN BRIGHTON

1. Put on your silliest hat, pack up some fish sandwiches and head off to number 64 Elm Grove, where you will need to part with a few quid to discover what the future holds from Mystic Margaret. Try not to be frightened by her make-up and listen carefully to the nuggets of wisdom she imparts to you.

2. Wander up to the top of Elm Grove and reward yourself with a quick cuppa at Beckie's café, where you can pretend you are in a Mike Leigh film or, if it's a *really* good day in there, a David Lynch.

3. From here cross over and follow Tenantry Down Road for a stunning view of the coastline as you pass through Brighton's shantytown. The curve of houses you can see far below are Roundhill Crescent, where notorious baby-eater Genesis P. Orridge used to live, while the strange little huts on either side of you are occupied by Brighton's flourishing Amish community. Keep your mp3 player well hidden at this point or you may have a bloodbath on your hands.

4. At the end of the road take a left and look for the entrance to Woodvale Crematorium – the chosen resting place of infamous occultist Aleister Crowley. This vast graveyard is remote and enchanting: if Buffy Summers ever came to town, this would definitely be her hangout.

5. Leave by the main exit at the bottom, and head into town. Your afternoon can be made complete with a pint in the Basketmakers pub, tucked away at the bottom of the North Laine. Search the tins on the wall to see who can find the strangest message inside, and then leave one of your own. After that it's either home for tea or popping about 30 mushrooms and flying to Neptune on the magic swan.

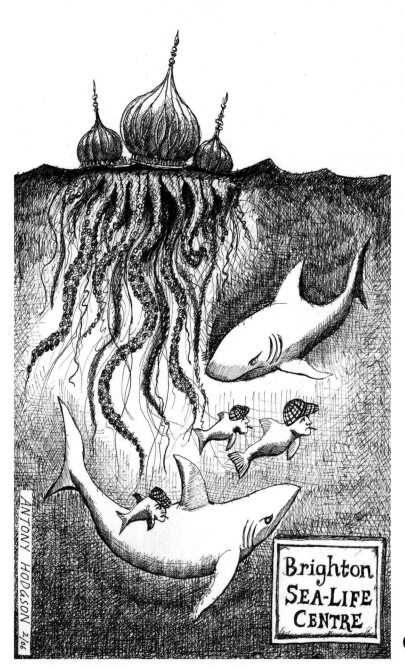

Brighton
SEA-LIFE
CENTRE

ANTONY HODGSON 2/06

The Sea

Despite the fact that Brighton receives millions of visitors every year, you'd be surprised how few take the plunge and venture – beyond the occasional paddle – into the sea. Is it too cold, is it fear of sharks, turds and toilet paper, or are they all just a big bunch of jessies? In an effort to encourage a few more of you out of the pubs and into the Blue, this chapter gives the facts about seawater quality and explores a few ways to go messing about in the water.

WHERE TO SWIM

Brighton Beach

A lot of people are understandably sniffy about swimming in the sea in Brighton but I have to confess that floating on my back in the water with the sun turning my skin the texture of a leather chesterfield still rates as one of my favourite Brighton experiences. True, it isn't the cleanest water around, and you may find yourself in the company of lobster-red revellers (try saying that fast) standing around up to their waists because they can't be bothered to queue for the (non-existent) toilets, but don't let a little wee put you off. At least it warms the water up a bit.

Hove Beach

A lot quieter than Brighton (that's a shock, I know) and well endowed with lawns, benches, grand seafront Regency buildings and multi-coloured beach huts to have a good old nose into as you stroll casually past. The charm of the beach hut I confess to finding still somewhat elusive – it's just a garden shed without the stack of pre-decimalisation porn and the half bottle of brandy, surely? Water quality-wise, maiden aunts had to cover their mouths with lavender-scented hankies in 2005 when, surprisingly, Hove had worse results than the main Brighton beach and failed to meet "guideline" EC compliance. It did reach mandatory compliance but you might prefer to take a dip here with your mouth firmly closed.

Portslade Beach

A left turn just past Hove Lagoon as far as the first carpark brings you initially to what an acquaintance of mine assures me is the *"swingers' beach"*, since she was approached by a gentleman of no fixed clothing at this very site and furnished apropos de nada with this apparently necessary information. Subtle. If you fancy giving it a go I'm usually there at about 6.30pm on a Tuesday. Progress further along the beachfront road here towards Carrots Café and, despite the industrial backdrop, the beach is actually quite pleasant and, whisper it soft, at low tide there's even some sand. It doesn't shelve as steeply as Brighton or Hove beaches so there's less mountaineering to do when you just want to get *out* of the water.

Shoreham Beach

Just a mile or two beyond Portslade, through Shoreham High Street, over the estuary and a quick burrow through the residential roads to the left, you'll find a remarkably clean and peaceful beach with sand and only light breezes much of the time, the downside being the utter lack of facilities. Mostly patronised by bewildered-looking families from southern continents who stand around near the water's edge with all their clothes on, regardless of the weather.

Saltdean

Five miles west of Brighton and home to more winners of the international What Do You Keep In *Your* Beach Hut?

competition. Although the water's fine, the best thing about this place is the Lido, where you can swim unravaged by the sharks that have plagued the area east of the Marina since escaping from some millionaire's underwater fantasy playground a couple of years ago.

And elsewhere

Though over twenty miles away, Eastbourne (like Hove without the glamour and excitement) and Littlehampton both have Blue Flag beaches, so if you're some sort of effete snob who demands such fripperies as clean drinking water, lifeguards, first-aid equipment and sand that isn't held together by some unspeakable odiferous gunk, then you'll be pleased you made the effort.

WATERSPORTS

Brighton Swimming Club

www.brightonsc.co.uk

Based at arch 250E down between the two piers, this is the UK's longest-established swimming club, formed in 1860 and still going strong. Many of its hardcore club members meet **every** morning at 7.30am for a dip before work. Only if the sea *"looks suicidal"* will they give it a miss. New members are always welcome, though they'll require you to wear a coloured rubber cap when going in, which might make you feel like a right charlie but is for your own safety.

Those members who brave the sea when it's below 40° – something that only happens occasionally – can pride themselves on being issued with a club certificate; its oldest member, Jim Wild, now 93 years young, recalls the time the temperature of the sea dropped to below 30° and he returned to the club with icicles hanging from his nipples!

Annual traditions include a big game of water polo down at the Marina, a chilly annual Christmas dip and a Boxing Day race. See website for more details.

The Brighton Kayak Company

185 Kings Road Arches (01273) 323160
Open all year round (for retail)
10am until "whenever"
www.brightonkayak.co.uk
£10 per hour for kayak rental

Found under the promenade between the two piers, The Brighton Kayak Company hire out single and tandem kayaks, organise banana boat rides and parasailing. They also hire wetsuits, have full changing rooms and showers, and sell beachwear and wakeboarding gear. You can even book parascending and other action sports, both locally and internationally, through these guys. All staff are qualified instructors.

Hove Lagoon
Western end of Hove promenade
(01273) 424842
www.hovelagoon.co.uk

Windsurfing, sailing, yachting and powerboating start at around £40 for a two-hour lesson with an instructor. Check the website for more details.

ROCKPOOLING

Past the Marina on the way to Rottingdean there are some fabulous rockpools where you can find edible spider and shore crabs, sea anemones, little fish and the occasional beached giant squid. If you're in the car, drive to Rottingdean (just follow the coastal road heading towards Eastbourne), head to the seafront and turn right. From Brighton Pier it'll take ten minutes to cycle or 30 minutes to walk.

IMAGINED CONVERSATION BETWEEN A FATHER AND SON EDIBLE CRAB:

- Son?
- Yes, Dad?
- Sit down Son, there's something I'd like to tell you.
- Yes, Dad?
- You know how all these years your mother and I told you that 'edible' meant found under big stones...

DOLPHIN SPOTTING

The Dolphin Hotline
Contact Stephen Savage 0777 3610036
www.seawatchfoundation.org.uk

There has been an increase in sightings of dolphins along the coast, in particular bottlenose dolphins and harbour porpoise. I must stress that to spot one is rare but the best time to see them is high tide between March and September. Between the two piers and around the Marina are your best viewing spots, and the website is there to help with identification. The most celebrated dolphin ever seen in Brighton was dubbed Smurfy because of his unusual iridescent colouring – he hung around the pier for a couple of weeks jumping at the Green Bagel and trying to poke his nose through it.

If you do see one, phone this chap above and make him very happy; he's currently tracking all dolphin and whale activity along the south coast.

75

SURFING

By shaggy blond-haired, Hawaiian-shirt-wearing Marcus O'Dair

Let's face it, Brighton is no surfer's paradise; the waves are infrequent, small and messy, the sea is dirty and the temperatures would send an eskimo running for extra thermal undies. As the title of a film about the Brighton surf scene noted, it's *Not California*.

But Brighton surfers, many of whom have surfed all over the world, are passionate about the local breaks. Yes, the waves are usually small, but they're good enough for several competition-winning Brighton surfers who are out there every chance they get. Yes, it's cold, but people surf in the Outer Hebrides, in Sweden, even in Alaska (the boundary between surfing and masochism being decidedly blurred). And, yes, it's dirty – but hey, what do you expect in Brighton?

The main spots

The two main local breaks are the Hot Pipes and the Marina. The Hot Pipes, near Shoreham Power Station, has a friendly atmosphere and, for once in Brighton, easy parking. This fairly gentle beachbreak is a good spot for beginners.

The Marina, on the other hand, is ridden mainly by shortboarders. It's a fairly fast wave breaking over a shallow chalk-and-flint reef, and suitable for more experienced surfers only. It used to have a reputation as a fairly heavy locals' spot and it's still a good idea to show a bit of respect for the regulars.

Other spots include the West Pier (especially on a groundswell), the Wedge (primarily a bodyboarding break) and Shoreham Harbour. Outside Brighton, check out Littlehampton and Eastbourne and, farther afield, East and West Wittering and Camber Sands.

THE SURFERS AGAINST SEWAGE CAMPAIGN FOR CLEAN SEAWATER IN BRIGHTON

The national environmental group Surfers Against Sewage have had a strong local campaign in Brighton for more than eight years. They are calling for full treatment for the 95 million litres of sewage that is discharged untreated into the sea off Brighton. That's 80 Olympic-sized swimming pools of raw sewage every 24 hours!

A few facts about the quality of Brighton seawater:

- Brighton is one of the only major coastal resorts in the UK without full sewage treatment.

- The discharge in Brighton currently breaches European legislation.

- Inadequately-treated sewage contains millions of viruses and bacteria which can survive for days and days in seawater – swallowing one of these pathogens can cause illnesses from gastro-enteritis to Hepatitis A and E.coli 0157.

- The most cost-effective, long-term and safe sewage solution for Brighton is full treatment UV (ultra-violet) disinfection. It is tried and tested, economically viable and used successfully by water companies across the UK.

If you would like to get involved in the local campaign to encourage Southern Water to provide UV treatment for Brighton's seawater visit www.sas.org.uk

Shopping

Brighton can be a shopaholic's paradise, particularly for lovers of antiques, fashion, jewellery, music, kitsch, glamour-wear, retro clothing and over-priced screen prints of Al Pacino. And with over 700 independent shops in the centre alone, the town boasts more unique boutiques per square mile than anywhere else in the UK. The most colourful areas with the best shops are definitely North Laine, Kemp Town and the Old Lanes. For the less adventurous, Western Road and the Churchill Square shopping centre have everything that you'd expect to find in a high street (including the crowds, lack of greenery and lunatic bus drivers).

North Laine is terrific, not only for its wide selection of 60s/70s clothes and record shops but also for unique boutiques like CyberCandy, stocking specialist and retro sweets; Wildcat, the world's largest stockist of body jewellery; and Pussy, offering stylish wares for the home as well as a good range of smutty books. Get into the swing of North Laine and you'll find yourself going home with a woolly mammoth ivory nosestud, a Mod suit, a chocolate-covered scorpion and a pair of thigh-high boots. And you only popped out for a loaf of bread.

Kemp Town too has an eclectic mix of boutiques, ranging from a wealth of second-hand places to gay clothes stores, poodle parlours and over 300 shops stocking butt-plugs and lube. The Old Lanes, while a lot less flamboyant than North Laine, are good for jewellery (particularly if trying to track down your great aunt's stolen necklace), antiques, cafés and new clothes shops. Think of it this way: if North Laine was Eric Morecambe, the Old Lanes would be Ernie Wise (with Kemp Town as special guest Danny La Rue).

And finally, before you rush off with your credit cards, don't get up too early! Shops here can open notoriously late (especially in North Laine) and not always at the same time every morning. So, do yourself a favour, have a late night on the tiles and get up at the same time as nearly everyone else here – around 11am.

While every city in England has an HMV and Virgin store staffed by spotty grungers who insist on playing Scandinavian death metal at full volume, Brighton has some of the best independent record shops outside of London, and because of the city's size you can get round them all easily in an afternoon. There is a long tradition of good vinyl shops down here which, like many of the characterful shops in this town, are an essential part of Brighton's appeal. So come and sample these marvellous enclaves of vinyl/CD and I guarantee you will go home with an armful of goodies, even if it means eating beans on toast till payday. I do each month and I've now lost three stone. Bugger Atkins all you fatties! – try the Record Diet!

DJ and vinyl junkie Andy Roseman

Across The Tracks

110 Gloucester Road (01273) 677906
Open 10am-6pm daily, Sun 12noon-5pm

A personal favourite. This shop is vinyl heaven and CD paradise with a fantastic selection of every genre from latin, pop and metal to rockabilly and blues. It even specialises in demos of bands old and new. Alan the owner has an encyclopaedic knowledge of music: what he doesn't know about labels, dates and names could be written in the space between Noel Gallagher's eyebrows. What's more, once he gets to know your tastes he'll get to uttering those words that'll be music to your ears: *"I've got something you might be interested in"*. Prices range from a quid for bargain 45s through to £80 plus for collectables.

At weekends a chap called Euan runs a small stall outside flogging soul, reggae, jazz and 78s. You can't miss him: he has the loudest laugh in Brighton and is usually surrounded by a swarm of eager collectors.

SHOPPING

Superb service, great choice and a favourite haunt of carrot-topped snooker-loopy record junkie Steve Davis, Across the Tracks is a 'proper' record shop in every sense of the word.

Borderline Records

41 Gardner Street
Open Mon-Sat 10am-5.30pm, Sun 12-4pm

Borderline has consistently stocked an amazing range of music since it opened countless years ago. It may be small but by avoiding chart music and the obvious mainstream fodder, its stock is a carefully selected and extensive range of re-issued jazz, soul, psychedelia, exotica, reggae, latin, soundtrack, electronica, post-rock and indie. Most is on CD but there is a smaller selection on records. Outside there are boxes of cheap CDs starting at £3 and vinyl offers galore. Staff are friendly and helpful and there're always some foot-tapping sounds being played. If you can find a bad record here I'll change my name to Barbara.

Edgeworld

Upstairs above Re-Load,
6 Kensington Gardens (01273) 628262
Open Mon-Sat 10.30am-6pm,
Sun 12noon-4pm

Easy to miss, which would be a real shame, especially for anyone with a passion for small independent labels or with tastes that lean towards *Wire* or *Plan B* magazines, or Radio 3's *Mixing It*. You'll find lo-fi, mellow country, post-rock and electronica here, and offerings from labels such as Pickled Egg, Drag City and Domino. There's also a fair selection of CDs, though the stock doesn't seem to change that often. If you want to hear some of the music on offer there's a tiny listening area in the corner for vinyl, or simply ask the friendly (and refreshingly unpretentious) staff, Colin and Dave, to play whatever you fancy. Edgeworld is also a good spot for finding out about some of the more low-key gigs in Brighton. They'll even stock your own CDs as well, if properly packaged. Mine's been sitting there for years.

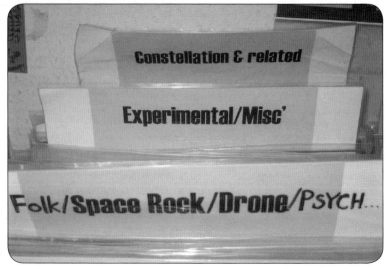

Essential Music
15-16 Brighton Square (01273) 202695
Open Mon-Sat 10am-6pm, Sun 12noon-5pm

If you ever lost your CD collection (ie had it nicked) your first port of call for replacing it would probably be here as value for money is the name of the game at Essential. All genres are covered, from indie, punk, rock, hip hop, soul and jazz to lots of weirdybeardy world music, with £5 as the usual starting price. In fact you'd be hard-pushed to find better CD bargains anywhere else in Brighton, even from most of the second-hand places. Listening facilities are also available, so why not come on a quiet afternoon and indulge in all those classic old albums you've always wanted to hear? The staff are quite bonkers too, and play a superb mixture of easy listening one minute and some crazy Euro pop the next. There's also a great DVD section with hard-to-find B movies, manga and kung fu films and some better-known Hollywood blockbusters. Highly recommended.

The Punker Bunker
Below Immediate Clothing, Sydney Street
Opening times Mon-Sun 11am-6pm (but according to its owner "*you can knock a couple of hours off either side, owing to the fat bloke upstairs being late*")

Run by Just One Life promoter Buz, this tiny basement shop caters for anyone with a passion for ska, punk, Two-Tone, metal, rock and underground punk rock. Hanging on to those old punk rock ethics, Buz is an eager promoter of live, noisy music in Brighton, sells all his CDs for a tenner or less, describes the Fish Brothers as "*beautiful people*" and discourages nu-metallers from visiting his shop. "*There are certain records I can put on to scare off the nu-metal kids,*" he comments wryly.

You can also buy tickets for all punk related gigs down here, buy yourself a badge that says *Fuck Off*, find adverts for local bands and learn all about the scene from Buz. Long may he reign.

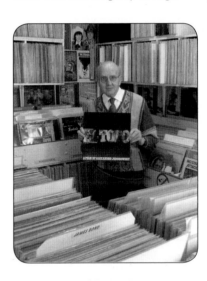

The Record Album
8 Terminus Road (01273) 323853
Open Mon-Sat 11am-5pm

Up the hill just round the corner from Brighton Station lies the Record Album, the oldest record shop in the country and a must for collectors of rare vinyl.

The shop specialises in all types of deleted recordings and one-offs, especially soundtrack albums, most of which are new or in mint condition, and the records that owner George sticks up in his shop window invariably reflect whatever movies are being shown on terrestrial TV that week. Don't expect to find a bargain. Prices start around £10 and go up to £75 or more for that ultra-rare electronic 50s sci-fi B movie soundtrack. George also supplies records to the BBC, theatre and radio and has an extensive mail-order service. It is easy to spend a couple of hours here, simply for the company of its owner. George always wears a shirt and tie, is impeccably polite and happy to share his passion for music with you, though ask him why he doesn't stock CDs and George will shudder and say *"uh, those ghastly little frisbees"*.

Rounder Records

19 Brighton Square (01273) 325440
Open Mon-Sat 9.30am-6pm,
Sun 10.30am-6pm

A first-class record shop offering discount CDs, a 50-50 split of dance and indie, the cheapest vinyl in town and staff whose discerning tastes you can trust. Rounder is also *the* place to come for tickets to local gigs and, if you subscribe to their 'weekly' e-mail not only will you be treated to the acerbic wit of Steve Sexton, but you'll also be kept up to date on the best gigs in town. Finally, remember to look out for the constantly changing graffiti round the back of the shop. It's all the handiwork of Warp/Skint musician Req.

The Wax Factor

Trafalgar Street (01273) 673744
Open Mon-Sat 10.15am-5.30pm

There is an unwritten law in Brighton that all good record shops be run by blokes called Alan. The good news is The Wax Factor is not only run by Alan Senior, who has been in the business 25 years and is a mine of information on everything you ever wanted (or didn't want) to know about rare vinyl, but his son Alan Junior trades here too. Alantastic!

CDs are on sale but it is the vast stock of (mainly) 50s to 70s vinyl that is so impressive. The walls are adorned with extremely rare and very tempting records of bygone days many of which would cost you a kidney or two should you wish to take them home and give them a spin.

Sure, they know the value of what they've got but there *are* bargains to be had and they frequently clear out stock for a quid upwards. The two Al's will also keep you abreast of new stock if they know your tastes and will endeavour to get you something no matter how rare or bizarre it is, though they draw the line at animal porn and Sting records.

Next door there's even a 50s style café complete with jukebox and diner furniture. The ideal spot to have a cuppa and bacon butty as you drool over your finds.

BOOKSHOPS

BIG GUYS

Borders

Churchill Square (01273) 731122
Open Mon-Sat 9am-9pm, Sun 10.30am-5pm
www.borders.com

When the rest of us are dragging ourselves out of bed, making strong coffee, lighting cigarettes and smearing marmite on the cat, these guys are up and open. Didn't anyone tell them that in Brighton no one even thinks about getting out of bed before 10am, never mind shopping? Still, that's crazy Americans for you*. They do, however, stock a fine array of books and CDs, have a small café upstairs, and the *very best* selection of magazines and spoken-word tapes in town. Also a good place for seeing small music performances and book readings – keep a look out for their monthly flyers for details.

Sussex Stationers

37 London Road, 114 St James's St,
55-56 East Street, George Street, Hove,
194 Western Road (01273) 206606
Open Mon-Sun 9am-5.30pm

Don't expect to find the latest occult offering from Julian Cope about elf magic or the history of shoelaces written in Esperanto, but if it's the most popular works of fiction/non-fiction you're after you'll find them here with discounts to rival even those rotten supermarket chains.

Waterstones

71-74 North Street (01273) 206017
Open Mon-Fri 9am-7pm, Sat 10am-6pm,
Sun 11am-5pm
www.waterstones.co.uk

The Brighton branch of Waterstones has always felt more like a friendly local bookstore than a chain and owes much of its success and popularity to its lovely manager Annie, who works hard to ensure that the stock here, as far as possible, reflects the true spirit of the town. Many of the staff, too, seem to have their finger on the pulse of what Brighton readers are looking for, demonstrating that with a little care and passion, a chainstore can still have a heart.

LITTLE GUYS

Brighton Books

18 Kensington Gardens (01273) 693845
Open Mon-Sat 10am-6pm, occasionally open Sundays

As well as offering a large selection of rare and unusual second-hand hardbacks (£90 for the collected works of Madame Blavatsky) and cheaper paperbacks (usually sitting in boxes at the front of the shop), Brighton Books is home to some wonderful characters. There's Simeon (the last of the famous Brighton shop cats), a friendly black tom who will greet you at the counter and rub himself against your chest to entice

*Saying all that, I've just noticed Waterstones opens at 9am too…

83

you into making a purchase and – on some days – local legend and king of charity shopping, Mr Stephen Drennan. Stephen's *Little Book of Charity Shopping* can still be purchased from the till here, along with its sequel and a selection of his lo-fi comics. If he's wearing a badge, playing a bizarre record and sporting a black rollneck, you can rest assured that all is well with the universe.

Simeon shares a joke with a customer

City Books
23 Western Road (01273) 725306
Open Mon-Sat 9.30am-6pm,
Sun 10.30am-5pm

Established for over twenty years, this is Brighton's biggest independent bookshop and favourite haunt of Nigel Richardson (author of *Breakfast in Brighton*). The kind of place you wander in to buy the latest McEwan and end up having a natter with the owner for half an hour about existentialism, City Books is a local bookshop that cares about its customers and seems to make an extra-special effort in properly

representing Brighton through its choice of stock and window displays. Well worth supporting.

Colin Page
36 Duke Street (01273) 325954
Open Mon-Sat 9am-5.30pm

This former 19th century baker's is officially Brighton's oldest bookshop and comes complete with all the trappings of the dusty, antiquated variety once frequented by JR Hartley, including a marvellous old spiral staircase at the back. Set up in 1975 by John Loska and his twin brother Stephen, the shop specialises in antiquated and rare books but, for the general buyer, always has a box of interesting paperbacks outside and a basement of hardback fiction and factual books ranging from history to the occult. It's also a popular haunt when the luvvies are in town. The likes of Stephen Fry and Simon Callow are former regulars, as are old-school politicians (*"the ones who still read"* quipped Stephen) like Denis Healey. A treat for the serious book collector.

Kemp Town Books (and Bookroom Café)
91 St George's Road (01273) 682110

One of only two remaining independent bookshops left in the city, Kemp Town Books has been here for over 35 years, run by the affable Darion Goodwin for the past twelve. Charming, personable and peaceful, this is everything a small bookshop should be; it even boasts a little café upstairs, playing host to evening courses in poetry, life drawing and other workshops at night. Priding himself on their fast-order service, Darion personally guarantees next-day delivery for 90% of orders (faster than Amazon!) or a free pint and cheesy chips from the Barley Mow next door.

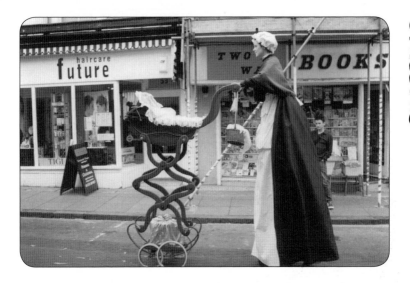

Two Way Books

54 Gardner Street (01273) 687729

Frozen in time since 1982, this singular bookshop must be the only place in England still selling Paul Young and Van Halen annuals. If pictures of David Lee Roth in spandex pants aren't your bag, they also do a nifty selection of old comics ranging from *Dr Who* to *Tractor Weekly*. Mix that with more bizarre stuff like shelves of Mills & Boon, Giles compilations and a few discreet piles of porn and you'll probably wonder how they make a living. Barbara Cartland or back issues of *Razzle* anyone?

The Wax Factor

Trafalgar Street (01273) 673744
Open Mon-Sat 10.15am-5.30pm

If second-hand books on the occult, drugs, philosophy, sci-fi, eastern mysticism and music are your bag then this is the place for you. The window display alone should be enough to pull you in as you drool over all the Crowley, Philip K Dick and Burroughs books. They have a pretty good selection of fiction here too, which is just on your right as you enter. More importantly perhaps they stock one of the best collections of second-hand CDs and vinyl in Brighton, with 7inches and CD singles in the basement (See *Record Shops*).

West Pier Books

Underneath the West Pier (or what's left of it) Open Fri-Sun

At weekends, when the weather is good, you'll find these guys down on the seafront. Run by local filmmaker Mark Keeble and 'Polack' Pete, West Pier Books hold a good collection of second-hand paperbacks with a slant towards cult fiction. Brighton's answer to the Persuaders, the duo can be seen at country fairs or whizzing around Brighton in Mark's black 70s Jag blasting out easy listening music. I really should get round to including them in the *Eccentrics* chapter one of these days…

GROOVY GIFTS & COOL THINGS FOR THE HOME

Blackout

53 Kensington Place (01273) 671741
Open Mon-Sat 10am-6pm

Off the beaten track in North Laine, Blackout still get long-term Brightonians stumbling through their doorway for the first time going "*ooh, are you new?*" despite having been here for over fifteen years. The shop's unique angle is kitsch-fashion-folk art and religious imagery and it has cornered the market in Tibetan baby carriers, fluorescent loo brushes, Virgin Mary ashtrays, plastic Hindu gods, recycled tyre tables and tribal jewellery. They have a policy of selling nothing black, hence the name, though I did find a black scarf on my last visit leading me to wonder if they have a secret goth in their midst. (Having spotted one of their staff, Sally, buying a Fields of the Nephilim album in Snoopers the other day, I think I've found the culprit).

Sally reminisces about her glory days playing penny whistle for Christian Death

As well as Sally, you'll find Brian and Cica on the prowl. Cica, being a *"vicious little bugger who hates kids"* is best enjoyed from a discreet distance while plastic fetishist Brian is much friendlier and will even get all lairy if you're carrying the right kind of plastic bag.

Castor & Pollux

164-166 King's Road Arches
(01273) 773776
Open Mon-Sun 11am-5pm,
winter months Fri-Mon 12noon-4pm

Named after the Roman gods of seafarers, C&P is an attractive beach-house boutique selling stylish books (*Girls Guide to Surfing* anyone?), furniture, art, flowers, pottery, cards and prints. Owner Mike clearly has a taste for quality; he's wisely avoided the kitsch in favour of the beautiful and everything on show is kind on the eye. In fact I've had *my* eye on those new Penguin bookcover deckchairs for some time now. More places like this down on the seafront please!

Sneek

34 St James's Street (01273 679648)

Over the past couple of years, St James Street has been upwardly mobile in a big way - to the extent where a shop specialising in chic interiors and design-based gifts now doesn't feel out of place. Opened two years ago by furniture designer Cathy Norcott, Sneek inevitably attracts its share of hip thirtysomethings but the atmosphere remains mercifully unpretentious. There is a particular focus on lighting and designer wallpapers, but they stock everything from books and cards to clocks, tea pots, key-holders and wine racks. The biggest customer attraction, however, is Heddy, Cathy's gorgeous black Labrador (sadly not for sale).

EM-Space

20 Sydney Street (01273) 683400
Open Mon-Sat 10am-6pm,
occasionally Sundays

Run for many years now by Kathy
and Janine, EM-Space specialises in
design-led gifts with a slant towards
cards and books, artists' sketchbooks
and beautiful traditional photo albums
(the ones where you add the sticky
corners).

Fossil 2000

3 Kensington Place (01273) 622000
Open Tues-Sat 10am-5.30pm (6pm Sat),
Sun-Mon 11am-4pm
www.fossil2000.co.uk

This unusual shop just off the beaten
track in North Laine has an incredible
collection of ammonites, trilobites,
fossil plates, crystal-growing kits for
kids and lots of other prehistoric relics.
Owner Denise mentioned to me
that if you want something specific
it's worth asking, as "we can get our
hands on most things", which made me
wonder whether she had won a strip
of Lyme Regis in a poker game. Prices
range from 20p for a stingray's tooth
to a £1,200 triceratops horn or even
an amethyst geode for £7,500! More
unusual, perhaps, is their collection of
flies in amber, beetles in treacle and
woolly mammoths in a tar pit.

Idlewild

64A Dyke Road (01273) 774401
Open Mon-Fri 9.30am-5.30pm,
Sat 10am-5.30pm
www.presenttopost.com

This quirky gift shop in the heart of
the Seven Dials stocks a colourful
collection of cards, children's toys, mini
piñatas, candles, mobiles, photo frames,
tins of sweets and more besides. Kids
with pocket money to blow can find
anything from creepy crawlies to
Miffy toys and if you're looking for an
unusual gift, the choices here won't
break the bank. Their excellent website
is full of more of the same and
provides an excellent service – ideal
if you need to send a gift-wrapped
present but can't be arsed to drag
your drug-addled body off the sofa.
Smart.

The Lanes Armoury

26 Meeting House Lane (01273) 321357
Open Mon-Sat 10am-5.15pm
www.thelanesarmoury.co.uk

Souvenir firearms and armour from all periods of history. Get your granny that old Vickers submachine gun she always wanted,or maybe a Luger for young cousin Donald. They also have Kentucky rifles, Zulu war shields, Napoleonic swords and even a helmet from the Iraqi war. A Tudor suit of armour would set you back around £20,000, though the less affluent can buy a cap badge for only £3. If the Ronnie Reagan picture isn't up then nag them to get it back on display as there's a good story behind it.

The Little Juicy Lucy Shop

17 St George's Road, Brighton
(01273) 697017
Open Tue-Fri 10am-5.30pm, Sat 10am-5pm
www.juicylucydesigns.com

'Juicy Lucy' began designing cheeky little fairy cards whilst sitting in her pyjamas in a flat in Kemp Town about ten years ago. Since then she's got dressed, made herself a nice cuppa and turned her hobby into an internationally successful business, supplying over a thousand outlets in the UK and abroad. And whilst on first appearances, this shop could be mistaken purely as a place for children, with its happy fairy cards, mugs and magnets smiling from the window, don't be fooled – many of the designs are really rather naughty! For a free fairy gift, take your *Cheeky Guide* along to the shop!

Oki-Nami Japanese Shop

12 York Place, opposite St Peter's Church
(01273) 677702
Open Mon-Sat 10.30am-6.30pm,
Sun 1pm-5pm

Unique in Brighton, Oki-Nami offers the lot - from lunchboxes and fresh sushi to woks, knives, noodles, calligraphy sets, kimonos, and Hello Kitty everything. It's a little incongruously located in the No Man's Land between London Road and Trafalgar Street, particularly as the shop is so colourful and well-designed

Now, which naughty girl didn't take her Prozac this morning?

compared to neighbouring burger bars and burned-out shops, but against my predictions it seems to be flourishing. It's easy to lose track of time in Oki-Nami as there are two floors of fascinating goodies, many of which will have you asking the shopkeepers, "*err, what is this?*". They also offer sushi lessons for £75 once a month. Loved the bizarre banjo music last time I came in. Recommended.

Painting Pottery Café

31 North Road (01273) 628952
Open Mon-Sat 10am-6pm, Sun 11pm-6pm
first Thursday of the month late night
www.paintingpotterycafe.co.uk
Prices start around £3 for tiles and eggcups

Abiding by the philosophy that everyone is a painter, the Painting Pottery Café is a place where, for a £5 studio fee, you can try your hand at decorating plates, mugs, eggcups and tiles. They will ply you with coffee, hot chocolate and teas for as long as you want, and will even glaze and fire your finished masterpieces. The late-night

Thursday sessions are especially worth attending, as food is laid on and you can bring your own booze. So, men, don't be surprised if after 14 cans of Special Brew you wake the next morning to find eight new eggcups sitting on your kitchen table, each crudely adorned with pictures of your own genitalia.

As well as being immensely popular with families and children, the recent arrival of open art and craft activities in the basement offers a chance for adults to learn how to throw pots and make clay sculptures, papier-mâché mirrors and jewellery through courses or one-off sessions and taster days.

Pardon My French

104a St George's Road, Kemp Town Village
(01273) 694479
Open Mon-Fri 9am-5pm, Sat 10am-5pm
www.pardonmyfrench.co.uk

Run by a lovely eccentric French lady, Mait Faulkes, Pardon My French is a cornucopia of luxurious boudoiresque items, often with a humorous slant. Products range from watering-can handbags, hot-water bottles with boobs and plates from Provence to old enamel signs with such messages as *"Chat Genteel"*, *"Lapin Lunatique"* or (my favourite) *"Attention! Chien Bizarre"*. The whole shop is jam-packed with curious and wonderful items which are, according to Mait *"things my friends like in my house that they can't find anywhere else. I'm not minimal, definitely not minimal!"*

Pussy Home Boutique

Little Pussy 3a Kensington Gardens
(01273) 604861
Big Pussy 3 Bartholomews (01273) 749852
Open Mon-Sat 10am-6pm, Sun 11am-5pm
www.pussyhomeboutique.co.uk

Cross the sexy glamour of Betty Page and the slick design of Frank Lloyd Wright with the cool sounds of Goldfrapp and you're beginning to get an idea of Pussy. Often imitated in Brighton but never equalled, this stylish and saucy boutique boasts a wonderful selection of cool furniture, chic and erotic books (such as the very popular *Big Book of Lesbian Horse Stories* and *Christie Report*), jewellery, *Moomin* crockery, Paul Frank, Tatty Devine, aussieBum pants and T-shirts. Pussy also stock, without doubt, the best cards in town. How could you resist their offensive range that include captions like *"You smell of wee-wee"* or *"Jesus Loves Everyone. Except for You, You Cunt"*?

They've got two shops in Brighton; Little Pussy (the original) in North Laine and Big Pussy in the Old Lanes, which has more of everything and a range of glamorous furniture in the upstairs room. Run by Nicki and her faithful sidekicks the whole gang seem to spend most of the day nattering with half of Brighton over a cup of tea and a fag, yet still manage, unfailingly, to have the best window displays in town. Nicki also has a great talent for predicting trends. Spot something unique in Pussy and, chances are, you'll see it in next month's issue of *Vogue*. Highly recommended.

Pottery sells modestly priced and beautiful earthenware ceramics, all made on the premises, from bowls and plates to more creative figurines and one-off vases. It's also worth coming in and asking about Peter's excellent ten-week pottery classes which, from word of mouth alone, have been full since they began.

Timeslip Videos

Bottom of Trafalgar Street,
Open *"eight days a week"* Mon-Sun
10am-6pm

Steering away from mainstream, big budget and blockbusters, friendly owner Mick has instead an excellent range of old classics (Hitchcock, Powell & Pressburger etc), cult movies and modern world cinema on DVD and video. And with prices ranging from the £4-12 mark, anyone with good taste in films is going to find something here to take home and cherish.

The Workshop Pottery

94 Trafalgar Street
Open Tues-Sat 9.30am-5.30pm
www.workshoppottery.co.uk

Run by Peter Stocker, this shop has been in North Laine an incredible 27 years and has survived a busload of crusties crashing through its window in 1994 and the notorious Southwick earthquake of '78. Peter still remembers the days when North Laine was an area that just sold items like work boots and maids outfits, and scruffy urchins would roam the streets shouting *"Coo! Ta mister!"* when you threw them a tangerine.

Of course, nowadays, the boots are a fashion statement, the maids' outfits are sold for kinky purposes and the scruffy urchins all play in local band The Mutts. But I digress; the Workshop

Yasher Bish

96 Gloucester Road
Open Tues-Sat 10am-6pm, Sun 12noon-4pm

Specialists in all things Turkish, Iranian and Afghani, from ornate backgammon sets, prayer rugs (£15) and goat-herders' bells to a wide range of colourful and very beautiful rugs. Upstairs is packed with original Anatolian pots, some over 100 years old, but still with that faint lingering smell of olive oil. And back by popular demand – the kitsch classic Mosque alarm clocks for only £12!

SPECIALIST CLOTHES SHOPS

From safari suits for him to rubber catsuits for her, Brighton boasts a fine collection of retro, exotic and club-fashion clothes shops, the majority in North Laine. If you want to get kitted out in something especially slinky for a club night or just want something new for the wardrobe, here's a selection of the best places to go.

Colonel Mike's

12 Kensington Gardens (01273) 687811
Open Mon-Sat 11am-6pm, Sun 11am-5pm

The gents who work here are a marvel to behold. A true anomaly among the painfully hip shopkeepers (and customers) in North Laine, they can be found stood to attention in various corners of the shop decked out in army jumpers, boots and trousers, looking for all the world like abandoned Action Men. But really they're very friendly and will attend your every whim, whether you need a Red Welsh Guards jacket for your new band attire, a Russian coat, assault boots for walking across the pebbles on the beach or a full RAF uniform for a fetish party. True, their *"British by birth, English by Grace of God"* T-shirts might raise an eyebrow but there are two floors of fascinating stuff to rifle through from parachutes and shoulder bags to camouflage clothing, and those with an eagle eye for a bargain might like to know they do the cheapest sunglasses and plimsoles in town – for a quid and a fiver respectively. You can even try on the silver fireman's suit, just for fun, as I'm prone to do now and again.

Get Cutie

33 Kensington Gardens
Open Mon-Sat 10.30am-5.30pm,
Sun 12noon-5pm

Celebrated for their beautiful prints and vast array of cool shirts, tops and T-shirts, Get Cutie are a halfway house between Top Shop and Simúltânê, and make beautiful, stylish one-off designer items that might have to be an occasional treat for those on student wages but won't break the bank for the tens of people on decent wages in Brighton. Recommended.

Gresham Blake

20 Bond Street (01273) 609587
www.greshamblake.co.uk

It's good to see someone encouraging the blokes in this town to finally get out of hoodies, jeans and trainers and dress with a little style. Of course style in this case comes at a price. Being a bespoke tailor in North Laine you can't expect Blake to be cheap but you can expect quality suits that give a nod and a wink to chunky English gangsters in 60s Britflicks. If you can't afford a full three-piece, treat yourself to a tie, cufflinks, socks or something from their special range of novelty sombreros.

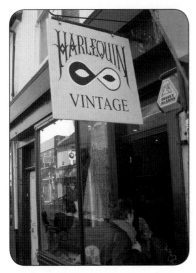

Harlequin

31 Sydney Street (01273) 675222
Open 10am-6pm Mon-Sat, Sun 12noon-6pm
www.harlequin-vintage.co.uk

Step into a world of old-time sartorial elegance: a place decorated with tricycles, gramophones, feathers, fans, a real fire, stained-glass windows and Victorian boxed butterflies, which sells such beautiful items as moleskin top hats, velvet jackets, flapper dresses, 1930s peasant tea dresses and kimonos. While it may raise an eyebrow that this unique little shop is to be found in the kitsch corridors of North Laine, it'll come as no surprise that owner Zoe Bedeaux ran Liberty's vintage section for fifteen years, as her knowledge of the quality and style of yesteryear is evident in every corner. Though really for the ladies, don't be disheartened chaps: Zoe promises a men's equivalent will be opening soon, replete with Victorian tea shop and waitresses in the correct kinky attire. Who wouldn't relish the thought of seeing all the North Laine slackers getting out of their saggy-arsed jeans and ironic T-shirts and into a good smoking jacket and pair of slacks? On a final note, if James is in the shop, get him to tell you about the cast-iron bath sitting in the window. Apparently his daughter was *born* in it! Presumably *before* it got put in the window, but then you never can tell in this town…

Hemp Shop

19 Gardner Street
(01273) 818047
www.thehempshop.co.uk

The oldest-running hemp shop in the UK selling a wide range of clothes, hempseed oil, pasta, Catch Henderson T-shirts, eco-luggage skin care and dreadwax. As approved by hemp-loving Woody Harrelson. And before you ask (as everyone does), no you can't buy a T-shirt here, take it home, smoke it and get high. God knows I've tried.

BUY YOUR OWN
FUCKING LIGHTER

Jump The Gun
36 Gardner Street (01273) 626777
Open Mon-Sat 10am-6pm, Sun 12noon-5pm
www.jumpthegun.co.uk

The UK's *only* exclusive Mod shop,
Jump the Gun has been established in
Brighton for nearly fifteen years now,
and is almost as synonymous with
the city as the Pavilion, clubbing, Chris
Eubank and arson. This well-loved
store boasts a handsome collection
of suits, shirts, parkas, Dr Martens and
coats for the dapper gentleman, all at
very reasonable prices (parkas start
at £75, shirts £40, suits £175-275).
The shop's two owners are brothers
Adam and Jonathan, who live and
breathe the Mod life – arriving to
work on Lambrettas, always dressing
smartly and nipping up Little East
Street every lunchtime for a bit of
how's your father. For those not into
the scene, Jump the Gun is still worth
a visit, for it is as much about proper
tailoring, quality garments, good
treatment and looking sharp as it is
about Mod culture. As Adam puts

it, *"We want our customers to go away
looking like a cross between John Steed
and Sean Connery. But be warned; if you
drink too much, you won't fit into these
clothes!"*

M-Store
37 West Street (01273) 323505
Open Mon-Sat 10am-6pm, Sun 11pm-5pm

Fashion items with a surf and
skateboarding slant from the likes of
Mooks, Insight, Paul Frank and Parka
Rock, all at painfully hip prices.

Paul Bruton Army Surplus
Viaduct Road
Open 10am-1pm and 2pm-4.30pm Wed-Sat

The two masked dummies that stand
guard outside this shop must rank with
the Pavilion and the West Pier as some
of the most famous monuments of
Brighton. Both creatures have posed
with innumerable tourists and even
appear on an album cover by some
obscure Scottish band. Like Colonel
Mike's, the stock in here is immense:
you can get kitted out in just about
any uniform you fancy, from the pith
helmet and khaki shorts style of *It 'Aint
Half Hot Mum*, to the German guards
in *Escape from Colditz*. And the dressing
booth is fantastic, but you'll have to go
in to find out why!

Route One

3 Bond Street (01273) 323633
Open Mon-Sat 9.30am-6pm, Sun 11am-5pm
www.routeone.co.uk

The guys in here are friendly, sell skating clothes of the jeans-hanging-off-your-arse variety and have a decent selection of boards, wheels, trucks etc. They are also pretty knowledgeable on the current scene and can tell you some of the better places to skate in Brighton.

She Said

Exclusive lingerie, corsetry, and erotic accessories (see *Sex, Fetish etc*).

Simultané Ltd

37 Trafalgar Street (01273) 818061
Open Mon-Sat 11am-6pm, Sun 11am-5pm
www.simultane.co.uk

Whenever Simultané* comes up in conversation amongst my female friends there is a perceptible change of atmosphere in the room, as if Johnny Depp had just walked in wearing nothing but a sock over his John Thomas. Designed and made by local designer Sarah Arnett, Simultané's clothes may not be pricey but they are, according to the ladies, to die for. With a slight nod towards 40s and 50s glamour, many of the garments here have featured in Vogue, sold at Liberty's, or been exhibited during London and Paris fashion weeks. As well as beautiful design, attention to detail and great cuts, another appeal of Sarah's clothes lies in the fact that all the prints here are designed in-house and are quite stunning. Simultané has a wide range of accessories, jewellery and homeware as well as a gallery and exhibition space for local artists and designers: check out the original artwork for old Mills & Boon covers!

Yamama

92 Trafalgar Street (01273) 689931
Open Mon-Sat 11am-6pm, Sun 12noon-5pm

A colourful range of interesting and fair-priced clothing with an urban-hippy slant, from baggy trousers and hemp clothing to shirts and skirts for the bohemian traveller-type.

**it's pronounced Simultane, not 'Simultainay', the
'é' is merely a poncy imposter!*

FATBOY SLIM'S

all season fashion tips

Hello! Norman 'Fatboy Slim' Cook here, come to give you some fashion tips! And I reckon I'm a bit of a style guru, because once I was watching What Not To Wear *with Zoë and she said: "You should be on this programme, Norman," so she obviously reckons I'd make a better presenter than them! So, without further ado, here's Norm's guide to how to look and feel good, whatever the weather.*

Summer

Summers in Brighton always remind me of being a kid. You know – deck chairs, buckets 'n' spades, weeing in the sea. Nowadays I spend my summers idling on the beach, pottering around the house listening to records, or even making my own by cobbling together a few R'n'B samples with a drum loop! No really! It's as easy as that!!!

And what could be more perfect for those long hot, sticky months than to slip into a cool, thin, colourful, 100% cotton Hawaiian shirt? They're comfortable, stylish, eye-catching, and make you look like a real 'Funk Soul Brother.'

Autumn

Now a lot of people see this time of year as an excuse to start sporting knitwear and favouring such autumnal colours as burnt oranges, dark browns and reds. This I believe is a terrible mistake! You wouldn't catch me going out in a snowstorm dressed all in white!!!

Take a tip from me – dare to be different! Why not go for something colourful, and striking? Like a Hawaiian shirt, say! And, when everyone else is turning up to those Halloween parties in black (yawn!), you'll steal the show with a dazzle of colour on your back!!!

Winter

Like many people I tend to suffer from the winter blues, especially during the long months from January to March. If I look out of my bedroom window in the morning and it's cold, miserable and grey outside, my spirits start to flag and, before I know it, I'm comatose in front of the box with a jazz mag in one hand and a joint in the other, watching Kilroy talk to middle-aged housewives about teenage pregnancy. God, do I get depressed!! Until, that is, I remember my faithful Hawaiian shirt! Once I've whipped off my jim-jams and got that cool cotton and splash of colour on my back it feels like a little bit of the summer has returned, leaving me with a rosy complexion and a chance again to face the world with a smile. I recommend you do the same. Magic!

Spring

Now during the 'rainy season', a lot of people favour waterproof coats with hoods. This, I believe, is a terrible mistake. And can be extremely dangerous! Did you know that wearing a hood can reduce visibility by up to 37%?!! If, for example, you were crossing the busy A27 between Worthing and Shoreham, your so-called 'sensible' hooded raincoat might protect you from the wet, but would offer precious little protection when you failed to notice the 30-tonne Juggernaught that was hurtling towards you, smashing into you at a 120 miles an hour and crushing your head like a ripe melon.

So don't be silly. Be safe!! Make yourself visible when crossing the road. Why not go out just wearing something brightly-coloured – something like, say, just for the sake of argument... a Hawaiian shirt?!! Sure you might get soaked, catch a cold, or worse, pneumonia, but at least you'll be safe.

Right – I'm off now;
I've got until tomorrow to write
a new album. Not a problem!!!
Praise you!!!!!
Norm

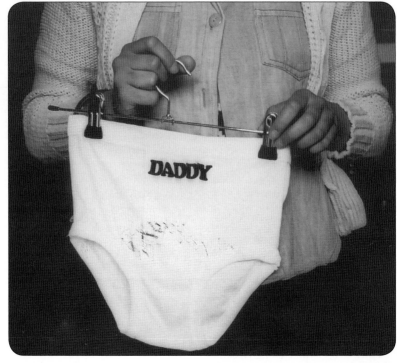

X 2 Zee
27 Western Road
Open Mon-Sat 10am-6pm,
Sun 11.30am-5.30pm

Boots and shoes of every colour, shape and size from thigh-high boots to glittery DMs and with a nod towards goth culture. They also do a rather odd collection of faded punk and metal band T-shirts. Curiously, I popped in last Christmas to find the owner sat in the middle of the shop with a half-empty bottle of spirits in his hand smoking a fat cigar, listening to loud music and having a thoroughly good time. In his inebriated state, he did sell me shoelaces that were eight times too big for my shoes but hats off to the man, he clearly knows how to let his hair down at work.

HIGH STREET STORES AND DESIGNER LABEL SHOPS

For the ladies there's a wide range of clothes and shoe shops around the Old Lanes including the likes of Nine West, Design Lab, Offspring and Morgan in Duke Street; French Connection, Jigsaw, Monsoon, Mango and Laura Ashley on East Street; Moist, Fat Face and Oasis in Duke's Lane. If you're looking for Miss Selfridge, Hennes and Warehouse you'll find them up by Churchill Square, along with most other predictable high street clothes.

Guys, err… Top Man and Hennes anyone?

Circe's Island
22 Trafalgar Street

Decorated with plastic birds, palm trees and fishing netting hanging from the ceiling, Circe's Island is an exotic cavern of vintage clothes and shoes. Unlike most other North Laine second-hand shops, the emphasis here is on the exotic and glamorous rather than the usual tatty denim jackets and Hawaiian shirts. If it's made of feather, fake fur, sequins, satin or leather, you'll find it here (if you don't mind the smell of roll-ups, that is).

Launderette
49 Grand Parade (01273) 692068
Open Mon-Sat 10.30am-6pm
www.launderette-exchange.co.uk

Vintage clothes shops are nothing new around Brighton but bubbly duo Tam and Clare have come up with a twist based on US thrift stores, whereby you can bring your old (clean please, they're not a *real* launderette) stuff in and if they want it then you get anything off their racks for half price. If your castoffs are too grim they'll still take them and pass them on to the Emmaus charity project, and they promise not to guffaw at your previous fashion gaffes until you've left the premises. The gear in here is a more modern take on retro stylings rather than the usual acres of velvet, and includes new creations from young designers at pretty reasonable prices; I've watched a couple of lady friends cooing over their label shoe selection, most of which didn't even look like they'd been worn outdoors, and starting prices were £20. As well as a humorous line in window displays they've got a keen eye for what's natty, so if you can't find anything you like in here, you're probably blind.

Shabitat

Lewes Road, opposite The Bear pub
(01273) 677577
Open Mon-Fri 9am-5pm, Sat 10am-4pm
www.magpie.coop/shabitat.php
www.leftover.co.uk

A dirty great sky-blue warehouse by
the Hangleton gyratory might not
be most people's first port of call
for intriguing second-hand clobber,
but the selection in the back room
of Magpie Recycling Co-op's HQ
is so mind-bendingly cheap you'd
be well advised to drop by before
you hit North Laine and lash out
a fortune on a garish orange tie
with an inexplicable stain. Coats are
three pounds, trousers two, and if
you've only got a quid you can still
get some headgear. Why this place
isn't mobbed every Saturday is an
enduring mystery – I can only assume
hardly anyone knows it's here. There's
also a smattering of 'reconstructed'
garments by Leftover, giving a new
lease of life to sweatshirts and skirts
via the clothcutter's equivalent of
gene splicing. The remainder of this
cavernous barn is given over to
second hand furniture, the pricing
strategy for which eludes me, ranging
as it does from £2 for a table to a
bizarre painting of Hattie Jacques'
disembodied head floating on 60s
wallpaper for £200.

To Be Worn Again

51 Providence Place (01273) 624500 &
Sydney Street (01273) 680296
Open 11am-7pm Mon-Sat, 12noon-4pm Sun

Hidden away just off Trafalgar Street
opposite St Bartholomew's church, this
is the biggest second-hand clothing
warehouse in Brighton. The stock
comprises the usual 70s shirts, leather
and suede jackets and paisley dresses
but as there's so much of everything
you're more likely to find something
suitable for a night at Dynamite
Boogaloo. Don't miss the backroom
with a great selection of coats, including
three-quarter and full-length fake
furs. It's usually quiet in there, even at
weekends: perfect if you're in the mood
for trying on loads of things. The shop
on Sydney Street also sells trainers,
bags and retro furniture upstairs. Nice.

Traid

39 Duke Street (01273) 746346
Open Mon-Sat 10am-6pm, Sun 11am-5.30pm
www.traid.org.uk

A welcome anomaly among all the
trendy clothes stores on Duke's Street,
Traid is a sort of upmarket Oxfam
whose policy is to favour certain
clothes styles for particular areas.
While many of their London shops
tend to focus on second-hand designer
gear, here the emphasis is on retro
and sportswear, though to be honest
they seem to have a good all-round
selection of fake furs, dresses, jackets
and accessories. What is unique,
however, is their Remade range: old
shirts, jackets and dresses, re-cycled
by adding slogans and different bits of
material to turn them into one-offs.
It's the fashion equivalent of sampling I
suppose…

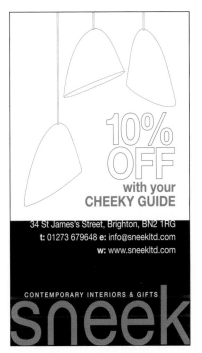
MUSICAL INSTRUMENTS

Adaptatrap
26 Trafalgar Street (01273) 672722
Open Mon-Sat 10am-6pm

This place sells a whole range of drums, koras, xylophones, singing bowls, old gongs, horns and many other exotic and strange instruments from all over the world. What's more, they don't mind you coming in and playing with them. Owner Les is helpful and will smoke an entire roll-up without taking it out of his mouth whilst offering advice on what to do if you've damaged your congas (ooh, missus).

The shop is littered with ads for music lessons so if you're sticking around Brighton and need that all-essential sitar teacher, this is the place to look. You'll also find out about workshops and gigs here, ranging from zither recitals to shamanic drumming weekends.

The Guitar, Amp and Keyboard Centre
79-80 North Road (01273) 672977
Open Mon-Sat 9.30am-5.30pm,
Sun 11am-4pm
www.gak.co.uk

Created from the barrow-boy charm of its haggle-friendly owner Gary who turned up in Brighton ten years ago with just a broken banjo and the gift of the gab. Since then he has built himself an empire which seems to dominate half of North Road, with separate shops for every imaginable instrument. There're the Drum Cavern, Bass Basement, Didge Depot and Bongo Boutique to name but a few. True, GAK has become a victim of its own success, growing so large that the intimacy between customer and seller has been lost, but despite that it still seems to have kept some of Gary's "*sod it, call it a tenner mate*" approach to life. Will accept body parts as down-payment.

Acoustic Music Company
39 St James's Street (01273) 671841
www.theacousticmusicco.co.uk

I gave up trying to review this place as when I came in the guy seemed to be on the phone for hours and didn't acknowledge my presence. And besides I'm getting to be an impatient bugger these days. But they do sell a rather magnificent range of handmade acoustic guitars and mandolins with prices ranging from the hundreds to the thousands. So presumably they're better than the ones in the Argos catalogue.

ChoccyWoccyDooDah

24 Duke Street (01273) 329462
Open Mon-Fri 10am-6pm,
Sat 12noon-4pm, Sun 10am-5pm
www.choccywoccydoodah.com

You'll forgive the ludicrous name
the second you enter, take in that
sweet smell of Belgian chocolate and
marvel at the most outrageous, over-
the-top chocolate cakes you've ever
seen. They've got spiky fetish cakes,
ones covered in realistic vegetables
(including carrots and cabbage), ones
with willies, roses, mermaids and more
besides. If you can't afford a cake
(their top-notch wedding cakes can
cost up to £1,000), they do gold coins
and Cuban cigars for under a fiver,
though their consistent bestsellers
continue to be the chocolate shoes
and solid chocolate dogs like Ruby, the
bulldog puppy. Head of Creativity here
is the infamous Mr Dave Pop, also
renowned for his kitsch songs and
live appearances at various Brighton
venues over the years. If you want to
show him your appreciation, you can
actually buy a DVD of his greatest hits
or marvel at his artwork that hangs
above the counter.

CyberCandy Sweet Shop

98 Gloucester Road
0845 801 8815
Open Mon-Fri 10.30am-6.30pm,
Sat 10am-7pm, Sun 11am-6pm
www.cybercandy.co.uk

Unique in Brighton, CyberCandy must
surely be the only shop to have seven-
year-old kids and 40 year olds standing
side by side, drooling over the items
on display. Sweetie lovers, you'll think
you've died and gone to heaven when
you come here. With everything from
retro classics such as Pez and Texan
Bars (yes, they've been 're-issued'!) to
special imports like almond M&Ms,
banana Kit-Kats and peanut butter

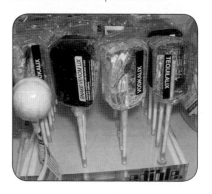

Twix, you'll be predicting an extra filling
or two before you even get to the till.
Check out the far wall, where they've
got more than 50 types of jelly bean,
including Bertie Bott's vomit flavour!

If esoteric sweets are more your
bag, you won't be disappointed with
their Swedish candy Plopp and Kack,
while lovers of the downright bizarre
can tuck into snake-venom lollies,
vodka-flavoured ants and amber-toffee
scorpions! And to think I spent my
childhood chewing on Fruit Salads and
Blackjacks.

Doggy Fashion
1 Grafton Street (01273) 695631
23 George Street, Hove (01273) 777555
Open Tues-Fri 8.30am-5pm, Sat 8.30am-4pm
Hove Tues-Sat 10am-5pm
www.doggyfashion.co.uk

Offering everything from home-knitted Spanish jumpers and beaded collars made by the Kenyan Masai tribe to diamante collars from Vegas, Doggy Fashion is nothing less than Harrods for dogs. Half an hour in this place and your furry chum could be walking out in style in a bespoke coat, sunhat, diamante collar and bow tie. After an hour he could even be sporting a Mohican, as they also offer a one-hour pooch pampering service. And according to the lady in here *"every time Beckham changes his hair, the request from the dogs' owners changes accordingly"*.

Thoughtfully placed in Kemp Town and George Street to cater for the gay crowd and the old ladies of Hove, Doggy Fashion has been a huge success since opening nearly ten years ago, and has featured in fashion magazines and celebrity dog shows.

Pet owners take note though: they only do **dogs**! The people who brought their rabbit in to be shaved and their budgerigar to have its toenails clipped had to be turned away. (Saying that, they're cool with kinky gentlemen who pop in occasionally to purchase collars and leads for their partners!). Go on, spoil your dog!

The Olde Rock Shop
West Pier, opposite Regency Square
Open Mon-Sun winter 9am-5pm,
summer 8.30am-late

Of the dozens of gift shops that litter the seafront, this one alone deserves a mention as the building is a period piece, has stood on the same spot for over 126 years and can be spotted in the many films made here from *Carry On Girls* to *Oh, What a Lovely War!* They sell all the typical tourist stuff from sticks of rock to snowstorms, fridge magnets and pottery lighthouses. And their seagull poo chocolates make great presents for kids.

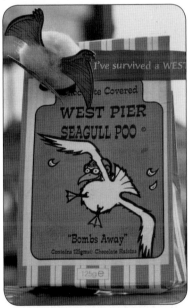

Taylors (Tobacconist)
19 Bond Street (01273) 606110
Open 10am-6pm, Sun 11am-5pm

A THANK YOU FOR SMOKING sign welcomes you as you enter, and the wide range of flavoured hand-rolling tobaccos (including chocolate), lighters and Cuban cigars reminds me why it took ten years to kick such a pleasurable habit. Go on, have a fag.

MARKETS

The Sunday Market
Behind Brighton Station
Open 6am-12noon

As much a part of this town as the Pavilion, a weekend in Brighton is not complete without a trip to the Sunday carboot at the station. It's *"Portobello on a budget"* as my friend Dermot succinctly put it. And while the serious bargain hunters arrive before seven, most sensible (and hungover) Brightonians roll up around ten. Sure, if you come at this time you'll have missed **all** of the bargains but you'll still get to peruse miles of tat, munch on a hotdog and keep your eyes peeled for your stolen DVD collection.

Having slimmed down in size since the pointless building of a Sainsbury's (within spitting distance of another **two** Sainsbury's) on the original site, the market is still packed to the hilt with record, DVD and video stalls, dealers in antiques and retro furniture, clothes sellers, food stalls and so much crap that you'll be either convulsed with laughter or so incensed you'll have a coronary as you spy second-hand tubes of haemorrhoid cream for £5, the leg of an Action Man for £8 and the cassette demo of a shit band you were in twelve years ago for £15.

One tip – don't be afraid to haggle; if something seems too expensive, say so. If the stall owner won't accept your generous offer of 50p for an original boxed Rolf Harris stylophone with wah-wah, take satisfaction in rolling your eyes, huffing, then walking off. If it was a bluff on their behalf they'll run after you and beg forgiveness…

Saturday in North Laine
Upper Gardner Street
Saturdays only 10am-4pm

This small weekly market in North Laine is nothing to get too excited about but get there early and you might pick up a cool pair of jeans, an old typewriter or a good book for a few quid. Get there after twelve and it'll be you and a hundred other people all huddled round a broken cine camera that's going for £60. But quality aside it's pleasant to wander down and peruse the junk, and a good alternative to being squashed in Kensington Gardens on a hot, busy Saturday afternoon.

Puny earthling, we shall soon destroy your planet - if only we could get out of these cursed pots

Old Post Office Market

Ship Street
Open Wed-Fri 11am-5pm, Sat 10am-6pm,
Sun 12noon-5pm
www.shipstreetmarket.co.uk

When the old Ship Street post office closed down and moved next door (for reasons I have yet to comprehend), it came as a pleasant surprise that the empty building was to be used as an indoor market. While the overall flavour of this place may be a touch too New Age for some people's tastes, there are plenty of curios in here, from designer clothes and jewellery stalls to homemade organic body products and animals made out of moss. In fact the emphasis here seems definitely on the handmade rather than the kitsch and retro and the whole place is more like a corner of Camden Market than Snoopers. Sadly the two-year countdown has already started to when it gets converted into (yes, you guessed it) luxury flats, so snap up those moss rabbits before they're run over by bulldozers and turned into doormats.

The West Pier Market
Weekends only

If you slept through the alarm at 11am for the station carboot sale, don't fret. A leisurely stroll down to the charred remains of the West Pier after lunch will more than compensate. Here you will find an eclectic array of stalls and friendly stallholders, flogging everything from clothes, books and sunglasses to painted eggs and sea monkeys (remember the miniscule creatures that used to be advertised in the back of old 1960s Marvel comics?).

Despite council grumblings, the West Pier market reflects much more of the personality of Brighton seafront than many of the other things built here. Any old seaside resort can have cafés and clubs on its seafront, but only in Brighton will you find chancers doing head massages, magic tricks and Tarot readings, writing on grains of rice (no, really) and selling bloody sea monkeys. And long may they reign. Take them away, and Brighton would turn into Skegness overnight.

FLEA MARKETS

Kemp Town Flea Market
31a Upper St James's Street
(01273) 328665
Open Mon-Sat 10am-5.30pm,
Sun 10.30am-5pm

Keep going up St James's Street and you'll find this garish, pink, two-storey building just after the road bends. There's the usual overpriced stuff in here but you might find some really unusual objects here and, dare I say it – the odd bargain?

There isn't much in the way of clothes, but there used to be a good stock of accessories for the house, like 60s lamps. Stock, however, seemed a bit thin on the ground last time I visited, and the window display was decidedly flaccid compared to past classics such as the skeleton in the deck chair. Is it still worth the trek from the city centre? I really don't know. If only the alligator lamp in there was for sale…

North Laine Antique Flea Market
Upper Gardner Street (01273) 600894
Open 10-5…ish, Mon-Sat…probably.
OK, truth is I don't really know

Being smaller and just off the beaten track in North Laine, this place tends to get overlooked in favour of Snoopers, its elder brother. Snoopers, of course, has the edge over all other flea markets in Brighton for its size, range of stock and vast collection of weird and wonderful retro items all selling at knock-up prices. This place is a little more like a jumble sale after the vultures have had their fill but still has the odd bargain for those in the know. Best visited on Saturdays when the outdoor market is on and there's more to see outside. I spotted *Allo Allo!* on DVD here for £18 on my last visit! Now *that's* funny.

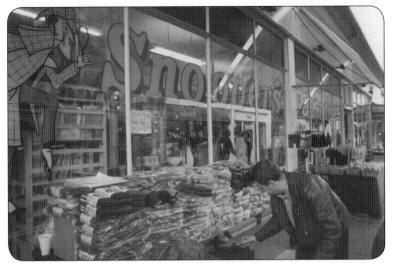

Snoopers Paradise
7-8 Kensington Gardens (01273) 602558
Open Mon-Sat 9.30am-5.15pm

Brighton's largest indoor flea market with two floors of stock which include a particularly good collection of 60s clothes, retro ephemera and furniture. It can't be denied that Snoopers is a cherished Brighton institution; somewhere to wile away an afternoon marvelling at the sheer size of it all and perusing everything from Victorian ephemera to second-hand undies.

However if you have a heart condition you might wish to keep away as you could find yourself taking the Lord's name in vain while uttering things like, "*Sixty quid......... for **that**?????*" or, "*I threw one of those away last year and they're selling it here for £200!!!! Aaaaarggghhh!!!!!!!*"

Then take a deep breath and thank the Lord that Snoopers hasn't yet been turned into a café bar or luxury housing. Amen.

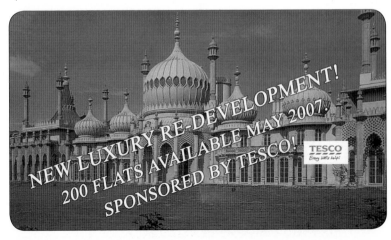

Cafés & Café-Bars

KEY TO CAFÉ LOCATIONS

C	–	City centre
H	–	Hove
HA	–	Hanover
K	–	Kemp Town
NL	–	North Laine
OL	–	Old Lanes
PC	–	Preston Circus
S	–	Seafront
SK	–	Skegness

Bill's @ The Depot (NL)
100 North Street (01273) 692894
Open Mon-Sun 8am-8pm, Sun 10am-4pm
www.billsproducestore.co.uk

A surprising but welcome export from the nearby *Wicker Man* island of Lewes, Bill's is a vision of the future for cafés the world over, overshadowing much that once seemed fresh and innovative in Brighton. Visit for the first time and it's like stumbling onto the set of an old Peter Greenaway or Jeunet et Caro film, such is the vast array of colours, sights and smells that greets you, not to mention the sheer scale of the place. Bill's is a café, delicatessen, epicerie, takeaway and greengrocer all rolled into one; great attention to detail is evident in its design, from the *Brazil*-style pipework that snakes across the ceiling to the beautiful etched windows at the front, though really it is the sheer volume of produce on display here that steals the show. There is food simply *everywhere*; from rows and rows of fruit and veg to pickles, sauces, oils and biscuits adorning the walls at the back; from fancy cakes like Ascot hats to the pies and pastries behind the counter.

In the centre of it all lies the café space: a jigsaw of wooden tables that can accommodate anything from two to twenty people, lending something of a canteen feel. Sit here and ogle the food, watch the chef wander out and choose the veg for his next dish and – if you end up sat on one of the long tables – make some new friends.

As well as the more obvious salads, pizzas, quiches, soups and tartlets on the menu, Bill's also does a nice line in comfort food: try the fish-finger sandwiches, Welsh rarebit, pancakes or the eclectic array of breakfasts. Or how about the rhubarb crumble smoothie – a pudding in a drink? The choice on offer means you'll never tire of visiting; there really is so much to sample.

Despite being located in Brighton's draughty old bus depot (hence the huge ceiling), Bill's thrives in winter and, should you feel a bit of a gust round your gusset, you'll find the staff whizzing around handing out hot-water bottles on especially cold days – another nice touch.

Unsurprisingly, this place is rather popular and space can be at a premium. Standing at the back waiting for a table during busy times can be a bit of a drag and you might find yourself in the way of those perusing the shelves or trying to get past to the loos, but you can do a little browsing of your own: marvel at the Dorset Knobs, Bill's own range of sauces or drool over the specials on the daily board.

A feast for the eyes as well as the belly and heartily recommended. **Top tip:** Try to get a table on the balcony, where the panorama of edibles is even more edifying.

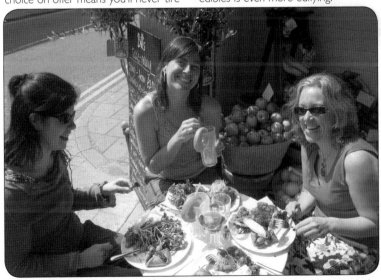

Cherry Tree (K)

107 St James' Street, (01273) 698684
Open Mon-Sat 8am-7pm, Sun 9am-7pm

Offering real oven-baked potatoes, mozzarella with everything, stuffed vine leaves and magnificent salads, this tiny café/deli in the heart of Kemp Town is an authentic slice of excellent healthy Mediterranean cuisine with dried food hung up around the place and staff chattering away in Italian and riding mopeds around and over the tables. And, speaking of tables, they've only got about four so it's best avoided at busy times unless you're prepared to wait. And if you do end up waiting (it's worth it), pester them to do something about their horrible ceiling.

The Cowley Club (PC)

12 London Road
Open weekdays 12noon-4pm (I think)
www.cowleyclub.org.uk

"Is it OK to take a photo? I'm doing a review for The Cheeky Guide to Brighton."
"I dunno mate, probably have to take it to the committee. I can let you know next Friday."

Welcome to the Cowley Club, a co-operatively-run anarchist café/ bookshop which takes its name from Harry Cowley, a local working-class agitator who campaigned tirelessly to improve the lives of his fellow workers until his death in 1971. The interior has a friendly handcrafted feel to it, with comfy mismatched chairs and panelled walls. Here you can buy zines, anarchist classics, books on anti-technology and feminism, pick up a copy of *Schnews*, have a tinkle on the piano or get your head stuck into such weighty tomes as *1983 Gender Issues in Patagonia*.

Mr Cyclops enjoys a nice cuppa at the Dorset

The café is open to all during the day and offers the best-value veggie food in the city, with most dishes priced at around £2. The cuisine can be something of a mixed affair, depending on who has volunteered to cook – a friend of mine ordered a platter of roast veg and was a tad nonplussed when a bowl of warm tinned spaghetti turned up. But usually it's good wholesome fare.

In the evening the bar opens. It *can* be a lairy affair here at weekends but during the week is a great spot for occasional live-music events: its homemade authentic atmosphere is ideal for intimate gigs. The only problem is, to come here in the evening you will need to be a member, and to be a member you'll need to have your name put forward by a current member. And thus the paradox of ordered anarchy doth prevail. An elite political organisation dedicated to ridding the world of elite political organisations... oh the irony... but as a pocket of resistance to Brighton's (and the world's) headlong drive towards cappuccino-snorting shopping addiction, the Cowley Club deserves our support. Harry would be proud.

The Dorset Street Bar (NL)
28 North Road (01273) 605423
Mon-Sat 10am-11pm, Sun 10am-8pm

A visit to Brighton really is not complete without eggs benedict, a coffee and a pose outside the Dorset. As well as offering a range of good beers, warm drinks and food – ranging from hot meat baguettes to mussels and a delicious seafood chowder – the Dorset has an enviable location on the corner of North Road and Gardner Street where, on warm summer afternoons, you can sit outside and marvel at the style gurus parading through North Laine. If you're local it's unlikely you'll pass an afternoon without spotting a host of familiar faces passing by to have a natter with (unless you've got no mates, that is) or even have a chance encounter with the smiley bloke who always carries a ghetto blaster and plastic bag full of CDs and takes requests (last time he nobbled me I asked for ELO's *Mr Blue Sky* and he had it!)

Top tip: Bring your own mayonnaise. For a place that knows how to be kind to its customers, their insistence on charging 45p for a dollop of the stuff seems a tad mean spirited.

THE COWLEY CLUB

Ethel ponders the consequences of her bourgeois existence before nipping off to Woolies to stock up on hairnets

Dumb Waiter (NL)

28 Sydney Street (01273) 602526
Open Mon-Wed 9am-6pm,
Thurs-Sat 9am-10pm, Sun 10am-3.30pm

Despite being decorated like the set
of a mid-90s sitcom, this laid-back
family-run café actually makes a
refreshing change from the transient
and overly trendy nature of North
Laine. True, it still seems to attract a
fair number of Brighton's dying breed
of dreadlocked, roll-up-smoking new-
age community but don't let their
bongo playing put you off your food
as this is still one of the cheapest
places in town for grub and does
a cracking breakfast for veggies
and carnivores alike – ideal for that
Sunday morning hangover cure. The
rest of the menu is straightforward
nosh: baked potatoes, soup, sausage
sarnies and some good puddings
(including treacle tart and custard).
Some evenings they're now open
for dinner, when the food becomes
slightly more adventurous, with exotic

burgers and salads, and you can bring
your own booze for a great-value night
out. There's also seating upstairs, a
couple of plastic tables outside by the
loos and a noticeboard for cello tutors,
eco-friendly plumbers and lonely-hearts
ads for non-smoking vegetarian cats.

Frank-in-Steine (C)

By the fountain in the Old Steine, at Grand
Parade (01273) 674742
Open 8am-8pm in summer,
9am-5pm in winter

Well, if your name's Frank, and you're
opening up a café in a converted toilet
in the Old Steine, what else *could* you
call it – 'Some flushers do have 'em'?

Not only is the Frankenstein motif
everywhere, from the napkins to the
mosaics and old movie posters on the
walls, but go downstairs and you'll find
a ghost-train style cage with a life-size
Frankenstein's monster inside. Sadly,
he suffers the indignity of sharing his
confinement with mops and cardboard
boxes, which rather take the edge off
the fright, though the barbed-wire toilet
seats might make you jump.

Along with Frankie, the two other
café mascots were Patsy and Clarence,
two weird orange frogs in a fishbowl to
the left of the counter, but one of them
has now passed on. If you own a child,
give it the task of trying to work out
the gender of the remaining one and
the required continuous staring into
the bowl should produce an unerringly
amphibious eye bulge. Or do it yourself
and unnerve the staff by ordering
a sandwich immediately afterwards.
Staying on the theme of kids, Frank-in-
Steine is very child friendly; they even
go to the bother of putting out boxes
of toys and bikes on the grass for kids
to play with, leaving you to relax, stuff
your face and have a crafty cigarette.

The grub here is your standard café/takeaway fare: chunky toasted sandwiches, cold sarnies, wraps, danishes and rolls for breakfast, coffee and juices etc. But while the food's nothing to shout about, Frank's remains one of the best places in the summer to escape the crowds, enjoy a spot of greenery and leg room and feel the soft spray of a nearby fountain on your chops.

Guaraná Bar (NL)

36 Sydney Street (01273) 621406
Open Mon-Sat 10am-6pm, Sun 12noon-5pm
www.goguarana.co.uk

"Europe's first Guarana Bar!" is the motto for this unique place in North Laine, which to most people (including myself) begs the question *"yes, but what **is** guarana?"* Well, having done my homework and sampled the stuff, I can tell you that it's a South American 'super-charged' natural energy drink, said to put a skip in your step and hairs on your chest. And very refreshing it is too (if you like the taste of wet grass). It is, however, just one of the many unusual and natural stimulating drinks and herbs on offer here. The closest comparisons I can think of for this place are the Smart Bars of Amsterdam as, alongside wheatgrass, coffees and other freshly-made brews, they stock an incredible range of smoking paraphernalia (grinders, pipes, scales etc), American Spirit cigarettes, herbal highs (Druid's Fantasy, Bliss Xtra), nutritional supplements, mild hallucinogenics (legal, of course) and aphrodisiacs. Ideal for those in search of a healthy pick-me-up or a mind-expanding experience, without the usual teeth grinding, bad trips and lousy comedowns. There's also a 30-seater café space upstairs. And before you ask, yes, it does attract more than the odd nutter.

Infinity Café (NL)

50 Gardner Street (01273) 670743
Open Mon-Sat 10am-5pm

This veggie/vegan café in the heart of North Laine was born out of Infinity Foods' incredible success and has the food to match. The menu is 95% organic, the coffee is fair trade, they offer a takeaway option, and there's thorough information on which items support your current intolerance, be it dairy, wheat, gluten, *Insight City News* or myxomatosis. Expect queuing at lunchtime, though you should always be able to find a seat upstairs and, besides, those salads are well worth waiting for – you can almost feel your body quiver with gratitude as you shovel them down.

Inside Out Café (NL)

95 Gloucester Road (01273) 692912
Open from 8am

Formerly Jack Horner's (yes, it's on a corner), Inside Out is one of the most convivial cafés in North Laine, boasting a good chef, an interesting range of well-cooked grub and the strangest toilet in Brighton. Open from eight o'clock every morning, this is the perfect spot to start the day with a good continental breakfast, eggs florentine, muesli and yoghurt or a more traditional full English if your belly is rumbling. At lunch you might be battling over the seats but it's worth it for their extensive array of panini, ciabatta and other mouth-watering breads with a whole range of fillings. Particularly impressive are their kids' menu (tiger toast is a winner with the ankle-biters), proper lemon pressé, chai latte and the delicious-looking cakes that sit in the cabinet by the door begging to be sampled.

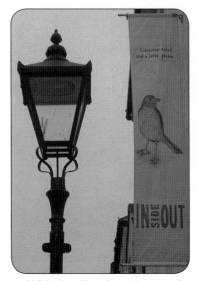

While the décor here gives a nod to the Spanish artist Cesar Manrique's love of cacti and mosaics, the two-way mirror in the toilet was the inspiration of owner James and is rather disconcertingly placed to give a full view of the café to anyone sitting down on the job. With that in mind, the obvious fun to be had here is to plonk yourself at the table closest to the mirror for the afternoon and whenever anyone goes to the loo, stare at where you think they're sat, look horrified and mouth the words, "*we can see you having a poo*". If they're new to the café they'll come out with a face like a beetroot sandwich. I know, I know, I have a childish sense of humour.

Jack and Linda's (S)

197 King's Arches
Open Fri-Sun 10am-5pm and weekdays throughout the warmer months

Located just to the left of the Fishing Museum, this is the place to stop for a seafood snack on Brighton seafront. Ex-fisherman and fisherwoman Jack and Linda have been here for over five years now, dishing out their mouth-wateringly delicious takeaway fish soup, smoked mackerel and potted crab, all at giveaway prices. The soup alone ranks amongst my top-ten favourite things about Brighton! Sit and slurp it in one of the upturned boats by the boardwalk and pretend you're in *The Poseidon Adventure*.

Mad Hatter (C)

35 Montpelier Road
(01273) 722279
Open Mon-Sat 8am-8pm, Sun 10am-6pm
(alternate Sundays 11pm)
www.themadhattercafe.co.uk

Spacious, colourful café on Western Road with a new-age slant (judging from its hippy/boho crowd and ads on the walls for tai chi classes and pre-anxietal wheat-free crystal unicorn therapy). The grub is a fair selection of healthy salads, toasted ciabatta, pizza, cheesecakes and various teas and cold drinks but, thanks to the *Alice in Wonderland* theme (look for the model of the Mad Hatter hanging over the counter) you might cringe when having to order a Tweedledum or Tweedledee from the menu.

Highlights include the outside seating area, where you can sit and soak up the sun and the bus fumes in summer; the open-mic nights; performances; and their regular diner Angela, an eccentric old lady who's often spotted in here clutching her teddy bear.

In the past I've sampled meals here which have ranged from delicious to utterly tasteless (and an avocado sandwich really should not hurt your teeth) but as it was changing hands the week before writing this, it would seem unfair to tarnish the new owners with past culinary crimes. A welcome addition to that raddled behemoth known as Western Road, could Mad Hatter be *the* place to spearhead a revolution to transform this tawdry part of town into the new North Laine? I live in hope.

The Meeting Place (S)
Hove Sea Wall, Kingsway,
right on the seafront! (01273) 206417
Open 7am to sunset all year round
(weather permitting)

Set up as a temporary kiosk in
1935, the council characteristically
dragged its heels in allowing planning
permission for this seafront café as
a more permanent structure and
the thumbs-up only came through
in 2002! Not one to miss an
opportunity, its owner soon had the
place rebuilt… five metres to the left,
thus craftily relocating from Hove to
Brighton (well who wouldn't, given the
choice?). For me, the Meeting Place
ranks amongst the ten best reasons
for living in Brighton: it's literally a
stone's throw from the sea, the views
are terrific, it's far enough away from
the piers to avoid the weekend
crowds and, on a warm summer
morning, is the perfect spot to have
breakfast, read the paper in your
pants, get a suntan and throw yourself
in the sea. Heroically it stays open
throughout the bleakest of winters

but, as it's a Brighton tradition to
make a pilgrimage here on Christmas
morning for a coffee, you'll even see
queues then. The food is classic caff
grub – jacket potatoes, toasties and
chips, milkshakes, cakes, cakes and more
cakes. The café to come to if you want
the traditional Brighton experience
rather than the designer one.

Mock Turtle (OL)
4 Pool Valley (01273) 327380
Open Tues-Sat 10am-6pm, lunch served
11.30am-2.30pm

This wonderfully-preserved traditional
teashop in the Old Lanes is rightly
cherished for its dazzling range of cakes,
speciality teas and more besides (The
Times included it in its top 50 teashops
of Britain). Sadly owners Gordon and
Birthe Chater, a lovely old couple who
set the place up over 30 years ago,
threw in their aprons early in 2006
but they assured me the new owners
would be keeping it much the same,
which I know countless Brightonians are
praying will be the case. If so, lunchtime
visitors can expect to be treated to
some legendary omelettes, Welsh
rarebits and pork sausages while those
dropping by in the afternoon can stuff
themselves silly with cream tea and
choose from over 30 cakes and biscuits.
Top tip: There's a bit more leg room
downstairs!

Cafe Nia (NL)
87/88 Trafalgar Street (01273) 671371
Open Mon-Sat 9am-11pm, Sun 9am-6pm

With simple décor, candles, a
commanding view of Trafalgar Street,
laid-back music from the likes of Jeff
Buckley and imaginative grub, this café
used to get top marks all round. A
cracking slice of cake is still yours for
the asking, although at £1.75 a more
expensive espresso than theirs will

take some tracking down. The bad news is that success (they opened a second branch in Shoreham recently) seems to have left quality and quantity as rather low priorities. Restaurants that charge you extra for a few veg to go with your rather overpriced main course have become all too commonplace, but when the main dish arrives undercooked and lukewarm on a cold plate *and* a small bowl of chips costs £3, you suspect somebody is laughing. And it's not you.

Red Roaster (K)
1d St James' Street (01273) 686668
Open Mon-Sun 8am-7pm

If you're looking for the perfect place to fritter away an afternoon reading or chatting, and you're a genuine coffee lover and smoker (the two *always* seem to go hand in hand), this independent coffeehouse at the bottom of St James' Street should be your number-one destination. As the only place in Brighton currently in possession of its own roaster (yes, it's red), their claims for providing the freshest and best coffee in town should be taken seriously.

As well as offering the chance to get high on coffee – in myriad flavours and cup sizes – Red Roaster sell yogi teas (herbal drinks that *actually* have flavour!), steamed milk, breakfast patisseries and baguettes, sarnies, ciabatta and salads for lunch.

This is also a great place to come and mix with a genuine cross-section of the Brighton community. You'll find students, foreign visitors, poseurs, gay men, mums meeting for baby chat, an inordinately large percentage of pretty girls and always one disturbing-looking guy, chainsmoking and staring vacantly into space (but this is St James' Street,

after all). There's even a piano in here which, sadly, doesn't get played, unless a drunk tramp happens to wander in (or was that Nick Cave?).

Come on a busy day and the queue can be a touch slow but you could while away your time admiring the owner's collection of coffee pots high up on the shelf around the back wall, checking out the clientele to see if there's anyone suitable for flirting with, or getting someone to bag the sofa by the window for you.

And keep your eyes peeled for curly-haired manager Michael Keane, a coffeehouse aficionado and mine of information about leftfield pop, useful to know should you be overcome with a sudden need to remember the name of the bassist from the Woodentops.

Top tip: avoid the leather sofa by the till – the sound of the coffee machine can be intrusive during busy times, especially if you're trying to have a conversation.

Red Veg (NL)
21 Gardner Street
(01273) 679910

(See veggie section in *Specialist Food*)

Rock-Ola Coffee Bar (NL)
29 Tidy Street   (01273) 673744
Open Mon-Sat 10.30am-4pm

Operating as an adjunct to The Wax
Factor record shop round the corner
on Trafalgar Street and run by Alan
Wax's missus, the Rock-Ola takes a
hefty stab at recreating the feeling that
Tommy Steele (ask your dad) might
be about to wander in off the street
and strum a few chords while playing
bongos with his quiff. The chromed-up
furniture and imported US sparkly
plastic seating, the novelty cruet sets,
and the posters and memorabilia
(my favourite being the James Dean
promotion for Thunderbird wine,
"the drink that loves to party") all
goose up the 50s/early-60s feel, while
much of the food echoes a simpler
gastronomic era with dishes such as
corned-beef hash, shepherd's pie and

apple-and-blackberry crumble. Even
the menu's in pre-decimal currency,
though your dad might have balked at
paying nineteen shillings for a flapjack.
Best of all, there's an ancient jukebox
stacked with period 45s that's totally
free, ideal for playing Crispian St
Peters' *The Pied Piper* eighteen times in
succession (though the staff *will* lob a
Betty Boop salt shaker at your noggin
if you do).

The Sanctuary (H)
51-55 Brunswick Street East, Hove
(01273) 770002

(See veggie section in *Specialist Food*)

Wai Kika Moo Kau (NL)
11a Kensington Gardens
(01273) 671117

(See veggie section in *Specialist Food*)

A HEARTFELT DEFENCE OF GREASY SPOONS

by lard-lover Brian Mitchell

There *is more to life than longevity, as the regular patron of the greasy spoon will surely testify. Sadly, Brighton, once caff capital of Britain, seems to have fallen prey to the same gimcrack gentrification and grasping redevelopment that is ravaging all our cities, with chains like Starbucks and Costa squeezing out the independent trader. Furthermore, for reasons I cannot fathom, rather than taking to the streets in violent protest, vast swathes of the country seem to be positively falling over themselves to pay £2.15 for a cup of milky coffee. While in the grip of this temporary insanity, however, it is comforting to know that there are still a few establishments that struggle to maintain tradition and a proper sense of what is truly valuable – like shepherd's pie at £3.75 – and, fortunately, Brighton is still rich in them. Below is my (wholly subjective) list of some of the best.*

Becky's (HA)
Elm Grove (01273) 628184

Possibly the remotest café in Brighton (situated as it is at the very summit of Elm Grove), Becky's is certainly the craziest. Part building site, part modernist pavilion and part Hitler's bunker, it is also perhaps the only café since *'Allo 'Allo* to boast live music. Indeed, it comes as something of a shock to spy, amidst the vinyl table cloths and miscellaneous sauce bottles, the state-of-the-art seven-octave keyboard and microphone set up as though in readiness for the Fabulous Baker Brothers. Lord knows what the various truckers and labourers that comprise its clientele make of all this. Perhaps they enjoy the odd slow foxtrot after brunch.

Though I cannot vouchsafe the quality of the music (having thus far been denied the privilege of hearing whichever low-grade Horowitz graces this joint. Maybe, inspired by *Shine*, they expect another rain-soaked David Helfgott to stumble in off the streets) I can, without reservation, recommend the food. Great breakfasts, a good range of daily specials, exceptionally friendly service and excellent all-round value make this Greasy Spoon at The End of The Universe more than worth the schlep.

Smiley's And Scottie's (H)
196 Portland Road and 111 Victoria Road, Portslade (01273) 422320

Having spent the past eighteen years roundly disparaging Hove and all her works in every conceivable medium, I now find myself in the somewhat invidious and (for me) unique position of having to admit that I was wrong. Hove, as I have only lately grown aware, has considerable charms, not least of which are these two, near-neighbouring cafes. They will probably both despise me for this shameless shilly-shallying, but I cannot in all conscience name a preference for either. Like the Bigendians and Littlendians in Lilliput, there is little to distinguish between them beyond their merely superficial idiosyncrasies. Scottie's has plastic roses, 60s' push-down-and-spin ashtrays, permanent Southern FM and an incongruous (given that one would expect some tartan about the place) Egyptian-themed décor. Smiley's has vinyl table cloths, 60s' glass ashtrays, permanent Southern FM and, again incongruously (given the average salary of its customers), a whole load of estate agent adverts for upmarket properties splashed along one of the walls. Beyond that, they both serve wonderful food (Smiley's bacon pudding is a revelation) at agreeable prices. Take your pick.

The Brunswick Breakfast Bar (H)
Brunswick Street West, Hove

Once upon a long ago, Brighton boasted two kinds of café – those whose walls threatened collapse under the weight of posters for gigs at the Richmond or Freebutt, and those festooned with garish, disturbing, care-in-the-community art. The Brunswick Breakfast bar, I am very glad to say, falls into the latter category. There are some truly awful paintings in here, including one that seems to be – and correct me if I'm wrong – a portrait of someone's arse wearing a pair of spectacles. Taking breakfast here is rather like dining in Tony Hancock's studio in *The Rebel,* only with, presumably, much better food than one might expect in a garret and a great deal more comfort. I love this place; it reminds me, as too few things do nowadays, why I came to this town and never wanted to leave. Oh – and the breakfasts are sublime.

Divall's Café (C)
Terminus Road (opposite the station) (01273) 328861

This would deserve a mention on these hallowed pages solely for being the only café I know that still regularly serves mashed potato, but there are many other reasons for this accolade: the choice of vegetables is unparalleled, the value exceptional, the staff warm and friendly, and the cryptic back-room oddly congenial. When it closed down early in 1999 my life simply fell apart; its re-opening in time for the millennium was a portent more propitious than any recorded in the *Acts of the Apostles.* (And try saying that with a mouthful of mashed potato – Ed)

Mac's Café (K)
30 Arundel Road (01273) 692621

My friends and I make trips to this place as some people take jaunts in the country. When I remember its existence and that, with only a little effort, I can actually go there, I am cheered up in a way mere nature could never accomplish. Admittedly, it does look a tad soulless with its plastic seating and spartan interior but don't let that fool you: I have achieved the heights of ecstasy eating their homemade steak pie and seen the godhead in their bubble and squeak – Mac's truly puts the transport in 'transport café'. Also, as it is conveniently situated opposite Lidl, you can, after a hangover-cure fry-up, simply scoot across to stock up on more cheap booze for your next massive bender – like holy water from Lourdes. Make your pilgrimage today.

NB The Market Diner is not included in this list because, being an all-night café, it properly deserves its own category. Nonetheless, drunkards everywhere give thanks to the god of greasy spoons for creating it.

Specialist & Veggie Food

SPECIALIST FOOD STORES

Archer's

128 Islingword Road (01273) 603234

A halfway-decent butcher's is as easy to find as a pheasant in pyjamas these days, but Archer's also has the distinction of being the only organic one in Brighton. As well as a range of fine meats and some organic groceries to save you the schlep to Infinity, they produce a sausage so mesmerisingly good it will spoil other sausages for you forever. Be sure to ask for theirs as they also bus some other types in from Chichester. And, forgive my nostalgic mood, but it is a treat to be served by a bewhiskered gentleman in a stripy apron; according to his wife, Brian Archer is the reincarnation of Ronnie Barker's Arkwright from *Open All Hours*, but if you enjoy quality banter and a chance to catch up on local gossip you won't be disappointed.

Bona Foodie

21 St James's Street (01273) 698007,
34 Church Road, Hove (01273) 727909

Just to clear up any confusion, Bona Foodie is a titular pun — a test, if you will, of the clientele's dedication to Radio 4 and all things homo: bona means good in Polari, the language of gay slang, and is pronounced "*bone-ah*" (not "*bon-ah*"), as in, "*that chicken is giving me a boner*".

Pronunciation lessons aside, Bona Foodie is one of Brighton's best delis, with a great selection of cheeses, olives, anchovies and a few delicious experimentations of their own. For under a fiver they'll knock you up the best sandwich you've ever tasted and, for slightly over, they'll let you sit down amongst their prettily packaged food and eat it. They also do a good line in desserts which should be dubbed Really Big Cakes — meringues, brownies, and the like in monster portions.

Raw Magic

Above the Hemp Shop, 19 Gardner Street,
Brighton (01273) 691011
Open Mon-Sat 11am-5pm
www.rawliving.co.uk

Owned and run by raw-food
enthusiast and author of *Eat Smart,
Eat Raw* Kate Wood, this pleasingly
homemade little shop lurks in the top
room of the Brighton institution that
is the Hemp Shop. An Aladdin's cave
of 'superfoods', blenders, dehydrators,
sprouters, kitchen equipment,
magazines and recipe books, this place
offers everything one would need for
a raw food way of life. The produce
on offer will induce responses ranging
from "*euuurrrgghh!*" to "*mmm, ambrosia
of the gods*". Try their goji berries,
etherium gold and spontaneous-
combustion cakes for starters, while the
raw chocolate blends will – to be frank
– get you nicely high without the nasty
comedown, leaving you still competent
to operate farm machinery.

For those interested in such things,
the modern raw-food movement
believes in the notion that cooking and
processing food damages and reduces
its nutritional value (thus sapping the
body's vitality and strength). It was
more or less started in California
(where else?) but can trace its
traditions back to the Essenes. Even
Jesus, in *Corinthians Eleven* is quoted as
saying, "*lo, if thou eateth living food, the
same will quicken you, but eateth dead
food and it will killeth you... and don't get
me started on Pot Noodles*".

SPECIALIST & VEGGIE FOOD

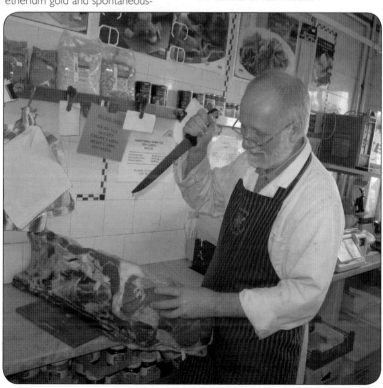

Brian Archer deals with another awkward customer

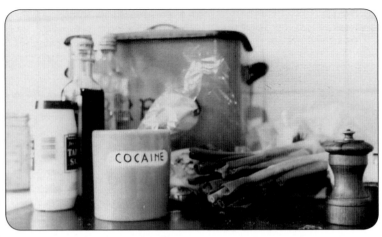

COCAINE

The Real Eating Company

86 Western Road, Hove (01273) 221444
Open every day 8am-11pm except Sun
and another day which I've forgotten

Five pounds ninety-five for a small bag of muesli? There, I've said it. Can any muesli *really* be this good? It's won awards, apparently, and there are certainly some interesting-looking pieces of dried fruit pressed up against the cellophane window. But when I say a small packet, I'm talking two bowls maximum. You could buy a decent piece of steak for that.

Exorbitantly-priced muesli aside, they do stock some interesting products, with the better ones residing in the chiller cabinet. They do an excellent range of posh smoked fish at quite reasonable prices and their mixed-leaf organic salad is superb. Probably a better bet is to take advantage of the restaurant/café facility and actually eat a meal here as they've earned all kinds of accolades from the broadsheet press for their in-house dining and, being far from the madding crowd (ie in Hove), it's often quite easy to get a table.

Shamanic Organic and Roar

Open Market and 30 Sydney Street
(01273) 689321 Open 10am-6pm
www.organicshamanic.com

This splendid Brighton institution has been running for many years as a stall in the Open Market and continues to do so, managed and owned by the terrifically named Peter Prudden, a friendly dreadlocked purveyor of rare herbs and spices. But while there has always been a psychedelic edge to Peter's trade (he specialised in the sale of magic mushrooms until Tony Blair put a stop to it), he also sells fresh local organic food, 'superfoods' and all manner of exotic edible plant life.

His new shop Roar is to be found between those two other outposts of the dedicated psychonaut the Guarana Bar and the Dumb Waiter and stocks various legal highs, health foods and clothes, as well as smoothies in a café space somewhat akin to the Greenfields at Glastonbury, with hammocks, cushions, piped chillout music and lovely elfish maidens serving your every desire, provided you've dropped enough herbal highs beforehand.

Taj Mahal

95 Western Road (01273) 325027
Open quite early-quite late

Riding on the success of its smaller sister shop round the corner on Bedford Place, the big, new shiny Taj opened last year to a fanfare of Bhangra-rap and jasmine incense, allowing a steady stream of shoppers to wander in wide-eyed amazement past the never-ending organic offerings, exotic fruits and unfeasibly large bunches of herbs. True, if you're after a loaf of bread you might have to settle for browsing the wall of extra-large flatbreads and wholemeal chapattis but if it's spices you're looking for, prepare to be completely overwhelmed. Those homesick for Japan will wipe away a tear as they consider seven types of fresh miso and every conceivable variety of seaweed, natto and umeboshi paste. And did I mention the Jewish section?

The organic grains? The ayurvedic products? The Indian sweets, Lebanese snacks and lasagne? Only the absence of polar bear claws and distilled gibbon drool lets it down.

Yum Yums

22 Sydney Street
Open Mon-Sat 11am-6pm

A rarity in Sydney Street (in that it's been there for over five years), Yum Yums is a traditional Chinese supermarket packed to the hilt with a fine selection of Asian goodies in bulk sizes. The freezers at the back store dim sum, pancakes and a host of other mysterious items requiring Chinese translation for identification. It's a little pricey but, as rents in Sydney Street are astronomical, who can blame them? You can even lose yourself for hours browsing the notice board, which would have you believe that everyone in Brighton wants to teach English, learn Cantonese or rent a room.

VEGETARIAN BRIGHTON

By Joseph Nixon

A typical vegetarian

If you're a vegetarian, a vegan or even a fruitarian, one of the best things about Brighton is that it's possible to live an animal-product-free existence with great ease. Unlike certain towns in this country, which will remain nameless (although Mansfield comes pretty close), you won't be met with a look of blank incomprehension if you request a veggie sausage in a café nor burnt at the stake for witchcraft, effeminacy and general oddness if you enquire about the possibility of a nut roast in your local (*"Aye, we'll be having a nut roast tonight alright. Fetch the flaming torches, Bert"*). **So** veggie-friendly is Brighton that I've seen clueless meat-eaters who request roast beef being turned away from vegetarian pubs with a cry of *"sorry mate, we don't do that sort of thing in here"*.

To anyone who, like me, spent his or her teenage years subsisting on a diet of burger-bar 'vegetarian specials' (a roll and salad, without the burger) or the ubiquitous restaurant veggie dish of the day (always, *always* bloody lasagne or some bland pasta dish), this city is a godsend. It's great living in a place with so many veggie-only eateries, where for once you'll be free of the paranoia (which secretly affects all vegetarians) that you'll accidentally be served a meat dish which you'll consume with relish while saying, *"bloody hell, these sausages are good. Almost like the real thing"*.

The best thing about Brighton veggie grub is that the eateries don't conform to the 'vegetarian food must be worthy, earnest, bland, look like a beige cowpat and taste like the contents of a lawnmower' rule. Some of the stuff on offer in Brighton looks and tastes so good that even your hardened carnivore mates might be tempted.

VEGGIE SHOPS

Bill's @ The Depot

100 North Street (01273) 692894
Open Mon-Sun 8am-8pm, Sun 10am-4pm

Worthy of mention for its great deli selection for veggies.
(See *Cafés* for more information)

Infinity Foods

25 North Road (01273) 603563
Open Mon-Sat 9.30am-5.30pm,
Fri 9.30am-6pm

Brighton's much-loved health-food shop stocks everything your (healthy) heart desires. Yogi teas, organic turnips, grains, nuts, seeds and tofu burgers all under one roof, and organic bread baked on the premises. Whether you're a veggie, a vegan or allergic to yak hair, you'll find something here to suit your palate. It's also handy for its notice board (if you're looking to share a room with a cat-owning, non-smoking vegetarian or need a lift to Belgium) and is a co-op too, so you can even feel saintly about shopping here.

Vegetarian Shoes

12 Gardner Street (01273) 691913
Open Mon-Sat 10am-5.30pm

Yes, very funny, I know you don't eat shoes (unless you're Charlie Chaplin). This shop sells leather-free shoes in various styles, from Doc Martens to Birkenstocks. They've also got trainers made from hemp, so I guess you could smoke 'em if you were desperate.

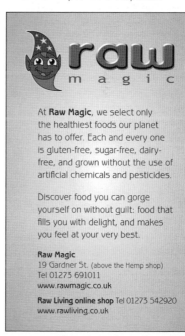

VEGGIE PUBS

The George
5 Trafalgar Street (01273) 681055
Food served Mon-Fri 12noon-9.30pm,
Sat-Sun 12.30pm-8.30pm

Brighton's most notable veggie and vegan boozer offers good food in light, airy surroundings. The extensive menu includes such old favourites as sausages n' mash, Thai fishless cakes, nachos, fajitas, burgers and (a rarity) tasty vegan puddings (including ice cream). Vegetarian beers and wines are also available, as are a selection of soya-milk coffees. Oh, and there's a beer garden at the back. The downside of this place is that when it's crowded (and sometimes, bafflingly, when it's not), it can take upwards of an hour for your nosh to arrive. So don't wander in for a bite to eat twenty minutes before an important meeting/appearing in court/getting married, etc. And, while I'm having a moan, many of the tables seem to have acquired an ingrained stickiness of such potency that your elbows and indeed plate may become welded to the surface – the staff once had to fetch an implement in order to chip away my used platter.

The Round Georges
14/15 Sutherland Road (01273) 603059
Food served 12noon-3pm

Once the frankly terrifying Sutherland – a watering hole even the Krays would have thought twice about popping into for a pint on a Friday night – this pub has recently had a makeover and is now dead trendy, and serves a good selection of veggie nosh. Proper home-baked pizzas are a speciality of the house but there are also root chips, frittata, mezze and a rare sighting of vegetable crumble.

FOR A SCRUMMY VEGGIE SUNDAY ROAST

The Barley Mow
92 St George's Road (01273) 682259

The Basketmakers
12 Gloucester Road (01273) 689006

The Earth and Stars
46 Windsor Street (01273) 772282

The Great Eastern
103 Trafalgar Street (01273) 685681

The Hampton
57 Upper North Street (01273) 731347

The Lion and Lobster
Sillwood Street (01273) 327299

The Shakespeare's Head
Chatham Place (01273) 329444

The Sidewinder
65 Upper St James's Street (01273) 679927

VEGGIE CAFÉS

The Sanctuary
51-55 Brunswick Street East, Hove
(01273) 770002
Open Mon-Sun 9am-11pm
www.sanctuarycafe.co.uk

This well-established and chilled-out vegetarian café has been one of Hove's best assets for many years now; it's spacious, offers tasty comestibles and has an intimate basement venue. There's a good range of salads, bakes, pies, pastas, soups and hot dishes of the day to choose from. It's all homemade, totally organic and, following a recent menu makeover, produced with a creative flourish though as the kitchen is small you can sometimes be in for a bit of a wait if it's busy.

Those with a sweet tooth and large disposable income will enjoy the excellent range of vegan and non-vegan cakes, and those who just like to get quietly pissed will enjoy the organic wines and beers. Incidentally, breastfeeding is positively encouraged, so you're well in if you're currently milky, or a pervy voyeur.

The Cella, downstairs, has suffered from a recent refit that unfortunately replaced its jumbly ambience with a rather cold office chic. Nevertheless, it's still host to many evenings of poetry, music and cabaret – Creative Liquid has a long-running monthly spoken-word offering, some of the better Brighton bands now gig here and my friend Denise swears she once saw an act here called Fish and Chip Strip, where a girl did a striptease and proceeded to smear herself with… yes, you guessed it. But this is Brighton after all. Sorry, Hove actually.

Wai Kika Moo Kau
11a Kensington Gardens (01273) 671117
Open Sun-Thurs 9am-5pm,
Fri-Sat 9am-10pm

This popular veggie café (pronounced "why kick a moo cow") now has only a single outlet left in Brighton. A second one, in the Old Lanes, decided to start serving meat, prompted by too many diners looking at the menu and going, "eurgh, broccoli"; it ended up with too many vegetarians going, "eurgh, dead animals," and promptly closed. Meanwhile, it's business as usual back at the North Laine branch, with a selection of burgers, pastas, breakfasts, tarts, rostis, tagines and risottos, as

Typical vegetarian family on holiday

well as a constantly refreshed variety of rather scrummy cakes. For a North Laine café they've got the right balance of style and atmosphere, with genuinely friendly staff who, after a couple of beers, will dance on request to old Motown classics. It's also useful to know that this is one of the few North Laine cafés to open *really* early. If you're partial to an early dip at the Prince Regent (as I am, occasionally), this, along with Inside Out, is one of the best places for miles around for a hearty post-swim breakfast.

For veggie/vegan restaurants, see special section in Restaurants

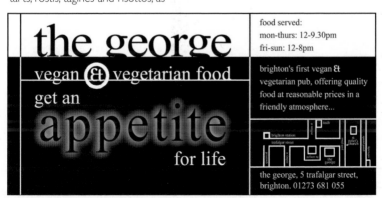

BRIG*H*TON'S BEST C*H*IPPIES

*Brighton has many advantages as a town, but really
good fish-and-chip shops is not one of them.
Perhaps it's the embarrassment of other,
more exotic eateries on offer that
has served to marginalise
our humble
national dish;
or maybe the
Bank Holiday
crowds allow
poor-quality
outlets to flourish.
Whatever the case, to
help you avoid a bad case of the runs after sampling fish
and chips from some of the more dubious outlets on the
seafront, detailed below are (in my opinion) the two best
chippies in Brighton. And yes, I am aware that we have a Harry Ramsden's...*

Bankers
116A Western Road (01273) 328267
Open Mon-Sun 11.30am-9.45pm

An excellent take-away and sit-down chippy on the high street, whose classic
60s décor will make you feel like you've walked into some kitchen-sink drama.
(In fact, thinking about it, it's quite reminiscent of the café where Rita works in
Billy Liar.) Bankers' fish and chips are near-perfect, they offer decent portions
for the price and the fish can even be cooked in Matzo meal (a Jewish
alternative to batter and definitely worth trying). If you're still feeling peckish
afterwards, *you are a glutton,* but I can recommend the cheesecake. Don't miss
the indoor guttering effect above the counter. What's that all about?

Bardsley's
23 Baker Street (01273) 681256
Open Tues-Sat 10.30am-2pm, 4pm-8pm,
closed Sun/Mon

Arguably the very best in town and well worth the long hike from the
seafront to the arsehole end of Brighton (off the London Road). Eat here
once and never again will you be able to face the polystyrene-flavoured fish
and cardboard chips they dish out on the seafront. For maximum effect it's
best to eat in. True, there are no French waiters to rush over and top up your
mug of tea or sprinkle yet more salt on your chips, but you can stare out of
the window here and reminisce about the old hairdresser Mr Cooper who
used to work opposite and do haircuts for 100p. Or you could even plan
what puppy you're going to buy from the pet shop next door.

Buddies

46-48 Kings Road, just down the
seafront from the Odeon (01273) 323600

Open 24 hours a day every day,
right on the seafront and yet weirdly
civilised, even at four in the morning
on a Saturday night when every pissed
lunatic decides it's time for a pizza and
a punch-up.

The Market Diner

19-21 Circus Street (01273) 608273
Open Mon-Fri 8pm-11am, Sat 8pm-9am,
Sun 8pm-6am

To be found on Circus Street, just
around the corner from the Art
Block, the Market Diner is one of the
most famous landmarks of Brighton's
nightlife. This is your classic greasy
spoon, boasting ashtrays made from
the foil of Mr Kipling's apple pies, a
near-legendary gut-buster and the
added bonus of being open all night.
This, purportedly, is to cater for truck
drivers delivering to the fruit market

in the small hours but, at the weekend,
its clientele consists mostly of drunks,
deranged lunatics, deranged lunatic
drunks and incapacitated clubbers. It
is, however, a must for that post-club
hunger and **the** place to meet and
socialise with dangerous people. And
hats off to the staff here – they're like
experts in linguistics. Not matter how
off your head you are, they can **always**
tell what you want.

The Brighton Bystander

1 Terminus Road (01273) 329364
Open Mon-Sun 8am-12midnight

Opposite the station, this greasy-spoon
café will deliver the goods if your taste
buds are none too discerning. Quite a
chilled atmosphere if you get a table
but don't let them rope you into giving
a hand behind the till, as I've witnessed
here on at least two occasions. It's also
a good place for picking up magazines
and flyers for local events, and a
perfect opportunity to amuse the staff
with the joke *"waiter, waiter there's a
flyer in my soup"*.

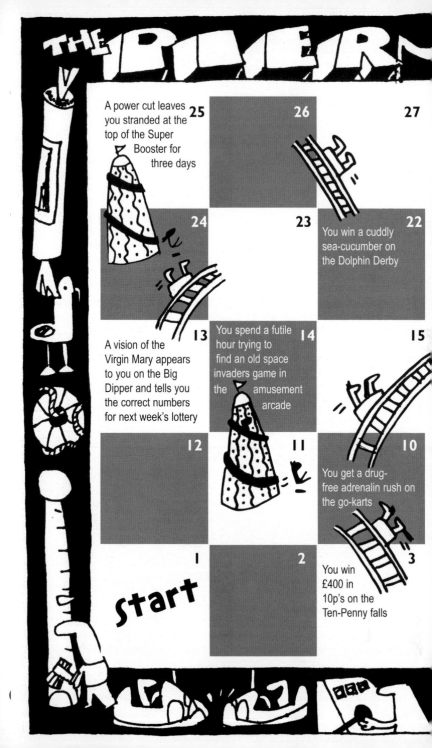

GAME

28

29 You sing 'Do you really want to hurt me?' in front of some mono-browed slapheads at Horatio's Karaokebar and get beaten up

30 *finish*

21

20

19 You fall into a deep slumber on the world's dullest ghost train

16

17

18

9 You jump off the pier and drown

8

7

4

5

6 The arcade swallows your kids for two hours allowing you to slope off for a crafty pint

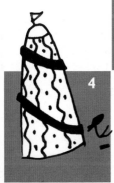

Restaurants

There are more than 400 restaurants in Brighton, with cuisine ranging from African, Mexican, Asian, soul food, Japanese and Lebanese to Cajun, French, Italian... even English. So, after all this hard work, not to mention putting on 327lbs in the process, I'll be very annoyed if you end up in McDonalds...

AFRICAN

Blue Man

142 Edward Street (opposite Amex)
(01273) 622885
Open Mon-Sun 6pm onwards
Kemias from £9.50, party banquets £20 a head

Set up a few years ago by Majid and Georgie, this authentic North African restaurant a little way up Edward Street is a real gem. Taking its name from the Tuareg (a tribe of Saharan nomads who, being supporters of Valencia United, only ever wear indigo), Blue Man serves a plethora of tasty dishes ranging from goat and turmeric or lamb with chickpeas and prunes to Algerian omelettes and even pigeon (of the wood, not Brighton, variety). Particularly recommended is the £20 banquet – perfect if you're with a large group and want a wide selection of dishes to sample. The meat dishes are superb: the lamb's liver with caraway, the Merguez sausages (lamb and chilli) and the roasted chicken are personal favourites. Veggies don't despair: there's grilled halloumi, bountiful salads, bread, fine couscous, cumin houmus, sferica (olive and herb bread) and plenty of tasty hot vegetable dishes. And there are still further pleasures, in the shape of homemade baklava, espresso with cardamom and shisha pipes.

As well as excellent cuisine, Majid and George have got the atmosphere spot-on too. Rather than fill the place with stuffed camels or spoil it with modern décor, the Blue Man feels authentic and characterful without being tacky. And little touches like the fez hanging over the toilet, the original desert artwork on the walls and the coloured lanterns mean you can really leave Brighton behind in here – not an easy thing to do in this town.

Top tip: It's bring your own booze.

Mint Restaurant/ The Mint Leaf Café

42 Meeting House Lane (01273) 323824
Open Sun-Wed 11am-5pm,
Thurs-Sat 11am-11pm
www.littlefish.ltd.uk
Main course £9-£14

Bringing some much-needed life to a quiet corner of the Old Lanes, Mint is an elegant and well-priced café/restaurant with a light North African/art deco slant that has beautiful big mirrors, fans and skylights. The food pays homage to southern Mediterranean tapas (raciones), with such offerings as sardine bruschetta and lamb kofte with minted yoghurt, though they also like to use organic and free-range meat and local food wherever possible, hence you'll find lemon sole and Sussex-bred sirloin steak on the specials board. It's child-friendly too, but rather than the usual lazy offering of offal and chips for kids, Mint would make Jamie Oliver proud with their "mini-me" versions of the menu. They're even committed to live music and performance: every week from Thursday to Saturday you can enjoy the acoustic sounds of everyone from Los Albertos to the banjo-wielding Fridge Magnets as you tuck into your tapas. Recommended.

..so the vicar said, *"Madam, I'm only testing your pomegranates!"*

AMERICAN/CAJUN/ SOUL FOOD

Momma Cherries Soul Food Shack

Little East Street (01273) 325305
www.mommacherries.co.uk
See website for new opening times and prices

Britain's only soul food restaurant, Momma Cherries serves up hefty portions of tasty, traditional Southern fare ranging from Southern-fried catfish and Brother Brian's pigs' feet to blueberry pie, all washed down with jugs of refreshing homemade lemonade. The menu alone merits a visit, for within its pages you'll find history lessons, poetry, photo collages, advice for diners (*"..read the menu in your best American accent. Think of a Southern Baptist preacher… let the energy flow"*) and even translations of such less-familiar American terms as:

Jello (jelly)
Biscuit (bread)
Small (medium)
Medium (large)
Large (huge)
Spicy (real hot)
Hot (have some water nearby)
Fanny (bottom)

Fact is, Charita and the gang like any excuse for a party. Halloween, Christmas and the Fourth of July are all celebrated here but the truly unmissable event is Thanksgiving, which Charita describes as an evening of *"giving thanks and pigging out"*. In the past she has had diners standing up and holding hands, while her mother (a 70-year-old Baptist minister) has blessed the food from her home in the States via the wonders of telecommunication. This is followed by a 'cabinet reshuffle', in which diners are split up and reseated to encourage mingling.

This, of course, is all a reflection of Charita's personality. Effervescent and larger than life, she is theatrical, ever-cheerful and even prone to burst into the occasional song. She even charmed Gordon Ramsey who, rather than criticise the food, simply told her to go out and entertain the customers more! In fact the tv appearance brought so much new custom that at time of going to print they were moving into bigger premises a few doors down the road.

On a typical evening Charita will buzz around the tables asking *"Y'all OK? You wan' mo vegetables, you wan' mo chicken? You just ask, honey!"* or regaling visitors with tales of her cheeky antics, such as the time she blagged her way backstage at the Theatre Royal to meet Huggy Bear, claming to be his long-lost cousin! For character and gut-busting grub, Momma Cherries is peerless.

Momma Cheery

CHINESE

Brighton Pagoda

Brighton Marina, West Jetty,
opposite the Seattle Hotel (01273) 819053
Open daily, 12noon-1.45pm and
6pm-10.30pm
Set menu £18-£25 per head

This can claim, without fear of contradiction, to be Brighton's *only* floating restaurant. There is no point in living if you don't experience the odd sensation of slurping good Chinese food as the waves rock you to and fro (unless, of course, you're the kind of landlubber who only has to *look* at a boat to start re-enacting the mushy-pea puking scene from *The Exorcist*, in which case this really isn't the place for you).

There are no quirks to the menu but the fare is surprisingly above average, given how cheap it is – you might expect to pay double for the ambience alone. The waiting staff can be incredibly pushy on a Saturday evening but be firm and they'll let you go at your own pace. A wonderful place to surprise somebody with – the lower deck is especially romantic for newfound loves. If you want to impress without breaking the bank, this exotic little one-off can be just the ticket.

China Garden

88 Preston Street (01273) 325124
Open daily 12noon-11.30pm
Main course around £10

If you were to judge this place by its décor it'd probably not fare well. It may look flash but, with the exception of the monogrammed carpet, as much effort seems to have gone into styling it as on the interior of my grey, 1980 Renault 5. This was probably the

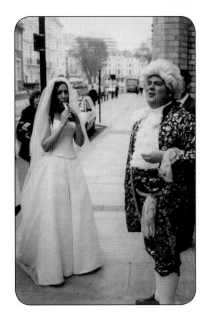

height of fashion 15 years ago but it wouldn't go amiss to remove some of the Athena pictures and have them quietly put down. Fortunately, however, the food here is such high quality, and the service so good, that to avoid this place for the sake of a few tacky features would be a real shame.

Having eaten here several times with large groups, I can vouch that everyone has savoured every morsel, from the hors d'oeuvres platter right through to the toffee banana at the end, with the food receiving nothing but glowing praise from all concerned. A far cry from the typical stodgy Chinese takeaways we've grown accustomed to.

Top tips: Try and get yourself a sea view, as the restaurant overlooks the charred remains of the West Pier. And if you're a veggie you'll need to ask for the special vegetarian option, as it's not on the menu.

ENGLISH/MODERN BRITISH

Blanch House

17 Atlingworth Street (01273) 603504
Open Wed-Sat 12noon-3pm,
Tues-Sat 7pm-10pm
www.blanchhouse.co.uk
Three courses about £30 a head

Tucked away as it is down a little-known Kemp Town side street and looking – at first glance – like any other residential abode, Blanch House is rather easy to miss. In fact this restaurant/hotel is so discreet that the first time I came to visit I knocked on the wrong door and got a very short-sighted old lady who, by pure coincidence, was called Mrs Blanche Hows. It wasn't until about halfway through my rice pudding, when her husband Ernie turned up from work, that we both realised our mistake but apparently this happens quite a lot, so if you do end up there accidentally, please do leave her a good tip as her gammon and chips is actually pretty good.

As for the real Blanch House's restaurant, if you judged it by the reviews on brighton-eating.com it'd not fare well but, having recently acquiring a new head chef, gone are the small portions and overcooked meat and back on the menu are sizeable chunks of well-cooked, tasty cuisine. Expect the likes of panfried seabass, ravioli of butternut squash, bread-and-butter pudding (yum!) and even apple crumble, all cooked well and beautifully presented. Worth noting are the cocktails here, described by GQ as the best in Brighton, which I'm inclined to agree with. Couple that with their excellent selection of wine and highly-entertaining and charming French and Italian waiters and it could be thumbs-up all round.

One small gripe however: the art-for-sale which adorns the walls and the piped cheesy euro dance music can spoil the atmosphere quicker than you can say *"I like having sex with small animals"* at your dad's funeral. And speaking of sex, if Eduardo is still working there, don't be surprised if he asks, *"Something for the weekend sir?"* in his broken English as you leave the restaurant – he models in his spare time and is the new face of Durex!

Conclusion? Bring your own CD, wear a Hawaiian shirt and you'll be laughing; this is excellent posh grub without the usual empty wallet and rumbling stomach at the end of the night.

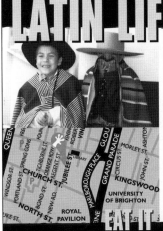
Harry's

41 Church Road, Hove (01273) 727410
Open Mon-Sun 9am-10.30pm
www.harrysrestaurant.co.uk
'Greedy breakfast' £6.35,
beef, steak, kidney and mushroom pie £7.65

Remember how in *The Beano* every week one of the characters would foil a couple of burglars (dressed in black striped shirts and carrying a bag of swag) to be rewarded with a slap-up meal of bangers and mash at the local nosh-up? This is a posh version of that restaurant, serving hearty, meat-heavy, traditional English dishes and old classics like jam rolypoly for afters (but unlike the ones you had at school, the custard isn't lumpy and Simon Timmins won't have flicked one of his bogies in it when you weren't looking).

Of course, there will be some amongst you who might scoff at the notion of traditional British grub, recalling the *Goodness Gracious Me* sketch where they all go out for an 'English' and try to order the blandest meal on the menu. *"Surely,"* you say, rising to your feet, *"running a restaurant that boasts a purely English menu is a foolhardy thing to do, on a par with opening a German comedy club or an Italian war museum?"*

Well, not Harry's. In fact, those among us who privately assert that apple crumble is a superior dessert to pannacotta, and that roast beef and horseradish sauce can never be supplanted in our affections by Mai Ped Pad, hold Harry's to our breast and whisper: *"Cry Harry for England and Saint George!"*

Generous portions, locally sourced and fresh ingredients (the fish is from Shoreham, the sausages from George Street), reasonable prices and beautiful simply cooked meals (the Sussex smokies and the liver and bacon are justly famous): truly, there is a little corner of Hove that is forever England. **Top tip:** Breakfast is superb and served until 4pm!

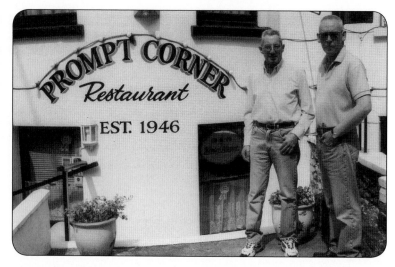

Prompt Corner

36 Montpelier Road (01273) 737624
Dinner served from 6pm,
Sunday lunch 1pm-4pm
www.promptcorner.com
Sunday lunch £10, main course around £10

Since its grand opening in 1946 by actor Bob Dean, Prompt Corner has continued to uphold and cherish its theatrical theme. When current owners Ken and Alan took over in 1979, they decorated the place with hundreds of photos of stars from the 30s to the 60s. Sure, there's a picture of Tom Cruise in here somewhere but, as one customer grumbled, *"he just doesn't belong here".*

And I know what he means. For it is the style and relaxed pace of this golden era of the movies that are evoked by the ambience of this restaurant. From the moment you step in and Ken greets you, takes your coat and sits you at the bar for an aperitif, you can actually feel time slowing down a pace and putting its feet up. Almost nothing has changed here since Alan and Ken took over. In a town of transience and ever-

changing fashion, Prompt Corner is a rare and almost surreal delight, reflecting a bygone era when style meant Lauren Bacall, not some floozy from *Big Brother*.

The cuisine is classically English (with a few French numbers thrown in for good measure) – plenty of steaks, fish and seafood dishes to choose from and the likes of chocolate pud and ice cream for afters.

Unsurprisingly, Prompt Corner has had more than its fair share of celebrity customers over the years, from Joan Collins, Frankie Howerd and John Inman to Cynthia Payne. *"She gave me one of her **luncheon vouchers,"** commented Ken, *"but I never used it."*

In fact, Alan and Ken have great tales to tell about some of their famous customers (make sure to ask Ken about the time David Blunkett popped in) and the two of them together make a great double act, Ken acting as foil for Alan's wry but good-natured quips. Ken has a wonderful way of floating around the restaurant – adjusting a napkin here, picking up an empty glass there – and there's a distinct air of the Peter Sellers about him.

Like all good places with a theatrical connection, Prompt Corner has its own resident ghost. The mistress of a Jewish landlord, she is said to have hung herself at number 37 (now the bar area) and while no-one has seen her directly, Ken said: *"Sometimes I'll think I see a shadow over someone's shoulder and presume a customer's gone off to the toilet, but when I look… there's no-one there!"*

For those who love Brighton as much for places like the Mock Turtle, the Colonnade Bar and the Pavilion as for its trendier clubs and bars, this restaurant will not disappoint.

The Saint

22 St James's Street (01273) 607835
Open Tues-Sun, 12noon-3pm, 6pm-closing
www.thesaintrestaurant.co.uk
Smoked-eel starters £6.50, crispy confit
duckleg £16.50, desserts £5.80

A haven for those with a more discerning palate and a welcome retreat from the lunacy of St James's Street, the Saint takes a rustic bistro approach to its English/continental menu and offers a superb range of meat, fish and vegetarian dishes. Or, to quote its affable chef, David Phillips, this is *"unpretentious post-modern cuisine, without a twist!"*

David (formerly of the Jolly Sportsman in East Chiltington) clearly cares about the quality of the food he cooks: 80% is sourced locally, the meat is all from Sussex, most of the vegetables are supplied by the Steiner bio-organic farm in Forest Row and the herbs are collected by wild foraging!

Inside, the Saint is deceptively spacious and modern, with soft candlelight, friendly (and rather attractive) staff and a gentle soundtrack from the likes of Sigur Ros and Goldfrapp – ideal for an intimate and unhurried meal.

If you're doing it in style, you'll want to begin by sampling a few cocktails; their own 'Saintly Cocktails' section has a few tantalisingly named brews, such as Salty Dog and Dicky Wibbly (which sounds like a medical condition for gentlemen who can't, er, perform), and once you're suitably loosened up by seven or eight of these, you'll no doubt be ready for food.

Typical dishes include confit of duck and salad of crayfish for starters; steak, pheasant or lime-infused, poached organic salmon for main and Mediterranean figs or sticky-toffee pudding for dessert. Tuck in and you won't be disappointed; the cuisine is stylishly presented, the meat and fish dishes juicy and tender, and the desserts very rich and satisfying (their organic apple, pear and honey tart makes me weep with pleasure). Just pray that after all this, the buttons on your trousers won't shoot off and land in someone's soup.

Top tip: The brown leather booths at the back are ideal if you're after an intimate meal for two.

Gratuitous *"that waitress fancies me"* photo

RESTAURANTS

The Strand

6 Little East Street (01273) 747096
www.thestrandbrighton.co.uk
Main course £15, starter £5.50

As 'strand' is German and Irish for coast, it may come as no surprise that the theme here is the beach. But rather than a Cockleshell Bay of portholes and deckchairs, the Strand's owners have come up with a wholly original design which utilised the talents of a few local artists: simple wooden furniture, a Barrier Reef bar area with gold-and-blue art installation and beautiful indigo fairy lights. Even the display of old knives, forks and spoons works surprisingly well.

Despite being a small restaurant they've wisely resisted cramming in as many tables as possible here. In fact, all the tables are of a decent size, making the Strand experience cosy and intimate but not intrusive. It's all very open too, with the bar in the centre and the kitchen staff on show – always a good sign.

Trying to get your head around the style of food on offer here can, however, be a little tricky. The owners describe it as Australian modern British but before you start thinking *"What, vertical columns of bar-b-q koala in lager sauce with Yorkshire pud served on big white plates?"*, they really mean Thai-influenced-Australian cuisine combined with modern English. Confused? It really doesn't matter, as every dish on the menu is a winner. When you're offered such perfectly cooked, mouth-watering delights as Thai fishcakes with sesame-and-coriander noodles, roasted fig and goat's cheese for starters or suckling pig with mashed potato and Calvados-soaked roasted apples for main, you won't care if it's Welsh, Canadian or Taiwanese. And

142

DAVE 'GORDON BLUE' MOUNFIELD'S "RESTAURANT-TO-TOILET PROPORTIONALLY REPRESENTATIVE INVERSE-VORTEX MANIFESTATION THEORY"

THE QUALITY OF A RESTAURANT'S TOILET FACILITIES IS DIRECTLY PROPORTIONAL TO THE QUALITY OF ITS FOOD. A FLASHY BUT ANNOYING AND NOT VERY WELL CLEANED OR MAINTAINED TOILET IS, THEREFORE, THE WORST OF ALL WORLDS. THAT MEANS YOUR FOOD WILL BE EXPENSIVE AND BAD. ON THIS BASIS ALONE I OFTEN MAKE IT MY DUTY TO VISIT A RESTAURANT'S TOILET BEFORE EVEN SITTING DOWN. IF I DO NOT LIKE WHAT I SEE, I MAY LEAVE. I HAVE SELDOM BEEN PROVED WRONG IN THIS RESPECT. THE INVERSE OF THIS RULE COMES INTO PLAY, HOWEVER, WITH RESPECT TO GREASY SPOONS: THE WORSE THE TOILET, THE BETTER THE FRY-UP. TRUE. I SWEAR TO GOD.

Photo by kind permission of Ali-Cats

working on the principle that you get what you pay for, the food here really is good value for money; the quality is consistently high, meat cooked to perfection and dishes always beautifully prepared. In fact it's thumbs up all round for the Strand. It's the perfect place for a romantic dinner for two, while a large gang could take over the upstairs room and have a ball.

FISH AND SEAFOOD

English's

29-31 East Street (01273) 327980
Open Mon-Sat 12noon-10.15pm,
Sun 12.30pm-9.30pm
www.englishs.co.uk
Grilled Dover sole £19, hot or cold seafood
platter for two £40

English's has, for countless years now,
enjoyed a reputation not only as *the*
seafood restaurant in Brighton but, for
many, as *the restaurant* in Brighton, full
stop. And I, for one, am not about to
disagree. Unchanged since it opened
in 1946, and housed in three old
fishermen's cottages in the Old Lanes,
English's is both an eat-at-the-counter
oyster bar (which still has the original
marble counter-top) and a high-calibre
seafood restaurant with an extensive à
la carte menu and weekly specials that
have been known to reduce grown
men to tears.

You *can* do English's for a modest
price (main courses range from
£10-£20) but, chances are, you'll get
carried way and opt for the deluxe
seafood platter, which will have you
delirious with joy when you spot it
being wheeled to your table like a mad
sculpture.

This restaurant also has many
appealing qualities quite apart from
the food. The Edwardian décor and
red velvet furnishings are thoroughly
charming, the journey up two flights
to the Ladies' offers terrific views of
Brighton and there are some nice
touches to the service – I love the fact
that the waiters present the desserts
on a silver tray to help you select your
choice.

If you are seated near the window
in the Red Room, have a good look at
the mural closest to you. The original
owner, Clifford Lee Jones, is the guy

Happy oysters just itching to be eaten

pictured holding a glass of wine. Look
carefully at the other characters,
however, and you'll notice they all look
strangely similar. Apparently the artist
could only afford one model, hence
the eerie *Boys from Brazil* experience.

Although from the outside English's
appears very posh and formal, this
belies a friendly interior. Sure, you'll
probably watch your manners if you're
sat inside rather than out, but it really
isn't the stuffy *"Certainly sir, whatever
sir requires, sir"*, type of establishment
that some imagine. And the clientele,
rather than confined to snooty suited
types, ranges from young couples
and seafood fanatics to flirty gay men
trying to chat up the waiter with
a French phrasebook (despite his
obvious Italian accent) and groups of
old duffers sitting around puffing on
cigars and swapping anecdotes about
going to school with Denis Compton.

Fashions come and go in Brighton
but sitting by the window of English's,
slurping on a bowl of lobster bisque,
eavesdropping on three old queens
on the table behind and watching the
plebs eating pizza at the restaurant
next door, has to rank in the top five
quintessential Brighton experiences.

The Regency

131 Kings Road (01273) 325014
Open Mon-Sat 9am-12midnight,
Sun 9am-10pm
Main courses £5-15

Yet another essential Brighton experience – sitting outside the Regency fish restaurant with a good plate of haddock, chips and mushy peas. And sticky-toffee pudding and custard for afters. Particularly recommended are their seafood platters: they're excellent value and the calamari can be chewed without having to take out dental insurance. From £5 for the basic haddock and chips to £15 for the Dover sole, if you're after an inexpensive sit-down fish-and-chip dinner with plenty of choice and a sea view, forget Harry Ramsden's and come here instead.

Curiously, the restaurant next door, the Melrose, has similar prices, menu and style, and I've never been able to figure out why the Regency is always much, much busier. Some friends reckon the food is better in the Regency but, having eaten at the Melrose on many occasions, I have nothing but praise for the place. Added to the fact that the

Regency has lost some of its charm since refurbishment, *and* that their eccentric waiter (the one who wears thousands of badges on his waistcoat) has defected next door, I'm beginning to *prefer* the Melrose. But then, being British, I'll always champion the underdog.

FRENCH

The Gingerman

21a Norfolk Square (01273) 326688 and
Drakes Hotel, 44 Marine Parade
(01273) 696934
Open Tues-Sat 12.30pm-2pm, 7pm-10pm
Two courses from £20

Local chef Ben McKellar has turned this unremarkable building in a quiet side street into a celebration of modern French cuisine. A small room, simply decorated, belies a purist approach, beautifully executed. From the fresh-baked rolls served with olive oil and balsamic vinegar on arrival to handmade petits fours, the attention to detail throughout the meal is consistently designed for inconspicuous pleasure.

Meat features heavily in the main courses, with creations such as pork

fillet with figs and squab pigeon on celeriac purée and, rather than going overboard on eclecticism, Ben's real strength lies in the intelligent perfection of his sauces. He has a rare ability to make simple cod or spinach taste divine.

INDIAN

Bombay Aloo

39 Ship Street (01273) 776038
Open Mon-Thurs 12noon-11pm,
Fri-Sun 12noon-12midnight
www.bombay-aloo.co.uk

This family-run restaurant has been around for years now and is terrific value for money as it's an all-you-can-eat vegetarian Indian buffet, including bhajis, salads, dips and curries with rice for only £4.95. Make sure to ask for the comments book at the end: there are some corkers in there including, my favourite, *"I luv your grub; had a fat poo afterwards"*!

They've also got a sister shop in Kemp Town (Bombay Mix) for meat-eaters, with meat and veg all-you-can-eat for £6.95. Mid-afternoon they're both even cheaper. Starve yourself for three days and clear them out.

Indian Summer

8 East Street (01273) 711001
Open Tues-Sat 12noon-10.30pm,
Sun 12noon-10pm
Kingsway, Hove (01273) 773090
Open Tues-Sat 6pm-10.30pm,
Sun 6pm-10pm
Main courses around £8

High ceilings, wall-mounted candles, the gentle strum of sitars on the stereo… these guys know how to create a seductive ambience; perfect for starry-eyed young lovers. But wait, won't all those bright-red tikkas and make-your-nose-sweat vindaloos have

our starry-eyed lovers reaching for the tissues a bit *too* early in the evening's proceedings? Fear not. The menu here forgoes the bog-standard Indian fare many punters might expect in favour of subtler, more ornate, European-influenced creations combined with traditional southern Indian cuisine. Expect grub that's more nouvelle cuisine than cumin naan. And that's no bad thing. Customers anticipating the usual fiery rumblings in their nether regions after a night out on the curry will be pleasantly surprised by dishes that include stuffed colocasia leaves, handmade dumplings, salmon steaks, almond marinades and tomato-encrusted mashed-potato crusts. The dessert menu continues in a similar vein; it's fair to say that dark chocolate sacher torte or vanilla-seed cheesecake with winter-fruit compote is unlikely to feature on the menu of your average high-street balti house. The wine list, meanwhile, is geographically expansive and finely varied, and the service is top notch. *"Our menu is designed with the more delicate European palate in mind,"* the waiter politely explained as he brought the hors d'oeuvres. Of course those with delicate European wallets be forewarned – an evening out at Indian Summer is a good deal pricier that your average curry house, but worth every extra penny.

In need of aperitif?

Planet India

54 Preston Street (01273) 275717
Open Tue-Sun 12noon-3pm,
Tues-Sat 6pm-10pm

Despite the existence of 200 million vegetarians in India, precious few have been inclined to nip over to Brighton to open a restaurant; it's taken a man from Luton to redress that balance a mite with a meatless menu and bargainacious curries like black chickpea or spinach-and-potato that'll barely set you back a fiver. Well, £5.39 for two of them with rice, to be precise, since this place has the oddest random pricing you've ever seen. It fair gladdens the heart to see underused figures such as 77p and £1.91 getting their moment in the sun.

To wash down your meal, may I suggest a bottle of the encouragingly named Thumbs Up, the Paul McCartney-endorsed fizzy pop made by Coca-Cola for the Indian market.

While delicious, the main courses do tend to lack a firmness of consistency but there are some fascinating and unusual starters to balance things out, like ketcheris (a sort of pea-and-coconut cannonball) and a couple of takes on bhel puri street food that have a wonderful fresh clean flavour.

Ambience-wise, it's a sort of cross between sub-continental transport caff and someone's kitchen (that's a good thing, in case you weren't sure), with framed family photos adorning the walls. And if that isn't relaxed enough, the owner will probably be padding about in shorts and bare feet, so you'll never feel underdressed, even if you've come straight from your job at Top Totty. Recommended.

ITALIAN

Alfresco

The Milkmaid Pavilion, Kings Road
(01273) 206523
Open Mon-Sun 10am-12midnight

Looking like something from a cool 60s Italian movie, Alfresco is an enormous glass-panelled building with a commanding view of the beach and a spacious round balcony on the first floor (which means you don't have to fight for a precious sunny spot during those two minutes of heat in the summer). While the building and its location are top banana the food certainly is not; it's the usual array of decidedly bland pizza and pasta dishes that any genuine Italian would turn their nose up at. Fact is, I had one of the worst meals of my life here one summer – the mussels were off and the pizza undercooked and cold. And I may not know *that* much about food but I'm sure that mozzarella is not actually meant to fizz in your mouth; the gaggle of surly teenage staff seemed to prefer loitering at the bar rather than acknowledging my frantic gestures that the cheese in my mouth appeared to have turned to Space Dust. The sad truth is that they really don't need to try hard here, this restaurant is in such a prime spot that it'd be full of tourists all year round even if it only served dogfood.

La Capannina

15 Madeira Drive (01273) 680839
Open daily 12noon-2.30pm, 6pm-11.30pm
Main course around £10

You'll be hard-pushed to find a proper Italian restaurant in these parts that can match La Capannina's high standards. It's a family-run place that simply sets store by doing things the Italian way. The restaurant itself is atmospheric, romantic and as authentic as they come. The menu is vast, the food top quality and the portions gargantuan. The only problem is whether or not to have a starter; it may leave you unable to tackle the main course without bursting at the seams. Unsurprisingly, La Capannina has a large fan base, so it's advisable to book ahead during busy times. Incredibly good value considering the standard of cuisine and service, this genuinely ranks as one of the best – you'd be mad to miss out.

JAPANESE

Sapporo

38-40 Preston Street (01273) 777880
Open evenings after 6pm
www.sapporo.co.uk

This stylishly minimalist gaff is part of the growing trend in Brighton for Japanese teppanyaki restaurants. For those who don't know, teppanyaki is simply an iron plate grill where food is cooked, but that really doesn't do it justice. 'Cooked by a charming, knife-juggling, egg-catching, fire-starting nutter' would be more accurate. For this joint is as much about theatre as it is food and it pays to be sat around one of the two teppanyaki tables, as this is where the action's at. (They do have a quiet dining area to one side but that's a bit like paying for tickets to a show then staying in the bar as the curtain goes up.) Your Hawaiian-shirted Japanese chef will then proceed to dazzle you with a display of speedcooking interlaced with

:07

FUN TIME-LEARNING JAPANESE

GOOD DAY(HELLO)-KON NI CHI WA
GOOD EVENING-KON BAN WA
START EATING-I TA DA KI MA SU
DELICIOUS-OI SI
THANK YOU-A LI GA TO
GOODBYE-SA YOH NA RA
CHEERS-KA N PAI
EXCUSE ME-GO ME N NA SA I
ITS YOUR ROUND-KO N KA I WA KI MI NO O GO

ENJOY YOUR JAPANESE EXPERIENC

knife play, catching of raw eggs flipped into his chef's hat, scallop-catching competitions (you open your mouth and he flips them straight in from the griddle) and – if it's your birthday – a beautiful Japanese-accented version of *Happy Birthday*, sung as he ignites vast sheets of flame inches from your nose.

With all these pyrotechnics you might expect the food to lose out; the opposite is true. It is quite stunningly good. On my last visit my lady friend was having mouth orgasms with every course (*"mmm... ooh that's SOO GOOOD!"*), and rightly so. The tempura here is refreshingly light, the sushi heart-rendingly fresh and subtle, and the beef stuffed with wild mushrooms worth committing a major crime for. The food seems to be unfailingly cooked to split-second perfection and the various sauces, wasabi and dips all superb and freshly prepared in the restaurant. And while it's not cheap, Sapporo does finally solve the age-old question, *"shall we go to dinner or see a show?"*

Moshi Moshi

Bartholomew Square (01273) 719195
Open daily 12noon–11pm
Tapas/sushi £12–£15

After establishing three successful sushi bars in the big smoke, Moshi Moshi demonstrated a new level of ambition by taking on the Curse of Bartholomew Square and winning. Ignoring the obscurity that has swiftly followed any attempt in living memory to set up a working eatery in this windswept graveyard of civic space beside the town hall, they demolished the old rotunda and started afresh.

The result is a sort of sub-007 screened cube, the entrance an opening fully fifteen-feet wide, with temperature cunningly controlled through a system of underfloor heating. First impressions are stunning: between wooden-slatted floor and textured red ceiling a great conveyor belt snakes around light rattan benches and a long bar. As you sit, you are faced with an endlessly renewed, slow-moving display of small plates containing colourful samples of sushi, sashimi, tempura and other delicacies. The simple beauty is that when something tasty-looking passes by, you pick it up. It may turn out to be pickled octopus with horseradish, but you can always hide it in your pocket if you don't like it. You can also order off the menu. Sushi set on stylised chopping boards, bento boxes (a double-decker starter and main course), seaweed-wrapped tamaki rolls and teriyaki combinations. Each table holds a jug of soy sauce, red-hot horseradish and plenty of lovely gari (sliced pickled ginger) to cleanse the palate.

Though wine is available, you can indulge yourself in a choice of hot or chilled sake, sake sours or Asahi beer. Thoroughly professional service is focused on guiding you through the unfamiliar experience. You are never committed here; you can as easily leave after a nibble as submerge yourself in a three-hour blowout.

This may not be Japanese cuisine at its zenith, but the food is good value and the belt makes for top entertainment: you can send notes to people you like the look of or, if you get your partner drunk enough on Tiger Beer, put on your best Bruce Forsyth voice, stick a cuddly toy and a set of steak knives on the belt and you should be able to convince them they're on *The Generation Game*.

LEBANESE

Kambi's

107 Western Road
(01273) 327934
Mixed grill £7, chicken shawarma £5.75

A favourite haunt for many years, Kambi's is the perfect size for bringing a group of friends to take the place over and share endless platters of dishes from the meat grills, falafels or side dishes like batata harra (sautéed potatoes with coriander, garlic and lemon) and rounding it off with a drag on the old hookah pipe. Be warned though, although flavoured with strawberries it's still tobacco at the end of the day. Just one puff and – if you're an ex-smoker like me – you'll be craving Marlboro Lights again.

Incidentally, a few years ago there used to be a band of musicians who occasionally dropped into Kambi's to play eastern European folk music. Knowing they did requests, my friend handed over a couple of quid for them to come over and embarrass me with a short serenade while I ate. Instead, bizarrely, they played *Happy Birthday* to *her*, and everyone in the restaurant joined in. She now has two birthdays a year, like the Queen.

MODERN CONTINENTAL

Hotel Du Vin Bistro

Ship Street (sea end) (01273) 718588
Open Mon-Sun 12noon-1.45pm, 7pm-11pm
www.hotelduvin.com
Main course £15

It can't be denied, the setting of this restaurant is magnificent. Spacious, elegant, candle-lit and decorated in a French colonial style, Hotel Du Vin's bistro has elegance, sophistication and (though I can't put my finger on why) a light sprinkling of the homo-erotic. Only the Russian doll-style champagne bottles in the centre seem weirdly out of place, belonging more to a tacky pub chain. Throw them away chaps, for goodness sake.

Unsurprisingly, this restaurant attracts those with a bit of money to splash around, though you'll also find starry-eyed lovers here, lavishing their attention and hard-earned cash on their new partners (on the proviso that tonight they'll get their jollies), and occasional gangs of American businessmen on all-expenses trips, talking louder than everyone else and swapping tales about their friends' tumours.

What will come as a pleasant surprise on your **first** visit here, however, is that the menu really won't break the bank. The main courses – cod, rabbit, lamb shank, sea bass, calf's liver and so on, while a little unimaginative, are all beautifully presented and well-cooked and at around £15 (if you go easy on the wine), won't break the bank. The trouble is, the wine *will* be your downfall; it's not called Hotel Du Vin for nothing. Unless you're the designated driver, mad or (worse) a Mormon, you simply won't be able to resist diving into their vast wine menu

Kumquat may.....

here – you'll find everything from wild-rabbit kebabs and lamb to sea bass and specialist seafood dishes, all cooked to perfection.

While restaurants of comparable quality can feel a little uptight, Due South strikes a good balance between posh and laid back. The candle-lit setting in the seafront arches is rather magnificent (the window seats are the ones to bagsy if you can) and the cuisine faultless, yet the staff aren't afraid to join in a bit of silliness or debate, and should you need somewhere to leave your bible you'll be pleased to know the rather unusual chairs in here are all former church seats with handy pockets to avoid getting gravy stains on your new King James. As well as caring about their food, Due South also participate in a seed-swapping event called Seedy Sunday and print a rather sweet A4 newsheet that covers the charity campaigns they are championing, tells you what's in season and has interesting little features on things like the history of broccoli. Top marks all round.

and, before you know it, the bill will have come to over £20,000 and you'll be doing the washing up here for the next 400 years. But it'll have been worth it.

Due South

139 King's Road Arches (01273) 821218
Open 12noon-4pm, 6pm-10pm
www.duesouth.co.uk
Main course £12-20

As the truism goes, simple ideas are often the best. And what could be a more straightforward key to success in Brighton than to set up a high-quality restaurant overlooking the sea with an emphasis on organic, fairtrade, free-range, seasonal menus and locally grown produce? As with the Saint, a staggering 80% of the food cooked here comes from within a radius of twenty miles around Brighton, with much of the veg grown on the bio-dynamic farms of Forest Row. Even their wine list includes a number of English varieties, which, though a tad sour, are surprisingly palatable. And they sure love their meat and seafood dishes

...I'm gonna have that satsuma or later

The Seven Dials Restaurant

1 Buckingham Place (01273) 885555
Open Mon-Sun 12noon-3pm, 7pm-10.30pm
www.sevendialsrestaurant.co.uk
Two-course dinner £22,
three courses £27.50

Since it opened in 2001, the Seven Dials restaurant has enjoyed overwhelming success. Winning awards and public acclaim – much of it through word of mouth – this former bank (and once, ironically, a Burger King) offers personable service, colourful and imaginative food combinations (black pudding and scallops, anyone?) and a cuisine that, while described as 'modern continental', has its roots in traditional English comfort food.

Owner/head chef Sam Metcalfe spent years honing his craft in a number of top London restaurants before doing the sensible thing and relocating to Brighton. You can see heartwarming pictures of him and his family on the stairs down to the basement, though who the bizarre photos on the doors of the Gents' and Ladies' depict is anyone's guess.

Dishes are beautifully presented and never served at a hurried pace. They do allow time to digest between courses here and don't make you feel they want you out as soon as possible. The menu changes every eight weeks or so but you can expect to find the likes of crab risotto, grilled halibut, Thai curried monkfish, roasted New England lamb, duck, wood pigeon and pheasant. And surely it's a mark of quality that they can do steak-and-kidney pie in an unpretentious way and get it so right that you'll swear (as I did) that it's the best steak-and-kidney pie you've ever tasted.

In summer, diners can opt to eat on the terrace, marvel at Sam's herb garden and meet some of the Seven Dials regulars, still pleased as punch to have an eatery of this calibre in their neighbourhood.

No Name

81-82 St James's Street (01273) 693216
www.sononame.co.uk
Main course around £13

Ever since Richard Gere, in the movies' least convincing portrayal of an architect ever, uttered the deathless line: *"there's a problem with the fenestrations"*, I've been examining windows for potential design flaws. This has led to some considerable time spent staring in through the expansive and apparently flawless windows of No Name, wondering why everyone seemed to be having such an uproariously good time. For some reason it always looks like it's Christmas inside, the ruddy-faced yeomen of St James's Street spearing huge chunks of sheep on their forks whilst bathed in warm light glowing round the brick interior. Now I've eaten there I can confirm

A pie is a man's best friend

that the food feels rather festive too; main courses like pan-fried pheasant breast on potato-and-apple mash or roast monkfish with a chilli, coriander and ginger salad arrive draped in rich satisfying sauces, while desserts are old fashioned and comforting puddings of the rice and sticky-toffee variety. One could complain about the wailing 80s divas moaning out of the sound system but doesn't, as the mood is generally chilled, the staff helpful and nicely thawed, and the toilets as shiny as a polar bear's nose. Christmas comes more than once a year here.

THAI/ORIENTAL FUSION

Sukhothai Palace

62 Middle Street (01273) 748448
Open Mon-Sat 11am-11pm, Sun 11am-10pm
www.spalace.co.uk
Main course around £8

"I've had, the Thai of my life, yes, I've never felt this way before…" as the hideous song nearly went. And they so easily could have been singing about this little charmer of a restaurant. The proprietess, a lady called Oy (I think that's how it's spelled), seems committed to the freshness and quality of her ingredients, which at the end of the day is what lifts Sukhothai up over the heads of most of the competition. (That and the ever-smiling, petite, gorgeous Thai waitresses, he said, receiving a nasty clonk round the head with a saucepan from his girlfriend standing over him as he writes this.) And while a cosy, homely atmosphere pervades, it always seems busy here, even at lunchtimes – which is the best advert a restaurant in this over-provided city can have and due in part to their amazingly good-value

I can recommend the smoked fish

two-course set lunch for a staggering £4.95!

The ideal spot for a sneaky midweek date, followed by a couple of pints at the excellent Hop Poles or downstairs in the snug of the Globe, all just a few yards away. And where else can you shout to the proprietor, *"Oy! What's for dessert?"* and get away with it?

Bali Brasserie
Kingsway Court, First Avenue, Hove
(01273) 323810
Open Sun-Fri 6pm-10.30pm Sat 6pm-11pm
Main course around £10

Found just off the seafront in Hove
and done out in wicker, bamboo and
plastic plants, this place is straight
out of *Love Boat* and *Fantasy Island*.
The ambience is made complete at
weekends by live music in the bar
from Gloria (or sometimes Mike),
who sits on a stool singing old
numbers from the likes of Nancy
Sinatra and Lee Hazelwood to
backing tapes, uttering such gems as
*"If anyone has a birthday out there,
come on up and we'll sort you out with
something reeeaal special"*.

A word of warning, though,
kitsch fans – even at the weekends
it can be pretty dead in the bar, so
I recommend this only as a place
for big groups. It'll really help if you
get dressed up, come en masse and
create the atmosphere yourself.
Incidentally, the food is Indonesian and
Malaysian. It's good, but a bit pricey.
"Look boss, de plane, de plane…"

SPANISH

Bodega D Tapa
111 Church Street (01273) 674116
Open Mon-Sat 12noon-11pm
www.d-tapa.co.uk
£3.25-£3.50 per tapa

Sandwiched inconspicuously between
two pubs right opposite the Dome, this
tiny little tapas bar shows how it should
be done; you sit at one of the four
tiny tables surrounded by shelves full
of much of the produce you're stuffing
in your face. The sheer mouthwatering
quality of the food and wine makes
you realise what's been missing from
other ostensibly similar experiences,
and there's no laboured pawing through
pages of menus as the dishes of the
day are written on a small portable
blackboard. And as if that's not easy
enough, you don't even have to choose
if you don't want to. Just ask and they'll
surprise you, sometimes with things
that aren't even on the board. Although
there are hot dishes such as paella
and fabada (a rich bean casserole), it's

Authentic Hassidic cuisine

Even the plates taste great at Bodega D Tapa

really the simple touches that amaze the palate, like the marinading of manchego cheese in startlingly great olive oil, or the 100-year-old sherry vinegar that transports olives to a different dimension from the 'open a jar and tip them into a bowl' approach you might be used to elsewhere. Other notable delicacies include the Iberian black ham (that's the pig that's black, rather than the ham) and the huge chocolate almonds.

Your genial host Genaro has an infectious enthusiasm for the ingredients, particularly the wine, oils and vinegars, which he imports weekly from his own family's production in Jerez. So longstanding is his passion for their sherry vinegar that as a child he used to secretly knock back bottles of the stuff, although I recommend you stick to half pints if you're a lightweight like me. Comestibles aside, there's a genuinely convivial atmosphere, Spanish in a way that doesn't require

straw donkeys or oak barrels suspended from the ceiling. Genaro drifts from table to table, tempting diners with vivid descriptions of the food, chatting about anything under the sun and trying to improve his grasp of colloquial English; I watched him carefully note down the word 'bonkers', a personal favourite of mine, after asking for its definition. Everyone seems to get drawn into everybody else's conversations and, added to the taste sensations on offer, you can't help but idiotically grin your way through your visit.

Although it's non-smoking inside, a covered terrace out the back is to be opened imminently for those who can't last the course without a fag. Drop in for a glass of their brilliant wine, buy a can of pimientos or a bulb of garlic, or keep ordering dishes until you burp; it's not expensive, it's not snooty, it's not fashionable, it's just bloody great.

VEGETARIAN

Bombay Aloo
(see Indian restaurants)

Food for Friends
17-18 Prince Albert Street (01273) 202310
www.foodforfriends.com
Main course around £10-14

In keeping with the constant gentrification of Brighton, Food for Friends – one of Brighton's long-established veggie restaurant/cafés – is another place to have received a makeover of late. Long gone are the canteen service, cheap stirfries, quiches that always made me fart and the down-at-heel hippiness that made the name so apt. Nowadays it's all neutral décor and fancy food. And while I'm not alone in missing what's gone and finding the new look a tad austere, it can't be denied that the food here is infinitely better. With a nod towards Terre à Terre, they've scrapped their school-canteen veggie grub in favour of such delights as tempura maki; tofu with brown rice, mushrooms and avocados; wok-fried veg and roasted organic almonds and even posh bangers and mash. And with vegan, gluten-free, macrobiotic and low-fat options on the menu too, no matter how 'Brighton' your diet is, Food for Friends can rustle up something tasty for your delicate palate. Despite their newfound sophistication I was heartened on my last visit by a group of girls at the table next to me reminiscing about the infamous 80s documentary on Tourette's syndrome. "Suck my cock, mother!" one of them shouted a little louder than planned, as we all turned around to stare.

PRESTON STREET

Despite the glut of restaurants in Brighton, if it's Saturday night, you're in town, hungry and have forgotten to book somewhere to eat, you could be in trouble. One of your best bets therefore is to head for Preston Street (which runs from Western Road to the seafront): it contains more restaurants per square inch than anywhere else on the face of the earth. They are of varying quality (so please don't blame me if your steak tastes like an old pair of Campers) but you do have an incredible choice of Chinese, steak houses, Italians, Japanese, Indians and countless others.

And if you don't like food at all, there's always Cheeky Chicken.

What *hasn't* changed at Food for Friends is the abundance of window seating. Sit by the big windows on a Friday night and you're guaranteed to have hen parties dressed as *Wonder Woman* and mulletted weirdos gawping at you as you wolf down your Japanese bar snacks. Are you on display for the pissed masses or are they your entertainment for the evening? Whatever the case, all this posh nosh and newfound sophistication means that Food for Friends is now more of a place you'd come for an intimate evening for two. Think Food for Dates rather than Food for Friends and you won't be disappointed.

Top tip: Don't eat your wasabi tofu square all at once or you'll have steam coming out of your ears.

Terre à Terre

71 East Street (01273) 729051
Open Tue-Sun 12noon-10.30pm,
Mon 6pm-10.30pm
www.terreaterre.co.uk
Main course around £10-16

With a deserved reputation for being one of the best restaurants in the UK, Terre à Terre has as much in common with standard veggie cuisine as Nick Cave does with George Clinton. The dishes here are totally unique, presented as works of art (many curiously reminiscent of Gehry's plans for the new King Alfred Centre) and the food so well cooked that you really *can* taste all the delicate flavours of the meal you ordered. Some might find the menu a trifle confusing – try the tonguetying or just plain ridiculous dish names such as Wotzyuzu Ithai Gnocchi, or Hellraiser and Cranberry

A typical vegetarian on his mobile

Kraut – but this is merely Terre à Terre's way of showing they have a sense of humour (something often lacking in a restaurant of this calibre), and staff are eager to explain and help you out with your pronunciation.

For newcomers, Terre à Terre's tapas is a perfect way to sample the variety of dishes on offer; they even do a Sweetie Tapas that comes with the warning: *"Do not approach alone and don't forget to share"*. Otherwise, you can expect the likes of wasabi cashews or pickled quail's eggs for appetisers, Truly Truffly Risotto for starters and lovingly created Beetroot Chevre Battenburg or Tiffin Tandoori Boudin for main course. It's hard to find fault with this place, as demonstrated by its endless accolades and awards but this is *The Cheeky Guide,* after all, so I hope they won't mind me making a personal plea for someone to paint over the splodgy wall décor, which somehow reminds me of those awful tie-dye bags and coats that hippy-drippy types used to sport in the 80s. This aside, Terre à Terre remains a much-loved and cherished institution. And if their Boozy Rum Truffles are anything to go by, their ever-expanding range of produce could be bestsellers in a few years' time too.

Looking forward to wrapping her lips round Terre à Terre's newest dish, The Errol Flynn

Watering Holes

Chances are that during your time in Brighton you might be tempted to pop for a swift half somewhere, so you'll be pleased to know that we have enough pubs and bars in the city to satisfy even the thirstiest of Glaswegians: from the tiniest (Queensbury Arms) and the tackiest (anywhere on West Street), to the campest and most flamboyant (Regency Tavern).

Over the past ten years, however, Brighton has seen a glut of new trendy pubs take over in the city centre, catering exclusively for a very young market. So exclusive, in fact, that there was a shameful incident five years ago when a 50-year old man was ejected from Polar Central on Queen's Road for being "too old" and "not trendy enough" (though unfortunately for them they picked on the wrong guy as he was a lawyer…)

This chapter contains, therefore, a carefully chosen selection of cool pubs and bars that not only cater for all you fresh-faced hipsters, but are also welcoming to the merely young at heart. Cheers. Or "Bottoms up", as they say in Kemp Town.

KEY TO PUB LOCATIONS

OL	**– Old Lanes**
C	**– City centre**
NL	**– North Laine**
HA	**– Hanover**
K	**– Kemp Town**
H	**– Hove**
S	**– Seafront**
PS	**– Preston Circus**
SD	**– Seven Dials**
D	**– Doncaster**

WHERE TO SAMPLE A BIT OF LOCAL COLOUR

The Charles Napier (HA)
Halfway up Southover Street
(01273) 601413

With maps of the British Empire on the walls, Latin-inscribed curtains, a collection of golf balls in a glass case, Spandau Ballet quietly playing in the background and a good pint of HSB on tap, the Napier remains a safe haven for the 30-plus crowd in Hanover who still carry their own personalised tobacco tins and do a good line in facial hairiness. Only the jarring presence of a TV and video game give any indication of a nod to modernity in this cherished time warp of a pub.

For warm afternoons and evenings they've got a sweet little beer garden round the back, though I'm reliably informed that Charlie the cat is no longer around, so you needn't worry any more about having moth-eaten felines launching themselves into your pint, more's the pity. The Napier is, however, extremely welcoming to all animals, as demonstrated by the fact that for several weeks last year it had its own resident pigeon which used to come in through the front door and stick around for a pint and a natter with Andrea behind the bar.

Top tip: If you're out with a friend, make for the yard of ale hanging above the doorway by the ladies, grab the two armchairs and you'll be immovable until chucking out time.

The Napier - still a popular pre-club haunt

The Colonnade (NL)
10 New Road (01273) 328728

This is the bar for the Theatre Royal next door. It's a wonderfully bizarre place at the best of times with the atmosphere ranging from that of a morgue to a Simon Callow party, with everyone throwing their arms around each other, shouting – *"Darling, I thought you were simply wonderful!"* The walls are decorated with signed photos of cheesy celebs (Roy Kinnear, Jeffrey Archer etc) which inevitably steer conversation around to trying to work out who they all are, and if anyone can remember the name of the bloke who played Eddie Shoestring.

While not to everyone's tastes, the Colonnade *will* appeal to anyone who doesn't mind sharing their pub with a man reading a Frank Muir book, a barmaid singing along to the *War of the Worlds* album, a load of hammy actors arguing over whose round it is and a grey-faced elderly gentleman in a three-piece suit who, completely unnoticed by all, passed away several hours ago.

And if none of *that* appeals, at least it's one of the few places in the centre of Brighton where you can pretty much guarantee a seat on a Friday night.

The Evening Star (C)
55/56 Surrey Street (01273) 328931
www.eveningstarbrighton.co.uk

One of only two independent breweries in Brighton, the Evening Star is the place to come if you're passionate about your beer. As well as offering such heavenly brews as the award-winning Hop Head, Old Cocky and American Pale Ale, their choice of bottled Belgian beer is unrivalled in Brighton, as are their **ten** hand pumps (seven for the real ales, two for cider and one for Horlicks).

True, this pub does have its fair share of real-ale types (those who smack their lips a lot and have a leather tankard hanging from their belt) and it's a rarity to see large groups of ladies in here, but if you're looking for somewhere to sample some genuinely excellent ales and true Brightonian hospitality, this place will not disappoint. The Evening Star is hugely popular at weekends when it adopts a kind of village-pub feel against a conversational background noise so loud you'll end up having to shout to be heard.

And finally, look for the brown bag on the shelf in the corner by the gents with *"Danger do not remove! Corporate crap may be unleashed!"* written on it. I'll leave you to discover what's underneath.

Dress code: Bad tache, mullet and beer belly for the guys, crew cut for the ladies.

Spats - go on, give him a cuddle

The Greys (HA)

105 Southover Street (01273) 680734
Sun breakfast 11am-12noon,
lunch 12noon-2pm,
evening meal 6pm-9.30pm Tues-Thurs, Sat
www.greyspub.com

This tiny but celebrated pub has been an institution in Brighton for as long as I can remember and is now even Egon Ronay listed, thanks to its larger-than-life chef Spats (easily recognised for his David Hockney-style glasses). The food is of course sensational, more akin to top-class restaurant nosh than pub grub. Expect such delights as lobster bisque, homemade patés, *Desperate Dan*-style cow pie with horns (!), strawberry-and-claret jelly and handmade coffee ice cream.

Despite its diminutive size, the Greys also puts on some excellent live events with a slant towards such pop, blues and folk heroes as Shirley Collins and John Otway, and storytelling and comedy from Peter Searles, Ken Campbell, Neil Innes and Monty Python's Carol Cleveland. Combine this with new beers on tap every two months and you have a pub that really has no need of lava lamps and designer furniture to create personality. Run by roguish landlord Mike Lance, the Greys attracts a hardcore following of Hanoverians and beer lovers, most of whom seem to be on first-name terms with each other. The last time I was in, I overheard an old guy at the bar saying to his mate: *"…so she's embarked on this four-year aromatherapy course… two years for each nostril"*. Highly recommended.

The Hand In Hand (K)

33 Upper St James' Street (01273) 602521

The place for lovers of real ale, the Hand in Hand is the other of the two remaining pubs in Brighton where the beer is actually brewed locally. Instead of spending £3 on a pint of gassy piss, treat yourself to a creamy pint of Kemp Town Bitter or try the Olde Trout (*"named after the landlady,"* according to the landlord). They also do a good line in German beers, chocolate and hard-boiled eggs.

A tiny one-room bar, the Hand in Hand is rather sweetly decorated with newspaper stories (Kennedy's assassination's up there somewhere), has a fully-working one-armed bandit by the door, naked Victorian ladies on the ceiling (pictures of, not real ones),

a rather pointless collection of ties and nearly always a friendly dog or two lolloping around.

A minor word of warning: The Hand in Hand is a very small pub so don't always expect a seat, especially at weekends when the mass of regulars (middle-aged, hairy beer-bellied types who always win at pub quizzes) is in. During the week, however, you should expect your own table and a chance conversation with a couple of beardy blokes about politics, holidays in Bavaria and real ale. If you want to spark a debate that the whole pub can join, ask why you can't buy turkey eggs.

Top tip: Come here for the beer, not to cop off with someone – this is strictly a non-pulling pub!

ANYONE FOUND LIFTING THE LID OR ADJUSTING THE VOLUME ON THE JUKE BOX WILL BE SEVERELY BEATEN BY BERT

YOU HAVE BEEN WARNED!!!!!!

ROCK-OLA 477

And if you use the toilet without buying a drink, the Heart and Hand's affable landlord Bert will force-feed you your own faeces

The Heart and Hand (NL)

75 North Road, opposite the Dorset (01273) 624799

This antiquated North Laine bar has, for as long as I can remember, been *the* hangout for Brighton musos, meaning that weekends in here can be like an informal identity parade of familiar faces from hip young bands (British Sea Power, Electric Soft Parade), has-beens (Spitfire, James) stalwarts of the music industry (Stereolab) and pint-sized frizzy-haired eunuchs (Leo Sayer). The reason for this is quite simple – the pub's famous jukebox, which features the likes of Love, The Electric Prunes, Scott Walker and Tim Buckley. Juxtaposed with the muso crowd, you'll find many North Laine traders, old-school antiques dealers, spivs and wrinkly old gits who look like extras from *Eastenders*. Or was that Peter and the Test Tube Babies?

Ranelagh (K)

2 High Street, on corner of St James's Street (01273) 681634

So I walk in here one Easter Sunday, to meet friends, and I'm confronted by two guys doing the Hokey Cokey to the orchestra break in the Beatles' Day in the Life (?!), while at one of the tables near the bar, a guy is shouting, *"I've taken more acid then every fucker in here. And anyone who says not is a fucking liar!"*

Welcome to another St James's Street anomaly. Sandwiched between gay bars and posh restaurants lies the Ranelagh, the last bastion of the pub drunk, the professional beer belly and sozzled old musicians with corrugated faces. Come and meet an array of characters, from friendly middle-aged blokes with ponytails and leather waistcoats to the kind of person one might simply describe as 'potentially violent'.

The music-themed décor ranges from the quaint to the naff, with albums stuck to the ceiling, pennies glued on the bar, banjos, guitars and accordions everywhere and a few dodgy photos and illustrations of old guitar legends on the walls. The Ranelagh does still pay homage to its theme, offering live music every Sunday, from boogie-woogie pianists to blues guitarists. And this, of course, is the time to experience the pub at its best. Otherwise, it's the perfect starting point for anyone foolish enough to take the challenge of a Tuesday night 'alternative' Kemp Town pub crawl.

The Regency Tavern (C)
32 Russell Square (01273) 325652
Food served 12noon-2pm every day

A colourful local with a genuinely eclectic clientele, the Regency Tavern has gay couples, locals, grannies, students and hammy old actors all mucking in together amongst the kitsch splendour of gold-leaf palm trees, bright-green wallpaper, plastic flowers and plaster cherubs. Part of the charm of this old Victorian boozer is the utterly OTT décor, which could

easily pass as a set from *The Avengers*. Even the gents is decorated with a glitterball and mirrored tiles.

If you're ever in for a friend's birthday (or your own, for that matter) make sure to inform the barstaff: they like nothing better than playing their flamboyant, operatic version of *Happy Birthday*, firing bubble guns in your face and giving out free drinks. And then, before you know it, the whole pub has joined in with the celebrations and you're arm in arm with some batty old Brunswick landlady, doing the hand jive.

In the last year, however, the Regency **has** changed hands and, while the décor and clientele have remained the same, it can't be denied that some of the personality behind the bar has gone. And whose idea was it to deck out the staff in Guinness logo T-shirts? They just don't **go** with the place. Gauche 80s shirts, jewellery and hairdos to rival Joan Collins? Yes! T-shirts? No. But it'd take more than a few underdressed torsos to spoil the place, so keep your fingers crossed that nothing else gets buggered with and come and enjoy the campest pub in Brighton.

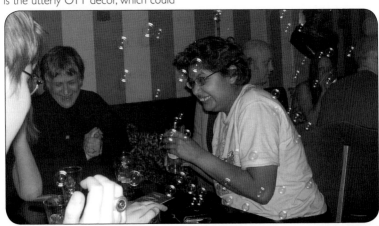

"I'm awfully sorry, that was a rather bubbly one."

www.0404.co.uk

FASHIONABLE DRINKING DENS

Ali-Cats (S)

80 East Street/Brills Lane
(on the seafront, underneath the Prodigal)
(01273) 220902
Films shown Mon-Sat 6pm, Sunday 5pm

Now erring on the wrong side of dingy, Ali-Cats is a secretive underground bar, hidden up an alleyway just off the seafront. Its clientele are a young indie-oriented crowd, who use it mainly as a pre-club hangout for the Pav Tav. The bar, with its underlit tables, sofas and futuristic lampshades, is a cross between a hip New York basement club and the Korova milkbar in A Clockwork Orange. Nice touches here include tiles set into the bar depicting images of Brighton from the 40s to the 60s, and the fact that every evening they show a cult film. Alas, as happens so often once a reputation is established, the place has been allowed to fall into disrepair and you now have a very real chance of injuring your coccyx if you fail to perch correctly on the edge of broken sofas and two-legged stools. Of the two cubicles in the gents, one door is hanging off its hinges and the other offers a grandstand view of the urinals via the enormous hole punched in the middle of the door. Or perhaps it's a new style of cottaging facility, it's hard to tell. At weekends, unsurprisingly, Ali-Cats gets very busy and claustrophobics may have a Charles-Bronson-in-The-Great-Escape moment, owing to the stuffiness and lack of light, but it's usually more sedate during the week.

Barley Mow (K)

92 St George's Road (01273) 682259
Food served 11am-10pm

This convivial Kemp Town local is the Michael Palin of Brighton pubs: an all-round good egg, thoroughly entertaining and prone to the odd bit of silliness. It boasts an old-school tuckshop behind the bar (selling the likes of Texan bars and flying saucers), has a heated beer garden, a quiz every other Thursday, free board games and roast dinners until 10pm! Plus it's the only pub in Brighton – or the world, for that matter – to have a 'sperm table'. That's all I'm saying on the subject.

The Bee's Mouth (C)

10 Western Road (01273) 770083

Once a gallery with a coffee machine, over the years it seems that lubrication has taken precedence over the flogging of paintings, resulting in one of the best new Brighton bars in years. Candlelit, with cosy booths and decorated with bold artwork, cheesegrater lamps, trumpet candleholders and spinning heads beneath the bar, this place feels more

Deep in the Bee's oesophagus something stirs

like a bohemian hangout from 60s Paris than a Brighton boozer, with only the expensive wine list on the blackboard at odds with its eccentric, down-at-heel décor. It's deceptively large too: once you're through the bar area, the Bee's Mouth carries on down some steps into another chilled-out area with a curtained corner for canoodling couples. Only the very brave would, however, choose to opt for the seating further down as the art seems to get more and more disturbing the further you descend, though it's worth exploring to find tables that could just as well be in the Parisian catacombs

If you're after an attractive arty crowd, a seat on a Friday (I suspect the occasional way-out jazz band puts off the masses), enjoy random encounters with strangers, take a slice of cake with your pint and don't mind a spot of live acoustic music, the Bee's Mouth is the proverbial bee's knees. Highly recommended.

Brighton Rocks (K)

6 Rock Place (01273) 601139
Food served 6pm-9.30pm, Sun 12noon-5pm

Sandwiched between a drama college and a rock school, and with a name like Brighton Rocks, you'd think a place like this would just wave a white flag, stick on the legwarmers and spandex, erect a piano in the corner and encourage its customers to break into spontaneous song/moshing whenever they felt like it.

In fact, nothing could be further from the truth: this place is a poser's paradise, with the emphasis on cocktails and global tapas, the décor New England beach house, and its clientele more aussieBum than Ozzy Osbourne. And not only do these guys know about cocktails and food, they also know how to have fun, and run the best street party in Brighton, the day after Pride.

Coopers Cask (H)

3 Farm Road, Hove (01273) 737026
Food served Sun-Thurs 12noon-9pm,
Fri-Sat 12noon-7pm
Sunday roast 12noon "until they run out"
(usually 4-5pm)

Let's face it, the words *good*, *pub* and *Hove* rarely crop up in the same sentence. Coopers however is the exception to the rule and has been a stonking success since opening five years ago, not least for its superb and inexpensive pub grub. Your only quibble with this place will be in wishing there was more of it as, being one of Brighton's smallest pubs, seating is always at a premium. Unsurprisingly, Coopers is rammed at mealtimes – if you are popping here for food at lunchtime, you'd best arrive early or you may find yourself eating your lobster in the ladies.

Dr Brighton's (S)

16 Kings Road (01273) 328765

Dr Brighton's shows off what this town does best by effortlessly blending a friendly, party atmosphere with a mixed gay/straight crowd, and is particularly popular at weekends with the pre-club punters (Revenge, the Honeyclub and the Beach are all within a two-minute walk).

As well as ogling the fish here, if you're ever stood up – or left waiting for friends – you can pass the time reading the trivia on the columns in the centre of the pub. Originally based on the theme of infamous drinkers (Dorothy Parker, Oliver Reed et al), it has since expanded to include odd titbits of information (discover what a hag fag is!) and stories of weird deaths (find out about the man who was crushed to death by elephant poo). Dr Brighton's even lays claim to the town's longest-running drinks promotion,

'Prescription', which they rediscovered in some 80-year-old documents about the pub. The perfect pre-club, seafront bar for the more discerning and a good place to take out-of-town hetero mates to ease them in gently.

The Eagle Bar (NL)

125 Gloucester Road (01273) 607765
Food served 12noon-9pm most days

Winners of the Food Pub of the Year Award in 2002, The Eagle is rightly celebrated for its nosh, which is superb. Owned by the same chaps who run the Hop Poles, this place attracts a similarly trendy crowd, has plenty of seating and, of course, prides itself on its cuisine. On a grumpy note, however, I experienced the worst service *ever* last Christmas when the surly twelve-year old who was serving (and clearly on a bad comedown), spent fifteen minutes talking to a mate on his mobile while everyone waiting at the busy bar got *very* pissed off. Later, when he brought my dinner he didn't bring any cutlery and when I asked for a knife and fork he leaned over the bar and pulled out a pair from the rack of *used* cutlery. When I confronted him and asked if he had any clean ones he replied arsily, *"No. Don't suppose we have,"* and shuffled off. And judging from friends' experiences in here of late, I'm not alone in being arsed around. Sort it out guys, love your food but employing arrogant knobheads is really not doing you any favours.

Oi fuckheads!
Who's the wanker
who ordered braised
auk on a bed of pureéd
moss? Come and get it
before I shit on it

Earth and Stars (NL)

Top of Church Street (01273) 772282
Food served Mon-Thu 12noon-3pm and
5pm-8pm, Fri-Sun 12noon-5pm

Brighton's most environmentally friendly pub, the Earth and Stars is carbon-balanced, has solar panels on its roof and used to pride itself on being 100% organic, from the beers, wines, soft drinks, peanuts and roast dinners to the floorboards, loo paper and staff. Ask for a pack of fags and you'll still get American Spirit, but they've been forced to cave in on the beers – alongside the Freedom organic lager are now ranked the labels of oppression, Kronenbourg and San Miguel. The food's mostly sandwiches now, albeit intriguing ones (chorizo, blue cheese and cornichons? No, I don't know what cornichons are either) but they do make an effort to use local ingredients, and organic ones where it doesn't represent commercial suicide. And that, in essence, seems to be the problem – that even in Brighton people aren't ready for the fully organic experience, even in a pub as lovely to sit in as this one. It's always been deathly quiet during the week and it shouldn't be.

The Fishbowl, as not featured in this book

Please get down there, and while you're at it, lobby the bar staff to bring back the unbranded drinks, and ask if their underwear is Soil Association approved.

The Fortune of War (S)

157 Kings Road Arches (01273) 205065

This long-established seafront pub gets stupidly busy during the summer weekends when it is literally mobbed by hundreds of visitors. In fact, be prepared to experience such a long and frustrating wait at the bar that you'll wish you'd simply gone to the off licence and headed straight to the beach instead with some cans. Come off-season during the day however, bag yourself one of the window seats with a sea view, ask them to turn the music down, and you'll discover that it's actually quite a charming bar.

The Globe (OL)

78 Middle Street (01273) 727114

This place has gone full circle from being a pleasant seafront local called the Globe to a garish turquoise hellhole (the Squid) and back again. Those blood-red walls and shelves of books downstairs even add a welcoming boudoir-cum-library feel to the place. Being so close to the seafront, however, all this newfound elegance instantly evaporates at weekends, as it still packs out with gaggles of blue-legged girls and blokes with FCUK T-shirts and parrot haircuts. Combine this with DJs playing music at impenetrable volumes and you'll be on your knees weeping for mercy. Like the Cricketers down the road, it's *much* better to experience the Globe mid-week when you can hear yourself speak, get a seat and enjoy the hard work that's gone into turning it back into a half-decent pub.

The Hampton (C)

57 Upper North Street (01273) 731347
Food served Tues-Sun 12noon-3pm,
5.30pm-9.30pm

This popular student hangout deserves
a mention for its décor, as it's been
rather imaginatively designed with a
Scandinavian slant, with lots of indoor
stonework, stripped wood, patterned
wallpaper and huge panoramic stills.
Visit on a Sunday for a superb roast,
bask in the courtyard on a summer's
evening with a jug of Pimms or drop
acid and spend the evening staring
at their giant poster of the Alps and
actually believing yourself to be:

a)   Heidi
b)   Goat Peter
c)   A goat

The Hop Poles (OL)

13 Middle Street (01273) 710444/710010
Food served 12noon-9pm weekdays,
Fri-Sat 12noon-7pm, Sun 12noon-9pm

As with the Coopers Cask (these guys
used to own it), the Hop Poles thrives
on a tradition of good-value quality
food, sweets behind the bar, table
service and a gay-friendly attitude,
while those with flexible necks can
also enjoy their wacky car hubcap
sculptures by the mysterious Ptolemy
– seek out the reptilian one.

The pub is popular with a young,
fashionable, mixed gay/straight crowd
and, unlike so many other pubs in
its close vicinity, does not attract
the weekend lager louts. They also
like a giggle in here – the recently
introduced pub quiz is almost
pantomime, featuring live music and
low-level pyrotechnics. Well, even
Metallica enjoy a night down their local
once in a while.

The Open House (PC)

146 Springfield Road (01273) 880102
Food served daily 12noon-4pm, 5pm-9pm

Worth a mention for being one of
the only decent pubs in this neck of
the woods (by London Road Station)
and still the best place for a post-film
discussion and pint after an evening at
the Duke of York's. The Open House
is decorated with colourful art (in
collaboration with the Fiveways artists
group), has a big beer garden and
three big seating areas, including one
non-smoking area which resembles
a living room (full of sprawling sofas,
paintings on the walls, empty beer cans
and pizza boxes). You'll also find gigs
upstairs and regular improv comedy
nights (including classes, if you need
to be taught how to make things up).
This boozer's only flaw is that the grub
isn't quite as good as it thinks it is. Still,
a meal capable of sentient thought is
remarkable in itself.

The spectacular view of Brighton beach, as seen from the window of the gents' toilets in The Setting Sun

The Setting Sun (HA)
1 Windmill Street (01273) 626192

Hidden away in the upper cranial cavity of Hanover, this little-known boozer can take a bit of finding for the uninitiated. True, service here can be slow at times and the seating arrangement a bit annoying – especially when you're trying to get to the patio at the back. And, despite the occasional presence of a bloke practising his banjo, it does lack a bit of charm. So why is it in here? The clue's in the name. For on a summer's eve, when the rich hues of twilight cascade over the shimmering channel and the sun's dappled beams singe the sky, the views of Brighton from the patio here are right champion.

Seek it out on a late summer's evening and once the sun's set you can pop off to another Hanover local or stick around and seek out the bloke who comes in sporting a flamboyant cravat. Last time I was here he walked through the door with an empty banana-milk carton, had it filled up with Coke, bought himself a cigar and promptly left. What's that all about?

The Shakespeare's Head (SD)
1 Chatham Place, on the corner of
New England Road (01273) 329444
Food served Mon-Fri 5pm-10pm,
Saturday 12noon-10pm,
Sunday 12noon-5pm

Leaving aside the general grooviness of this salon de bière, there is now another excellent attraction in the form of the exclusively sausage-and-mash menu, featuring such locally made epicurean delights as chorizo and pork-and-apple, a staggering nine different types of mash and six gravies including madeira-and-thyme. They do have chicken chipolatas too, which I personally regard as a crime against nature, but you can't expect perfection.

Pogo-ing bar staff are not unusual – they do like their music in here, though there's a veto on *Moon Safari* as the landlord got fed up hearing it in every other Brighton pub for years on end; should you accidentally start whistling *Sexy Boy* when you go to the bar, you may receive a sound thrashing with a string of bangers.

Apart from that, it's generally so laid back in here that every day is like Sunday (except that on Sunday you can't order sausages), and they've even got board games for when you've finished reading the paper. I once had an argument playing Jenga in here with a friend who was blowing on the wobbling tower of blocks during my go to try and make it fall over. We eventually agreed that 'atmospheric' disturbance not generated by the human body, such as a draught under a door, was all that was allowed, upon which he promptly opened a window and a howling gale swept through the room… well, you can guess the rest.

WHERE TO GO FOR A GOOD NATTER

Basketmakers Arms (NL)

12 Gloucester Road (01273) 689006
Food served weekdays 12noon-3pm,
5.30pm-8.30pm, weekend 12noon-4pm

Cherished by long-term residents, the Basketmakers is simply a damned good local with no frills, no pumping music, no trendy lagers, no vile artwork on the wall and plenty of decent pub grub. And, hidden away in the backstreets of North Laine, it's a place that weekend revellers rarely stumble across.

Part of the Basketmakers' unique charm lies in the thousands of old tins that cover the walls from top to toe, in which you can leave messages or look for any that have been left. I hid one in the Huntley & Palmers dundee-cake tin (though I can't guarantee it'll still be there now), found another with the message *"Ruth Hutt licked my face"* (?) and have discovered some other bizarre drawings and notes (see right) in old pipe-tobacco and biscuit tins. If you visit the pub it is your sworn duty to continue this fine tradition, particularly if taken with the urge to write fruity comments about the bar staff. My very latest find, incidentally, was the photo of this woman…

…with the message on the back: *"please help us find this woman"*. So the hunt is on.

And while you're at it, does anyone know Ruth Hutt? I'm quite partial to a spot of face-licking.

The Battle Of Trafalgar (C)

34 Guildford Road (01273) 882276
Food served weekdays 12noon-2pm,
weekends 12noon-4pm

Once the hangout for Brighton's theatrical types (possibly thanks to its close proximity to the original Nightingale Theatre at the bottom of the road), the Trafalgar is a relaxed, spacious local with plenty of seats, a suntrap beer garden and lots of lovely old theatre and comedy posters from days gone by.

The clientele and staff here have always been a friendly and mellow bunch; the chance of witnessing a fight in this place is about as likely as Elton John's hair growing back of its own accord. The bar billiards table has now sadly gone (the manager told me it was broken but a cheeky local chipped in that it was due to "*cost-cutting*"!) but if you like your bar snacks decidedly old-fashioned, as good locals go it's one of Brighton's finest.

Proof that drinking beer gives you the strength to lift entire vehicles

The Cricketers (OL)

15 Black Lion Street (01273) 329472
Food served weekdays 12noon-3pm,
weekends 12noon-5pm

One of Brighton's oldest pubs (it even earns a mention in *Brighton Rock*), suitably decorated with red Edwardian-style furnishings, old gramophones, ornate table lamps, stags' heads and wallpaper that'd make your granny blush.

The upstairs room, recently redecorated, is now distinctly at odds with the downstairs as, typically, it's had all its character ripped out, despite the Graham-Greene-used-to-drink-here theme. Gone is the wood panelling and the red-velvet boudoir décor that made the perfect backdrop to a professional can-can routine I once had the pleasure to watch here.

Though best avoided at weekends when it's stuffy, uncomfortably busy and populated by away football supporters and blokes who wear their shirts over their belts to hide their beer guts, on a quiet weekday the Cricketers transforms back to an eccentric aunt's front room where you can bag the window seats by the trophy cabinet, or sit at the back and marvel at the gaudy furnishings.

The Great Eastern (NL)
103 Trafalgar Street (01273) 685681
Food served Mon-Sat 12noon-11pm,
Sun 12noon-10.30pm

Another unspoiled Brighton pub with old wooden tables, shelves of books at the back, newspapers, friendly barstaff and a genuine mix of clientele from students to beardy old men (I even saw a vicar in here one Sunday necking a pint of Guinness).

If you're coming for the night it often pays to arrive early as seating is limited; the tables facing the bar can get a bit cramped if it's busy, while the big tables at the far end of the pub are perfect if you're bringing a crowd. The Eastern is also popular for its pub grub and does one of the best (and cheapest) Sunday roasts in Brighton. Also recommended are their S&M nights on Wednesdays. Fetish dress code is optional but a love of sausage and mash compulsory.

Hotel Du Vin Bar (OL)
2-6 Ship Street (01273) 718588

If you're looking for somewhere with a touch of sophistication and excellent service, and you don't mind paying well over the odds for a drink, Hotel Du Vin's bar is just the ticket. For an intimate evening with a small group of friends the setup here is perfect: the wide, open bar area is subtly lit and there are plenty of leather sofas and armchairs – once you've found a good spot you needn't move for the rest of the night as they offer table service and will even bring olives and pistachios for you to munch on. The French – when not slouching around and being surly – clearly know a thing or two about customer service, as all the staff here seem to be from across the water (or can pull off the accent)

and have the knack of treating you like royalty.

Unsurprisingly, the bar attracts moneyed types, particularly middle-aged geezers and their trophy second-division footballers' wives. Tacky punters aside, as my friend Rob said, *"a girl brought on a date here can rest assured she's fancied very much indeed"* (though she might be a little disappointed if you only ply her with drinks and skip dinner!)

With the exception of some of the cheesy clientele and the tacky wine-bar muzak, Hotel Du Vin has style; perfect if, after years of slumming it round Brighton's grotty boozers slurping lager, you welcome the idea of slipping into a cool suit/dress/ Superman outfit and spending the night sat on a comfy leather sofa drinking cocktails instead.

AFTER-HOURS DRINKING

With the change in licensing laws in 2005, most Brighton pubs now stay open until midnight or 1am at a weekend. Should you wish to continue drinking after this time, you'll have to hit the clubs or try places like Sumo (9-12 Middle Street), or Heist (top of West Street) which stays open *"until the last customer goes home"*. If you still need a drink after that, consult your doctor.

The Lord Nelson (NL)

36 Trafalgar Street (01273) 695872
Food served Mon-Sat 12noon-2.30pm,
Sun 12.30pm-3.30pm

Halfway down Trafalgar Street the Nelson is often overlooked, even by long-term residents, which is a pity as – together with the Great Eastern, Trafalgar and Basketmakers – this really is one of the best locals in North Laine. With tobacco-stained walls, *Sooty* collection box, ancient piano, pork scratchings, food *"like granny makes it"*, a mismatched collection of stools in the main bar and an unspoken policy of conversation taking priority over music, the Nelson has been spared the makeover treatment and remains a cherished old-school drinking establishment. It also has a terrific reputation for its food, which is really top notch. Sunday roast is a lavish serving of roast and veg (and they do a tasty nut roast for veggies) with crumbles and the likes of spotted dick and custard – of heroic portions

– for pudding fans afterwards. It's also popular with the Brighton & Hove Albion football crowd (hence all the photos on the walls) and still does its longrunning Tuesday quiz with cash prizes and free bottles of wine. Come here of a wet afternoon, sit down with a pint of Harveys Armada, bangers and mash and a copy of *The Argus* and, within a few hours, you'll be shouting *"Come on you Seagulls!"* in a genuine Brighton accent.

Curiously, for years now a Dungeons & Dragons group has been coming to the Nelson every Monday night dressed up as wizards and goblins and losing themselves in their Tolkienesque fantasy world, though how welcome they are is another matter. An innocent enquiry to the barman recently – *"Do you still have the Dungeons & Dragons here on a Monday?"* prompted him to roll his eyes, throw his arms in the air and say, *"look mate, it's got nothing to do with us all right? They just keep **bloody** turning up"*.

Another overzealous Dungeons & Dragons player makes his way to the Nelson

The Lion and Lobster (H)

Sillwood Street (almost Hove)
(01273) 327299
Food served 12noon-9pm, and they don't
scrimp on the portions either

As many pubs in the city fall victim to the modernisation process, the Lion and Lobster remains a true traditional seaside boozer with psychedelic beer-stained carpets, seafaring tales from salty old dogs, burned-out clubbers in their late 30s, an ocean of paunches and an absolute fog of tobacco smoke. On football nights they celebrate in style, with TVs in every corner and plenty of beer- and testosterone-fuelled "ooooohh"s, "aaaaahhh"s and "the referee is a mong"s. It's even a B&B on the sly, which is invaluable if, at the end of the night, you just can't face leaving.

Walmer Castle (HA)

Queen's Park Road (01273) 682466
Food served Mon-Thurs 6pm-9pm,
Fri 5-9.30pm, Sun 12noon-8.30pm

Cosy and convivial Hanover pub with some rather tasty grub courtesy of Fi's Kitchen. In fact, owing to their stone-based ovens and unusual toppings like Billy Gruff (goat's cheese and sun-dried tomatoes) and jerk chicken, the staff's claim that "*the Walmer does the best pizza in Brighton*" may not be too far from the truth. Along with the fish tanks, fairy lights, Lucky Strike machine, mellow back room and colourful décor, it is the staff – and their pride in the place – that makes the Walmer so welcoming. Get chatting with Grant behind the bar (usually wearing a woolly hat or three) and you can find out about the Walmer's commitment to National Pirate Day (hence the silver-foil knives still hanging up behind the bar), learn the names of the fish (which mysteriously seem to keep

changing) or get him to make you a hot toddy on a cold winter's night and you'll see why the Walmer hasn't needed to change its formula for the last ten years.

FOR A CRACKING SUNDAY ROAST WITH ALL THE TRIMMINGS

Seven Dials: *Prestonville Arms/Shakespeare's Head*

North Laine: *Lord Nelson/ Great Eastern/Earth and Stars/The Eagle*

Kemp Town: *Barley Mow/ Sidewinder/Brighton Rock Beach House/The Stag*

City centre: *Regency Tavern/ Hampton/Western Front*

Hanover area: *Hartington/ Dover Castle/The Hanover/ The Walmer/Pub With No Name/Greys*

Hove area: *Coopers Cask/ Lion and Lobster*

Old Lanes: *Hop Poles*

Preston Park area: *Open House*

(See pub reviews above for more details)

DISCOTHEQUES

Home to the famous Zap Club, Ocean Rooms, Audio, Honeyclub, Catskills Records and Skint, Brighton's club/DJ scene boasts everything from cool underground jazz and retro to house and garage nights, as well as hosting the biggest gay club on the south coast. Combine this with regular visits from big-name DJs, plus our own Norman Cook, and it's not surprising that Brighton's clubs are packed every night of the week. What other town can boast more than 30 clubs within walking distance of each other, and most a stone's throw from the beach?

One of the very special things about Brighton's nightlife is that, unlike so many other UK cities, the clubs here do not merely represent weekend escapism from drudgery and boredom. If anything, some of the best nights here are mid-week and even Sundays are starting to become fashionable. Clubbing in Brighton seems nothing less than a shameless celebration of living in a party town, which is probably why upbeat and carnival-type music, like big beat, Latin jazz and 70s disco are particularly popular here. And with celebrated club nights like Dynamite Boogaloo, Wild Fruit and Born Bad, the scene has a glitz, glamour and kinkiness that Manchester, even in its heyday, could never have provided.

Audio

10 Marine Parade (01273) 697775
www.audiobrighton.com

Probably the only club in town that virtually insists you wear trainers and a T-shirt, Audio has its finger firmly on the pulse of what's hot, or even just glowing gently; it also has a magpie tendency to nick everyone else's best nights, having clawed up Dynamite Boogaloo, Stompa Phunk and the Tru Thoughts crew. In Supercharged they already had a sublime weekly breaks event and it's now become the kind of club you can show up to almost without bothering to check what's on and know it'll be good, which is no small achievement given the dilution of dance music over the past few years.

When they opened in 2004, kicking off the current Brighton obsession with club refurbs and name changes, they divided the old Escape Club into two separate venues, with Above Audio as a separate, less hectic bar experience – you can still move between them but you have to go back outside to do it, which I'm sure is purely to ensure unhealthy clubbers get an occasional dose of sea air to restart their vital organs. The hippest club in town, in a good way. Highly recommended.

A CHEEKY TALE

If you look above Audio you'll see a flat which has a commanding view of the beach and, in particular, the phone box in front of the club. Two guys, Mark and Bruce, used to live up there and some nights after the club had almost cleared out, they'd ring up the phone box, wait for some inebriated clubber to answer, take a note of how he was dressed and then play these weird 50s adverts down the line. It would start with some cheesy music and then go –

"Hi, and welcome to the world of Lux soap, a new powder that'll get your clothes whiter than white"

– and then a different voice would say –

"You are wearing a red shirt, jeans and a blue hat."
Click

You can't see my bra in this, can you?

Babylon Lounge
Kingsway, Hove (01273) 207100

No club adjoining Hove's bowling greens and lagoon will ever be cool, particularly when it so closely resembles a school gymnasium. That said, Babylon Lounge does offer decent soul and goth nights and hen-friendly male strippers every Friday (see Adonis Cabaret review in *Sex* chapter). The rest of the time it contents itself with bog-standard student nights, salsa classes and midweek sessions hosted by part-time garage DJs from as far afield as Brighton.

Top tip: Unless you live in darkest Hove, you'll need to get a cab here. I'd recommend paying the driver an extra quid to wait around for a couple of minutes as, after a quick nose around inside, you *may* choose to make a sharp exit.

The Beach
171-181 Kings Road Arches
(01273) 722272
www.domainmysteriouslyallowedtolapse.co.uk

It's been a long slow descent for the Beach since its glory days hosting Fatboy's Big Beat Boutique, and the final warning sounded in 2004 when Bedrock packed up and went home. Despite the marvy brick arches and pillars, there's no getting away from the fact that most nights in here come served with a fat wedge of stilton, so much so that I swear I slipped on a carelessly discarded Jacob's cream cracker last time I ventured in. Still, if you want to get pissed and lurch about to Visage, don't mind me, go on in.

B'lo (formerly the Joint)
37 West Street (01273) 735284

Another day, another refit and a *really* crap new name but otherwise this place hasn't changed all that much. There's more chrome and more

...and she chose to spend it at Babylon Lounge??!!

speakers, and they get a gold star for stocking some decent bottled ales behind the bar, while their stock-in-trade of alternative electro-goth, metal no-wave industrial disko is still very much in evidence with classic night Detournement firmly in place and some interesting live bands clad in purple plastic and scary boots. If you've got a spider's web tattooed on your eyelid you'll fit right in. That's not all they do of course, as Boogaloo Stu still drops by to parade his Cavalcade of Pop, and the inevitable house nights also crop up. The stairs here are just made for a dramatic entrance, as somebody proved to me one night when they executed a series of forward rolls all the way to the bottom, culminating in a floor surf straight out across the dance floor. Completely deliberate of course.

Emblematic fragrance: Brasso and Windolene.

Brighton Gloucester
27 Gloucester Place (01273) 688011
www.thebrightongloucester.co.uk

Despite some minor Botox and a slight name change, the Gloucester seems destined to live on forever as a cheap, cheerful, come-as-you-are club, responsible for more unwanted pregnancies and regretful *"Oh no, did I really slam-dance to the Sisters of Mercy?"* recollections than Brighton's other clubs put together. Expect every musical taste to be catered for here, from 70s and 80s to house, indie, nu-metal, nu-goth, nu-gothmetal, old-gothmetal, quiteoldbutnotasoldasold-gothmetal, and so on. Inside, the Gloucester is a split-level funhouse with a dance floor straight out of *Saturday Night Fever*, and while some nights it's full to capacity, on others there'll just be a few punks sat in the corner eating jelly. Even the clientele here are an unpredictable lot – everything from gangs of teenagers from Crawley to gaggles of secondary-school teachers who've popped down here *"just for old times' sake"*. Until you've been here twenty times, skidded in a puddle of vomit, danced like a loony to Abba and been chatted up by a fifteen-year-old, you're still a newcomer in this town.

Knobbly knees contestant at B'lo

Casablanca
2 Middle Street (01273) 709710

This club specialises in Latin jazz and jazz funk, and is particularly refreshing in that it has live bands at weekends and not just DJs. With such a strong DJ culture here, you forget sometimes what a pleasure it is to dance to live music, especially when the bands really know how to let rip. You'll turn up, look at the outside, and go *"oh God, no"*, and yes, it is cheap, but you will have a good time despite yourself.

The club has two floors and while it's a bit annoying that you can't take your drinks between the two, the top half is basically just a bar (with a naff car theme), so I'd recommend sticking to the downstairs bit. Shame that the dance area is between the bar and the exit, but if the funky music and those horns don't move you to dance, you're in the wrong city.

Dress code: flares, corduroy cap, goatee.

The Church (formerly Club New York, The Shrine, The Loft, The Attic Conversion)
Dyke Road (01273) 208678

Housed, amazingly, in what was once a church, this is now a place of worship for salsa devotees, some of whom *can* actually dance. Essentially operating as an ongoing 24-7 salsa lesson, this place runs classes most evenings, with a club night straight afterwards.

The teachers are very good, the regulars super-friendly (and often gorgeous) and the vibe noticeably sparklier than most house nights in town. Two mid-size dancefloors hold the action and, if you're lucky, some sharp-dressed, swivel-hipped Mediterranean sex bomb will hold you up in the middle of it.

Creation
78 West Street (01273) 321628

Formerly the Paradox, this place has always tried to take itself more seriously than the Event II (just across the road) but, being located on West Street, it is, of course, fighting a losing battle. Full of weekend revellers in their late teens, Creation is a gigantic multi-levelled club, with three dancefloors, cosy corners and paid podium dancers. It operates a seven-nights-a-week mix of chart hits, club classics and more specialised garage/R&B nights, not to mention the famous Wild Fruit. But it ain't classy. No sirree. Take a bodyguard and a mask to filter out the aftershave that can kill a girl at twenty paces.

Dress code: G-string/thong.

Concorde 2
Miles from anywhere, Madeira Drive
(01273) 606460
www.concorde2.co.uk

Built out of the ashes of the Water Rats (a one-time greasy bikers' hangout), the Concorde 2 took over from where the original Concorde left off by specialising in live music, cracking club nights (from reggae and punk house to hip-hop and dirty acid techno) and odd one-offs, such as the UK Air Guitar

Championships. While the Concorde works far better for live music than club nights it's always fantastically relaxed, reasonably roomy, and you never have trouble getting a drink at the bar. If you are coming along though, for goodness sake, try and wear something that doesn't clash with the paint job.

Engine Room
5 Preston Street (01273) 728999
www.engineroomclub.com

Confusing as the concept of live death metal may be, that's one of the delights on offer in this hardcore rock/punk/glam/goth den. It's a sticky little basement with lots of odd corners and anterooms to hide in, red gothic-arched seatbacks and huddles of fetishistically adorned groovers, who may accidentally poke you in the eye with an exocet-shaped piercing but will apologise unreservedly and offer to mop up any blood afterwards. On some nights there's so much PVC in here that the squeaking and rustling almost drowns out the music, yet still there's a curiously inclusive feeling that welcomes even the most conservatively dressed. If you're lucky you might get to see a professional pole dancer using the facility in front of the stage, but if not then feel encouraged to have a go yourself – they offer prizes for the rudest gyrations. Watch out for organiser Neil wafting around in his floor-length coat like a big black crow.
Emblematic fragrance: Wet eyeliner and Castrol GTX.

The Event II
West Street (01273) 732627

The largest club in Brighton, popular with students, virgin clubbers, hen and stag parties, 'weekenders' and the under-twelves. It is, of course, a blatant meat market but the nights are generally cheap, unashamedly glitzy and irredeemably tacky. Party tunes throughout the ages (plus a big nod to the previous week's *Popworld*) create the soundtrack, while the vast dancefloor is a sea of loved-up teenagers, all on the pull and sporting the latest in Top Man/Top Shop fashion. If you really insist on coming here, I can't help you.

Funky Buddha Lounge
Kings Road Arches (01273) 725541

If you like your clubs intimate then this is the one, its two parallel tunnels holding the bar and dancefloor like a giant Twix. Well they've made all the other chocolate bars huge, it must be the turn of the Twix soon, surely.

The Bud, as nobody calls it, has lost some of its cachet recently, what with Audio snaffling their best night; bland-o-rama smooth soul is starting to prove more popular and garnering a crush of lovely secretaries and gents who feel they're not dressed without a proper shirt and shiny loafers.

A fantastic place to pull, as it's so small you can't help snagging your signet ring on a lady's foundation garments 'by accident' and then finding a beautiful, crazy relationship unfurling before your eyes as you attempt to disentangle each other – *"you won't believe how we met, it all started when Darren suddenly found his arm trapped in my culottes"*.

Emblematic fragrance: Denim.

Funky Fish Club
19-23 Marine Parade, underneath the Madeira Hotel (01273) 698331
www.funkyfishclub.co.uk

Like a cow standing alone in a field of sheep, the Fish is so unpretentious it barely seems to be a club at all in Brighton terms. Insisting on a strict diet of 60s and 70s soul and 'classic' rock, it has no truck with name DJs and attracts a wide-ranging crowd who come to have fun rather than pose. Admittedly, it does have the strong flavour of a wedding reception with its state of the ark lighting, white tablecloths and occasional pensioner, but there's a friendly vibe about the place, even if they will still insist on testing the theory that you can dance to *Sweet Home Alabama*. Ladies, expect to be chatted up by visiting insurance salesmen staying in the hotel above, who will attempt to make conversation with opening gambits like, *"Oh, yes, I've always been a big fan of Diana Ross and the Pips"*.

What to drink: Babycham with an olive in it.

MOST EMBARRASSING REQUESTS

1. KYLIE - The Locomotion
2. ABBA - Dancing Queen
3. DJ CASPER - Cha Cha Slide
4. SPICE GIRLS - Wannabe
5. CHRISTINA AGUILERA - Dirty
6. GUNS & ROSES - Paradise City
7. LEO SAYER - You make me feel like dancing
8. BAYWATCH - Theme from Baywatch
9. S CLUB 7 - Reach
10. OPERATION BLADE - Bass in the place London

The Jazz Place
10 Ship Street (01273) 328439

Priding itself on being *"the world's longest-running weekend jazz club"*, the Jazz Place has changed little since it opened nearly twenty years ago. It's still a poky basement with two tables, five chairs and a dancefloor the size of a Persian rug. In fact, the only thing that ever seems to change here are the posters on the walls. But the Jazz Rooms remains a terrific club night and really packs in the weekend crowds – a friendly, straight-laced bunch, intent on sweating it on the dance floor to the Latin-jazz-salsa-afro beats spun by Russ Dewbury and co.

Not *just* the Jazz Place, on Tuesdays it's also the reggae place, as it has been home to the excellent Roots Garden for almost as long as Russ Dewbury's jazz nights. Laid-back, welcoming and even offering a free cloakroom, this is one of the best clubs in town. Serious jazzers, award yourself ten points if you recognise which Miles Davis album the colour scheme down here is taken from.

Dress code: Flares, corduroy cap, jazz dot*.

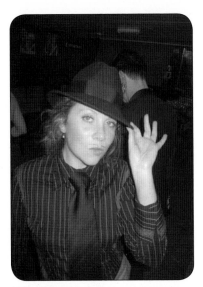

The Honeyclub
214 Kings Road Arches (01273) 202807
www.thehoneyclub.co.uk

Now expanded into something like 86 rooms, the Honey is suddenly among the biggest clubs in town though, given that the company includes places like Creation, that isn't necessarily a positive. If mainstream hardhouse, techno and trance are your bag and you still think glowsticks are pretty cool you'll find satisfaction here, though the way the door prices are going, recourse to a blag may be required. What the sound system seriously lacks in fidelity it makes up for in denture-rattling volume and this is where many of the pretty people come out to play, so if you're after a bit of deaf eye-candy this'll suit. Incidentally the new décor is mostly grey – if that's a colour *you* can get excited about please write to *The Cheeky Guide* with an explanation. And be nice to the gentleman who runs the concession table in the loos and he'll give you a special squirt of cologne 'down there'.

*That bit of fluff that grows below the bottom lip

KooKlub

10 Pool Valley (01273) 888000
www.kooklub.co.uk

Arising from the ashes of one of Brighton's lesser-known haunts, The Music Club, this is something of an anomaly among the seafront nightspots: a refurbishment that has involved more than a can of Dulux and some seatcovers. From the expensive leather loungers, the separate cocktail bar, the well-appointed sound system and the absence of drinks promos, it's clear that they're aiming at the better-heeled clubber, even if it is proving something of a struggle to get the music right – one night it can be packed to the rafters and another there's tumbleweed rolling across the dance floor. If that comes together, this could and should become one of the grooviest clubs in town. Grapple with their huge range of confusing dress codes at your peril though: *"we prefer dirty and filthy"* shouldn't encourage you to turn up in the sweatshirt you wear for decorating the kitchen, yet somehow it does. At least if you do bother to don your flashiest cleavage-flasher you'll feel that the luxurious surroundings merited the effort.

The Ocean Rooms

1 Morley Street (01273) 699069
www.oceanrooms.co.uk

A tip of the brim first to the sound system downstairs, which has experienced possibly the greatest sonic upgrade of any Brighton club in recent times. And a wipe of the rim for the gents toilet, which *was* sleek and svelte and is now getting rather tatty (bring back the toilet attendant I say) though, saying that, I'd still rather fall unconscious on the floor here than most club 'bathrooms'.

The Ocean Rooms is slightly trendier than its seafront brethren (despite the naff and clichéd quotations they insist on sticking on the front of the building), as are its punters, proving it with their Pimpbitchdisko weekends that alternate Ibizan legends such as Circoloco with cooler electro nights hosted by the likes of the painfully hip DFA Records.

There're three floors here, each with their own bar: the main basement room is spacious and lovely, the ground-floor one feels strangely claustrophobic and the VIP room on the top floor is rather like going to heaven (no, the *real* one) without all the fuss and bother of dying first. It's all white, except that by cunning rotating lighting schemes it often becomes other delicious shades, with the result that you can look up suddenly from a particularly embroiled conversation and wonder how someone changed all the furniture round without you noticing. In fact, rather than crashing out in the gents, I recommend the white loungey platforms up here – they're a lot softer and nobody will stand on you whilst fiddling with their trousers.

Emblematic fragrance: Chanel Allure.

Brighton clubs boast only the crème de la crème of modern disc jockeys

Sussex Arts Club

7 Ship Street (01273) 778020
www.sussexarts.com

A club you join (and they make you take a temporary membership on the door) rather than an actual dance club, this merits inclusion for the monthly residencies of 60s girl-group obsessives Da Doo Ron Ron and kitsch glamour-mongers Margot's Parties, both essential nights. The ancient building didn't really need a makeover (though the air conditioning's very welcome) but they've given it one anyway and now there's a pointless balcony at the back of the ballroom. Fans of fine Victorian porcelain can still get their kicks in the gents though, where the urinals are so massive you can play hide and seek in them.

Tavern Club

Castle Square (01273) 827641

This place has been a popular spot for indie music ever since Brighton's legendary Basement Club imploded after one of the DJs left a Shed 7 record playing all night by mistake.

The Pav Tav (as it's sometimes known) is basically a function room above a pub, but has enough character to suit the style of the club nights here. Subdued lighting, a wide bar and a few sofas make it intimate and friendly, and the indie nights are always heaving.

Every Friday, 200 nicotine-stained, pasty-faced kids in need of a good square meal drag their skinny bodies down here for Kick Out The Jams, to demonstrate how much they really can't dance, while Saturday's long-running 60s/retro night, Pod, remains ever-popular with the kind of crowd who sport huge lambchops, do their shopping at To Be Worn Again smoke Golden Virginia and know *all* the lyrics to *Forever Changes*.

Strict dress code: Dyed black hair, skinny-rib T-shirts and trainers. If you're ginger, don't even try.

185

The Volks

Pier end of Madeira Drive (01273) 682828
www.volksclub.co.uk

Hidden away off the main clubbing drag, the Volks is a bit of a gem for it's unsniffy attitude and discerning choice of sounds. White Rhino do a dynamite breaks night here (and help to save real rhinos, aaaah, environmentally sound clubbing) and there's a host of other specialist fixtures from jungle and afro to D&B, grime and psytrance. The main room upstairs is surprisingly airy, unlike the downstairs which is about the size of a sheet of A4, packed with excessively friendly people (I left a friend on his own in here and when I came back he hissed *"people keep smiling at me"*) and run by tasteful DJs who, for a change, know how to build a room up rather than throwing the entire bucket of bricks at it from minute one. If there's one carp de diem, it's that there's hardly anywhere to sit down, but then I am getting on a bit. For a taste of the original Brighton underground clubbing experience, this is the one.
Emblematic fragrance: Sweat/patchouli.

Ultra-strong earplugs for ultra-deaf clubbers

The Zap (formerly The Zap)

189-192 Kings Road Arches (01273) 202407
www.thezapbrighton.co.uk

Given its steady decline from *Screamadelica*-associated heyday into tedious disco and party-anthem sludge, it was inevitable that the Zap would have to reinvent itself or die trying. It was almost the latter when a refit and rebranding – to Union, oh dear – kept the punters away in droves, so it's rewound to the trad-house nights and themed costume parties like the Pussycat (recently reclaimed from the Concorde 2) and changed its name again to… er… the Zap.

The lighting now lurches wildly between almost pitch black and POW camp searchlight depending on which of the many rooms and corridors you're lost in, so an unwelcome surprise may await you if you've pulled what you think is a hottie in a dark room and then decamp to a bright one. Still, even if your new friend turns out to be a health hazard, at least the floor no longer is one, leaving your attention free to wonder at the incongruity of the giant jellymould chandeliers.

AT A GLANCE...

Chart/disco/party tunes: *Event II/Creation/The Beach*

Drum'n'Bass: *Zap/Pressure Point*

Easy listening/soundtrack/lounge/retro: *Hanbury Ballroom/ Prince Albert*

Goth/industrial: *Engine Room/Brighton Gloucester/B'lo*

Hip-hop: *Enigma/Pressure Point*

Breakbeat: *Audio/Volks/Concorde 2*

House/garage: *Audio/Ocean Rooms/Honeyclub/Zap*

Indie/rock: *Brighton Gloucester/Tavern Club/Engine Room/ Concorde 2*

Jazz/funk/salsa: *Casablanca/The Church/The Jazz Place*

Northern soul/Motown: *Funky Fish/The Jazz Place/Sussex Arts*

Reggae: *The Jazz Place/Volks*

70s/80s: *The Beach/Brighton Gloucester/Creation/Funky Buddha*

Techno/trance: *Honeyclub/Volks*

Electronica/krautrock/underground pop: *B'lo/Ocean Rooms/Hanbury Ballroom*

Legendary
BRIGHT⊚N CLUB NIGHTS

Supercharged
Audio, Wednesdays

Breakbeat supreme led by Krafty Kuts and a slew of big breaks bananas.

It Came From The Sea
B'lo/Komedia, monthly

Bleeding edge 'experimental disco', projections, sweets, more smoke than a dragracing track, and the hippest crowd on two skinny legs.

Wild Fruit
Creation, monthly

Bigger, gayer, glammer and more outrageous than the rest. So good you won't even notice it's held at Creation.

Detournement
B'lo, every other Saturday

Electrofunkrockscarfwearingindiepunkfringeflopping trendniknoise.

Pussycat Club
Zap, monthly

Any excuse for themed dressing up from *Starsky & Hutch* to the Mad Hatter's tea party.

Stick It On
Hanbury Ballroom, monthly

Play your five favourite records to an adoring crowd of your own mates, then watch everyone else have a go.

Da Doo Ron Ron
Sussex Arts Club, monthly

60s girl-group sounds, lack of snobbery compulsory, beehive optional.

Shitsmacker
The Shed, every seventh Wednesday

Gardening tips, birdsong and soiled breakbeats mixed by DJ Compost and his mum.

Positive Sounds
Audio, monthly

Tech-house and anything deeply funky from the renegade crew with their own magnificent handbuilt white rig.

Born Bad
Engine Room, monthly

Dirty girls in pvc and tattooed blokes with quiffs moshing to rock'n'roll in an underground scout hut.

Vavavavoom!
Info from Stella Starr:
msstarr@supanet.com

Based in Brighton – the UK's unofficial Capital of Kitsch – Vavavavoom! has been at the forefront of the new burlesque movement since 1997. Dreamed up as a *"vision made flesh"*, it's a reincarnation of every old-style Hollywood nightclub you've seen in the movies and always wished you could party in. Much copied but never bettered, it has blossomed from the most glamorous party in town to a vast burlesque empire. Look out for special events during the year, performances by the Dimestore Jive Revue – Vavavavoom!'s swingin' jivin' big band – and even a new School of Burlesque, based at the Rox Dance School.

I'LL MEET YOU AT, ER, WOSSITCALLED?
The ever-changing names of Brighton clubs...

The Zap → Union → The Zap
The Richmond → Pressure Point
The Joint → B'lo
Escape → Audio
Beachcomber → Honeyclub
Passion → Funky Buddha Lounge
Secrets → Storm → V2
Cuba → Club Blue → Arc
Zenons → Core Club
The Music Club → KooKlub
Catfish → Funky Fish
Revolution Disco → Event → Event II
Sherry's → Pink Coconut → Paradox → Creation

DYNAMITE BOOGALOO

Every Thursday at Audio
www.blueyellow.com/boogaloostu

In total contrast to the po-faced house nights that dominate Brighton's club scene, Dynamite Boogaloo is a fabulous *Tiswas*-style party of high camp, glitzy pop and lewd comedy, all the work of larger-than-life hosts Dolly Rocket and Boogaloo Stu (more often than not sporting a huge quiff, glittery suit and furry boots). If you're a Boogaloo virgin, be prepared for a surprising (and possibly shocking) night out, for as well as boogying to classic disco tunes and listening to Stu and Dolly croon their way through a couple of numbers, you may even find yourself participating in a few outrageous game shows, courtesy of Stu.

Penny Up the Crack is still one of their most popular games, in which contestants have to clench a penny between their buttocks, carry it across the stage and drop it in a bucket. It doesn't stop there, though. The rounds get harder as participants have to carry a pickled onion and then, finally, a raw, egg. Another classic is Parsnip Dildo Football: two contestants each wear a pair of knickers onto which is attached a parsnip (roughly sculpted into a dildo). A couple of audience members then sit with their legs open as goal posts and the contestants have to try and knock a potato through the posts using their dildo!

After fourteen years of success, Dynamite Boogaloo still doesn't appear to be running out of steam. Kept fresh by Stu's ever-growing medley of bizarre and slapstick game shows, the night always promises something new and outrageous for its audiences, ever-hungry for decadent behaviour. Although some weeks it does get out of control, as Stu once explained to me…

"I remember one night we're playing Penny Up the Crack when this contestant, rather than carrying the thing between his legs, dropped his trousers and

*actually **shoved** the pickled onion right up his bum-crack. We had to restrain him from 'dropping it' into the cup on the other side of the room as it wouldn't have been a pretty sight. Or smell. God, it must have stung though! Another time we were playing my take on musical statues – when the music stops, the participants have to pose in a lewd sexual act with someone from the audience. One night this guy pulled his trousers down and stuck this girl's face right into his crotch. It was disgraceful – I don't think she even knew him."*

"So he was disqualified?"

"No, he won. Of course."

Entertainment

CINEMAS

See the latest Hollywood blockbuster on Friday night, a David Lynch film on the Saturday, then a documentary about Voodoo S&M on the Sunday. Here's how.

WHERE TO SEE THE LATEST BLOCKBUSTER

The Odeon
West Street 0870 5050007

The biggest cinema in the town centre and, with the Event II nightclub next door, handy if you're taken by the urge to snog a few teenagers after the film.

Cineworld
The Marina 0871 200 2000

Eight screens and all the latest movies from Tinseltown. You won't find anything adventurous in their billings, and it is located below the multi-storey carpark in the Marina but, as far as modern cinemas go, it serves a need. Judging from my last few visits here, this place is, however, vying for Dirtiest Cinema of the Year award. At weekends (and during the week too) you may find yourself ankle deep in popcorn, teabags and litter. The fact that it seems to be run by disaffected teenagers has nothing to do with it, obviously.

CHEEKY FACTOID #478

I read somewhere that the reason popcorn is synonymous with cinemas is because when long feature films first started to be shown in the 20s, the cinema owners were afraid that their audiences would get hungry if made to sit still for over an hour and would leave. The cheapest, simplest solution was to make popcorn which, naturally, they gave out free. Nowadays we'll happily pay £10 for a bag of the stuff. Oh, the irony.

INDIE CINEMAS

Duke Of York's

Preston Circus (01273) 602503
Cheaper tickets Mon-Thurs before 6pm
www.picturehouses.co.uk

To be found at the end of London Road, this building is bright yellow and has a large pair of stripy legs sticking out over the balcony. It's easy to miss, however, as all the houses on the street have copied the idea and now there are hands, elbows and feet sticking out all over the place as far as the eye can see.

Having celebrated its 90th birthday in September 2000, the Duke's can claim to be the oldest independent cinema outside London, and shows a fairly wide selection of cult, art house and world films. It has a nifty little bar and balcony upstairs and, rather than the usual cinema junk food, offers a selection of cakes and hot and cold drinks. The auditorium itself looks magical, with coloured lights around the screen, and those blue velvet seats have to be the most comfortable in Brighton. Thoroughly recommended for *all* movie enthusiasts.

Tip: If you fancy seeing one of their late-night cult screenings at the weekend, buy your tickets in advance as they often sell out.

DUKE OF YORK'S TRIVIA

* The Duke's was originally built for theatrical impresarios Violette Melnotte and Frank Wyatt. Violette, always known to staff as 'Madame', was the archetypal iron fist in a velvet glove and, when one of the actors at the theatre gassed himself, she apparently instructed her solicitor to reclaim the cost of the gas from his estate.

* The Duke's famous legs once belonged to a cinema in Oxford known as 'Not the Moulin Rouge' and, every Sunday at 3pm, they do the Can Can.

SPECIAL FILM NIGHTS

Final Cut

Hanbury Ballroom, St George's Road,
Kemp Town
www.finalcut.gb.com

This short film-screening event
takes place on the last Thursday
of every month and provides an
opportunity for local and national
filmmakers to show their work to
Brighton audiences and fellow auteurs.
Established in May 2002, it has grown
to become the largest film event of its
kind on the south coast and is a must
for anyone who makes films or is
simply passionate about the medium.

THEATRES

Brighton's Little Theatre Company

Clarence Gardens (01273) 205000

Founded in the late 70s by Syd
Little (of *Little and Large* fame), this
converted chapel tucked behind
the Pull and Pump has been home
for many years now to an amateur
company which covers everything
from Ayckbourn to Shakey. Avoid
the back seats – there are low-slung
beams that can obscure the view
– and keep a look out for Syd; he still

pops up occasionally to see the odd
farce, but has porked out a bit now and
looks more like Eddie.

Gardner Arts Centre

Sussex University Campus, Falmer
(01273) 685861
www.gardnerarts.co.uk

This late-60s purpose-built arts venue
looks like it's straight out of some
ancient TV comedy drama starring
Peter Davison as a bumbling lecturer
who wins the hearts of his rebellious
students by accidentally turning up
drunk and naked to one of his seminars.
My fantasies aside, the Gardner Arts
is a large multi-purpose venue up at
Sussex University, with a gallery space,
cafe-bar and 400-odd-seater theatre
space which plays host to everything
from comedy, theatre and dance to cult
films and occasional live music.

Cigarette girl Heidi Heelz tempts you with a
high tar Toblerone at the Kroon Kat Lounge

The Komedia
Gardner Street (01273) 647100
www.komedia.co.uk

Impossible to miss, owing to the fact that its outrageous red lighting turns Gardner Street into an enormous brothel every evening. That aside, god bless the Komedia; I've had countless unforgettable evenings here seeing everything from Julian Cope to Count Arthur Strong's live radio show, getting suited and booted and jiving to a live swing band at the Kroon Kat Lounge, or simply having a late night drink and listening to Glen Richardson on keyboards take any request from the audience.

Once, during a Voodoo Vaudeville show, I even saw a man called the Great Electra plug himself into a Van de Graaf generator, stand on a chair, pull down his trousers, stick a fluorescent strip up his arse and light it up. Happy memories.

While the Komedia don't seem to be very serious about theatre any more (I guess it doesn't pay the bills), they *are* serious about comedy and cabaret, and this venue remains *the* place to come for stand-up, sketch shows and live radio recordings. True, the prices of events here can be a little intimidating at times but whether it's a cult music event, weird local cabaret, magic shows or stand-up comics, it's usually worth the gamble. Favourites to keep a look out for are Voodoo Vaudeville, the Kroon Kat Lounge, Melting Vinyl gigs and good old Glen Richardson singing and playing Bohemian Rhapsody all the way through, note-perfect, in a cockney accent.

The Sallis Benney Theatre
University of Brighton, Grand Parade
(01273) 643010
www.brighton.ac.uk/gallery-theatre

Dead as a dodo for six months of the year, out of the blue, the Sallis Benney will have a sizeable world-music, theatre or dance season and then suddenly go back into hibernation again. It's like a drunk relative who's woken up at your party and dances their way across the living room only to collapse unconscious in the kitchen moments later.

Worth keeping an eye on during the summer term, as all the performance-art students put on free events here for a couple of weeks as the final part of their degrees, before settling down to lives of unemployment.

Dimestore Revue singer Mark Stoller, another victim of faulty venue wiring

The Joogleberry Playhouse
14-17 Manchester Street (01273) 687171
www.joogleberry.com

Established by sister and brother Sue and Geoff Popper in 2003, the Joogleberry has become a unique and indispensable late-night club venue for music, comedy, salsa, spoken-word events and bizarre cabaret.

It has a laid-back and welcoming café/restaurant space upstairs for those who want to drop by during the day or evening for food, but downstairs late at night is where the real magic takes place. Step in here for the first time and you'll feel like you've stumbled across some magical 60s basement club from Eastern Europe, all candle-lit, with a simple cabaret table set-up and decorated with fabulous nighttime scenes of houses with little lights twinkling in the windows. Sue and Geoff really have created the perfect environment for an intimate evening of entertainment here, be it the legkicks and catsuits of regular performer Fake Bush, the Wednesday-night flamenco team strutting their stuff, the dark brooding Sunday night sounds of local band the Desperate Ones adding new dimensions to Brel and Nick Cave, or an enthusiast raving about Russ Meyer films at the Catalyst Club. Highly recommended.

A typical Russ Meyer enthusiast

The Nightingale Theatre

29-30 Surrey Street (above Grand Central
pub, opposite Brighton Station)
(01273) 702563
alister@prodigaltheatre.co.uk

After many years in the wilderness,
the theatre once described as
"Brighton's best-loved venue" is back.
Look out for youth-theatre workshops,
touring companies and dance in
this newly refurbished (and very
swish) 40-capacity theatre space, all
choreographed by resident company
Prodigal Theatre. It all sounds great,
right? So come on guys, pull your
fingers out in promoting the stuff.

New Venture Theatre

Bedford Place (01273) 746118
www.newventure.org.uk

This converted school does about
nine productions a year, usually
covering more challenging stuff, such
as Pinter or Potter, than its diminutive
rival down the road. They also cultivate
new writing, so if you don't mind them
'deconstructing' your dialogue, pitch
up with your most inscrutable work.
Amateur dramatics at its finest – and
all housed in a rather beautiful building.

Theatre Royal

New Road (01273) 328488
www.theatreroyal.co.uk

For the more conservative theatregoer.
The Theatre Royal may offer a
predictable array of farces, thrillers
and musicals starring Tom Conti, Jason
Donovan and Elaine Paige but for an
authentic old-style theatre experience
it can't be beaten. The auditorium is
stunning; they've got plush red-velvet
seats, 20p binoculars and private boxes
for those who really want to do it in
style. I once saw Barbara Windsor in
the nude here, but that's another story.
Dress code: Loafers, slacks and
cardie. Monocle optional.

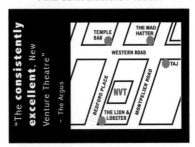

ENTERTAINMENT

197

COMEDY /CABARET

The Treason Show
Monthly at the Komedia (01273) 647100

Packed with songs, sketches and digs at the usual suspects (the police, celebrities, Tony Blair, crap TV) the performances from this comedy team are fast-moving and well executed.

Far from groundbreaking satire by the likes of *The Day Today* team, the Treason Show follows the well-worn paths laid down by shows like *That Was the Week That Was* and *Dead Ringers*. The show is split into two 40-minute performances and, although there'll be plenty of times when the slickness of it seems to outweigh the comedy, the pace of the show will leave you little time to dwell on the shortcomings of a particular sketch as seconds later you'll be hit by a cracking one-liner in the next. Look out for occasional guest appearances by *Monty Python's* Carol Cleveland.

The Krater Comedy Club
Weekly at the Komedia (01273) 647100

Running most weekends at the Komedia, the Krater closely follows the tried-and-tested Jongleurs format of compere and three acts. Regularly hosted by local comedian Stephen Grant, known for his speedy delivery, the Krater is unquestionably popular but does, however, demonstrate the frightening lack of original material from most of the comedians currently trawling the national circuit. Attracting stag and hen parties in their droves (a growing Brighton epidemic), this is hardly a discerning audience but at least they don't seem to mind listening to men and women in their mid-30s drone on about their pathetic sex lives in the name of humour. With moronic heckling and mobile phones going off every ten minutes, this is my idea of hell – but then maybe I just can't take a joke.

Brighton comedy group Spymonkey, much too funny for the Krater

Voodoo Vaudeville

Komedia (every three months or so)
(01273) 647100
www.voodoo-vaudeville.com

"Think of a nurse in a short PVC outfit. Give her a syringe, put a monkey mask on her and get her to inject a three-piece-suit-wearing gorilla to make it do a striptease." That – according to creator and host Chris Cresswell – is Voodoo Vaudeville.

A kinky Victorian freakshow for lovers of real pantomime, cabaret, comedy and dance, this is Pontins cabaret seen through the eyes of Lewis Carroll, where giant rabbits abound, ghostly puppets give acerbic advice to the audience, glamorous girls do teasing (and often hilarious) dances, dominatrixes wander through the audience meting out punishments and Chris and the team ham it up on stage and generally have a ball.

Ever-evolving, Voodoo Vaudeville has performed around the globe in recent years, but its spiritual home is still the Komedia, where it appears every few months or so in various guises. Regulars will be heartened to know that Baby Warhol is still around to give advice to the needy, there's a disco at the end and, yes, you can all still join in the snake dance. Recommended.

Dress code: Victorian gothic with a kinky twist.

SPOKEN WORD/DEBATE

The Catalyst Club

Joogleberry Playhouse
Second Thursday of every month, 8pm-late
£3 admission
www.catalyst-club.com,
mailing list: david@cheekyguides.com

Set up and hosted by that dashing, modest chap D Bramwell Esq, the Catalyst Club is a night for those who enjoy a bit of debate and learning with their glass of wine or beer, as each month the Catalyst plays host to three different guests who speak for fifteen minutes on something they're passionate about. This might sound like going back to school: it is people standing at a lectern, after all, usually with slides and notes, but because the Joogleberry is such an intimate venue, the speakers so engaging, the audience intelligent and the host so damned sexy, it seems to work rather well and doesn't feel pretentious or dry.

Talks range from anecdotal stand-up (such as the gentleman whose brilliant and funny talk on *The Persuaders* was really about his 70s childhood), to the challenging ("*Why we should all go to church*" and "*Debunking Quantum Physics*" raised an eyebrow or two) to the fascinating and bizarre (zombies, giant squid, occultism, Tin Tin, naturism… need I go on?).

There's usually a Q&A session at the end, where the audience (and often the barstaff too) chip in with their comments. And, if that's not enough, each night has a different musical theme with free CDs given out by guest DJs. But rather than blow my own trumpet too much about the night, I'll leave you in the capable

hands of satisfied punter Tom Sheriff:

"The Catalyst Club? It's the only night out in Brighton, or perhaps anywhere in the UK, where you can get thoroughly pissed, get free stuff and go home knowing more than you ever thought you could or would need to about such unlikely topics as the history of the martini, the life of Herman Goering and why toast always falls butter side down."

Café Scientifique

www.cafescientifique.org/brighton

At time of going to print this science-debating club was still meeting down at the Aquarium Terraces once a month for a talk from a guest scientist (usually clutching his/her latest tome) followed by a one-hour Q&A and a whip-round to pay for a new corduroy jacket and a comb-over.

The whole event is very relaxed and informal and can – at times – spark some fascinating debate. Check website for current details.

Comedian Dave Mounfield reveals his secret passion for rayon Y-fronts at Catalyst Club

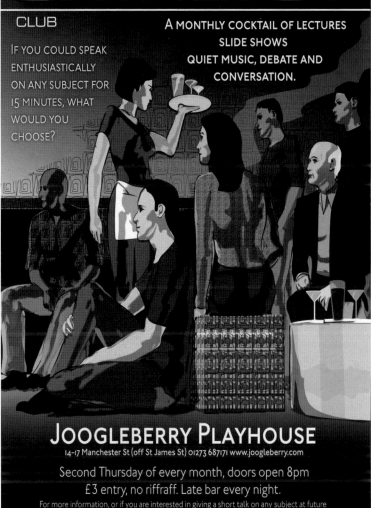

The Cheeky Guide to Brighton presents:

THE
CATALYST
CLUB

A MONTHLY COCKTAIL OF LECTURES
SLIDE SHOWS
QUIET MUSIC, DEBATE AND
CONVERSATION.

IF YOU COULD SPEAK
ENTHUSIASTICALLY
ON ANY SUBJECT FOR
15 MINUTES, WHAT
WOULD YOU
CHOOSE?

JOOGLEBERRY PLAYHOUSE
14-17 Manchester St (off St James St) 01273 687171 www.joogleberry.com

Second Thursday of every month, doors open 8pm
£3 entry, no riffraff. Late bar every night.
For more information, or if you are interested in giving a short talk on any subject at future
Catalyst Club nights, contact david@cheekyguides.com

GAMBLING

The Greyhound Stadium
Nevill Road, Hove (01273) 204601,
box office 0845 702 3952

With Blur now up to their elbows in
nappies and writing gloomy art-rock
albums about getting fat, you can go
to the dogs and have a laugh without
feeling that you have to be ironic
about it. It's a few quid to get in and
the minimum bet is a pound. Forget
trying to figure out how the betting
works, just pick the dog with the
silliest name, use the touts outside for
better odds, watch out for the lasagne
and you'll have a terrific night out.

The Grosvenor Casino
9 Grand Junction Road (01273) 326514
Open 12pm-6am daily (4am Saturday)
Bar open until 5.30am daily, 3am Saturday
(12am Sunday), food from 5pm-4am
www.grosvenor-casionos.co.uk

Having recently moved from its old
long-term home by Brighton Station
to a swankier residence, this casino
has gone decidedly upmarket since
the days of the grotty psychedelic
carpets and tiny bar. There are now
automated roulette tables, a £2,000
jackpot fruit machine, higher minimum
stakes, live entertainment at weekends
and a bar which stays open longer.
True, it's still full of guys with strong
aftershave trying to impress their
white-stilettoed ladies, and swarms
of Chinese businessmen with money
to burn, but with their massively
popular Texas Hold'em poker room,
the Grosvenor now seems to be
attracting a student crowd as well.

Membership and entrance is still
free and the good news is that it no
longer takes 24 hours to validate
your ID – turn up with any decent
proof of identity and you're straight

in. The live roulette tables start at 25p
a bet and pontoon and poker start
at £2, but there are other tables with
higher stakes if you're feeling brave.
Alternatively, you can just watch the
professionals in action and munch on
the free sarnies. And did I really hear
the desk-girl say "*Good Evening, Mr.
Paradise*," to one of the regulars as I
was leaving once?

Stanley Brighton International
6-8 Preston Street (01273) 725101
Open 2pm-6am daily (4am Saturday), bar
open until 5.30am daily (12am Sunday)
Free 24-hour membership and free
admission
www.stanleycasinos.com

Taking itself more seriously than the
Grosvenor, as you step in and hear the
lilting tones of Phil Collins and Philip
Bailey singing *Easy Lover* you'll realise
that this place means business. Like
the Grosvenor, the decor reeks of the
80s, with mirrored walls, fake-wood
panelling and a clientele to match
– for whom the mullet is still not a
fish. Downstairs no longer has the bar
area with the world's biggest telly that
would suck you in whatever was on
(once, against my will, I got drawn into
a documentary about Doug McLure
and didn't get out for hours). They do
table service now – a much better
arrangement – though you can pop
down there still for poker tournaments.

Set in the gorgeous surroundings of the Royal Pavilion Estate, Brighton Dome boasts three top venues - the Concert Hall, Corn Exchange and Pavilion Theatre and also hosts the annual Brighton Festival in May

With a world-class programme featuring the best in live music, theatre, dance and comedy it's no surprise that Brighton Dome is the South Coast's leading arts venue, and Brighton Festival is the England's biggest International arts festival!

Tickets / Information 01273 709709
www.brightondome.org
www.brightonfestival.org

The Music Scene

Let's begin with a couple of jokes...

Q. What do you call someone who hangs around with musicians?
A. A drummer.

Q. How do you know a drummer is knocking on your door?
A. The knocking speeds up.

And while I'm on a roll…

A bass player's girlfriend comes home to find him giving a particularly painful Chinese burn to their ten-year-old son. She begs him to stop and asks why he's inflicting pain on their loved one.
"Because he's de-tuned one of my bass strings," he says angrily.
"But there's no reason to treat him like that!" she exclaims.
"Yes, but the little bugger won't tell me which one it is."

VENUES

The Prince Albert
Trafalgar Street (01273) 730499
www.myspace.com/theprincealbert

While the multi-chambered downstairs bar remains ever popular with edgy, frazzled clubbers and bewildered flotsam, the venue upstairs has found its second wind in recent times. Largely thanks to the relentless tenacity and vision of booker Will, the Albert is coming together, bit by bit, as a great room to suit many moods – just as it used to be many years ago. Regular nights of the splendid ilk of Sweden Made Me and Bleeding Hearts have settled in nicely, their loyalty to the space evidence enough of its growing importance and flexible ambience. In contrast with the spit-and-sawdust fleapit that is the Freebutt (which is not a criticism, by the way!), the Albert has removable seating, a decent PA, charming star-curtain backdrop, a mirrorball and occasional candlelight. The range of nights here is wildly eclectic and often free, so there are few in Brighton whose tastes and pockets are not well served at some point during most months.

The Brighton Dome, Pavilion Theatre and Corn Exchange

Church Street/New Road
(01273) 709709
www.brighton-dome.org.uk

After a £22 million refurbishment, which included the installation of a state-of-the-art sound system and new bar area, the Dome is back, offering classical concerts, world music, comedy events and a plethora of big-name artists from Ken Dodd and Lou Reed (not on the same bill, more's the pity) to Arctic Monkeys. Just round the corner the cavernous Corn Exchange

offers what is, essentially, a rectangular Dome – but with a worse bar set-up and standing-only layout that has seen the likes of The Go! Team, Calexico and Grandaddy (RIP) pack the place.

The Pavilion Theatre, however – a great room on the right night – remains frustratingly underused for rock and pop and seems to have faded from the Brighton venue map, somewhat. Why is this? We need to be told!

The Brighton Centre and East Wing

Kingsway, Brighton seafront
(01273) 290131
www.brightoncentre.co.uk

Fancy parting with £50 to see a fat, ageing superstar drag his flaccid arse and ravaged carcass around an airport terminal? Oh, you do? Then welcome to the Brighton Centre, another of those vile purpose-built conference hall-type venues found in every large town or city, and seemingly fashioned after Heathrow Airport. Talk is in the air, however, of it being ripped down and replaced, so keep your fingers crossed. For good measure, also cross your toes and pray the council doesn't allow it to be replaced with something equally hideous.

In a strange Russian-doll kind of way, the East Wing is a slightly smaller but equally featureless room for those acts that can't fill the Brighton Centre but want to capitalise on its corporate décor and lack of character.

As with the Pavilion Theatre, I can't remember the last gig I attended here – it too is sadly underused in a city crying out for mid-sized venues. Someone, somewhere, needs to sort this out.

Concorde 2
Madeira Drive, Brighton seafront
(01273) 606460
www.concorde2.co.uk

Operating just below the radar of the Dome complex but still putting on intriguing and up-and-coming acts you actually may have heard of, this is an excellent live venue, even if the view-blocking antique iron posts on the right can mean that you don't see the face of the keyboard player all night. (See *Clubs*)

The Freebutt
Phoenix Place (01273) 603974
www.zelnet.com

Not a sexual favour, as tediously suggested by just about every visiting US band, but a tiny, magical venue, tucked up a side street behind the Phoenix Gallery. The Freebutt has,

over the years, put on thousands of gigs of every musical description, from ska to indie to hardcore, and is still the only venue in town where you can see a band most nights of the week (Wed-Sat). You still have to strain your neck half the time to see who's on stage, but they *have* improved the PA now so that not every band sounds like a Butthole Surfers album being played inside a kettle. If you're in a guitar band and looking for somewhere to play, this will probably be your first port of call. Join the ranks of legends who have helped make this scruff-hole a beloved institution. Upstairs, the Penthouse is a small chill-out room with a bar and the odd shagged sofa, serving as home to uber-hip club nights that are often packed with scruffy young things in need of a good square meal and a hug.

The Hanbury Ballroom
83 St George's Road (01273) 605789
www.zelnet.com

Located in the wilds of Kemp Town, this building was once a mausoleum for a rather eccentric Brighton pagan but is now a multi-purpose 120-ish-capacity venue offering everything from club nights to jazz, live bands and films. They also show footy. Marvellous.

Restored to its former glory in 2001, the ballroom boasts a beautiful domed ceiling adorned with bearded, shisha-smoking mystics, willowy ladies holding chalices and a Celine Dion lookalike playing the clarinet. The years have, however, taken their toll on the rest of the room. Despite continuing and valiant efforts that have included a brand new wooden floor, the pounding its patrons give it mean it's always in need of refurbishment: the walls need a new coat of paint, there are holes in the furniture and whoever chose to

hang that *bloody awful* blue picture above the stage should be shot. Five years it's been there. I pity the poor bar staff that have to look at it every day. A photo of Kirk Douglas's dimple or Shane McGowan's teeth would be preferable. Please, Hanbury Ballroom, take it down and burn it. And do invite me along.

Furnishings aside, the Hanbury genuinely is a local treasure, and the favourite Brighton venue of many. It's home to Brighton's longest-running jazz night every Monday, some of the town's legendary club events (such as Stick it On), regular gigs from the likes of Melting Vinyl and the Gilded Palace of Sin (who, it is rumoured, actually have their own pewter goblets and camp stretchers tucked behind the bar), occasional comedy and even regular film events.

If you DJ, play in a band, perform stand-up or fancy putting on something yourself, this is the place to try it out. They're a friendly and helpful bunch too – because they are 'music people'. And, to cap it all, there's even a cosy adjoining bar, which can be handy if you turn up too early and don't want to have to stand outside in the rain with your records, penny whistle and laptop.

HEALTHY CONCERTS
www.healthyconcerts.com

Whatever you think of Nizlopi's *JCB Song* (and I try to think of it as little as possible), their career has an unusual genesis in the Gigs In Digs scene, where acoustic performers play in people's gardens and living rooms. This concept was invented in Brighton as Healthy Concerts in 1994 by Paul Chi, who wanted literally to bring the artist and audience closer together, and cut out the background noise and fag smoke of pubs and clubs. The idea has since spread across East Sussex, seems particularly popular in the Bristol area and even popped up in the USA under the label House Concerts. Anyone can volunteer their home as a one-off venue, and there's a BYO policy on booze, although some venue owners are particular about what type of drink you bring, presumably to keep the Special Brew crew at bay. Talking is forbidden while musicians are playing, which you will either view as po-faced and overly reverential or a huge boon that allows you to concentrate on the music. There's also the occasional after-party, which can be, erm, not so healthy.

Wholegrain baguette Flying V

LOCAL PROMOTERS, MOVERS AND SHAKERS

Melting Vinyl
Contact Anna (01273) 325955
www.meltingvinyl.co.uk

Groovy Northern lass Lady Anna 'eh-up' Moulson has been beavering away in Brighton for many years now as a top promoter, and is responsible for some of the best gigs in town; everything from garage pop to twisted electronica comes under her wings. To her credit, she arranged the first-ever UK shows for the White Stripes, the Strokes (at the Lift, now Polar Central; yes, it was insane) and the Vines, and has put on gigs from the biggest (Turin Brakes), the quirkiest (local all-girl classical ensemble Ptthh!) to the smallest (Danish one-man band Midgetboy). With the lack of good venues an ever-growing problem in this town, Anna has applied a bit of lateral thinking recently and, as well as doing regular gigs at the Albert, the Freebutt, the Pavilion Theatre and the Dome, she has put on events in local churches, the Duke of York's cinema and even Fred's old allotment shed in Peacehaven. Go to Anna's events and expect way-out sounds, electronic pioneers, lo-fi, punk and some of the coolest bands on the planet. Support this lovely lady. It would be awfully quiet in Brighton without her.

The Gilded Palace of Sin
www.thegildedpalaceofsin.com

The clue is in the name. Set up five years ago with the express intention of bringing country-based/influenced music of any sonic approach to Brighton, TGPoS have earned themselves a thoroughly deserved but totally unexpected international reputation. Their care for acts and punters, an acute attention to detail and unnerving passion for the music they promote has won many friends, impressed by their drive to present great-value, top-quality shows. There's a punk DIY

Eee baa gum, Anna Moulsecoomb looks forward to another groundbreaking promotion

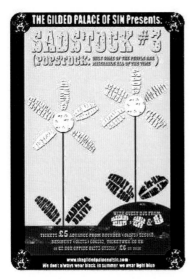

notorious for not mincing his words, was instrumental in bringing the grunge scene to the UK (he spent the late 80s hanging out in Seattle with Kurt and co) and has remained a fervent, verbal champion of cutting-edge, underground pop, always one step ahead of his peers. While not exactly a local promoter, Everett is prone to DJing at the odd club night in Brighton and on totallywired.com, providing the perfect opportunity to hear lots of noisy all-lesbian Japanese grunge-core bands, or whoever his latest flavour of the month happens to be. More importantly, it's actually in Brighton that Everett publishes his magazine *Plan B,* employing talented local illustrators and writers. While his style can be verbose, pretentious and childishly vicious towards anything remotely mainstream, if you're looking for someone in these bewildering post-Peel days who *genuinely* champions new and exciting music, you could do worse than seek the help of this man.

ethic, coupled with an obsession with bringing Brighton only the very best of what they see as Americana. They have an uncanny knack of unearthing future legends just as they set off and they heartily support the local scene. You can expect anything from bluegrass to power pop to future folk to acoustic misery at GPoS nights. There's plenty of country, of course, but the church is broad even within that genre. They also have a catch-all offshoot called Be A Ham to indulge much wider passions that have thus far ranged from the avant-orch pop of Efterklang to the visceral punk pop of the Thermals. Always unpredictable and never, ever dull.

Everett True

While some might dismiss Everett as the archetypal drippy indie kid who never grew up, it cannot be denied that his contribution to the music scene in the last two decades has been remarkable (and I'm not talking about that awful single he released in the 80s). This one-time NME journalist,

THE MUSIC SCENE

LOCAL RADIO STATIONS

FIP 90.5-91FM
www.fipradio.com

While not strictly local (in fact not even British), this cool, Parisian radio station has been broadcasting from a secret location in Brighton for years now. Advert-free and genuinely eclectic, FIP knocks spots off English music radio stations by offering everything from classical to jazz to underground pop and heavy dub reggae, all interspersed with the occasional lilting tones of a spaced-out Frenchman. FIP are also prone to playing whole albums at a time (not just singles) and have eight favourites each month they like to promote. In the evenings, French jazz does tend to take over but, trust me, that's no bad thing. The acronym, incidentally, stands for France Inter Paris.

Juice FM 107.2FM
www.juicebrighton.com

Back from the grave and with a new lick of paint, Juice now boasts some pretty excellent evening shows throughout the week, playing an eclectic mix of rock, jazz, funk, hiphop, dancefloor anthems and occasional live music. And to kick it all off in the morning they've even splashed out on slaphead comedian Terry Garoghan.

Totally Radio
www.totallyradio.co.uk

This local online station showcases non-mainstream specialist music and local bands (via Peel-style sessions at the Levellers Metway Studio) and utilises the cream of Brighton DJs and promoters to broadcast a truly varied, modern and exciting range of musical styles – the kind you won't hear on your FM radio. The on-demand shows are around an hour long and feature such local heroes as Boogaloo Stu (Dynamite Boogaloo), Russ Dewbury (Jazz Rooms), Dave Morrison (Gilded Palace of Sin) and Everett True (*Plan B*). Totally Wired, the station's homage to new Brighton music, has its own website (www.totallywired.co.uk), can be heard on Juice on Sunday nights and also offers resource facilities to local bands – printing, duplicating and mastering CDs. Totally Radio plans to launch on digital radio, which means you will be able to listen to it anywhere in Brighton if you have a digital radio or a metal plate in your head.

BBC Southern Counties FM
104-104.8FM

Local news for local people, Southern Counties offers the tried-and-tested formula of traffic reports, bland music, intrusive adverts and Alan Partridge-style presenters. At its best, however, it does probe and discuss local issues and serves the community (well, the Brighton middle classes, anyway) And there is plenty of exposure for local bands through demo panels and live sessions on fervent supporter Phil Jackson's show, so it's not *all* bad.

LOCAL PODCASTS

BrightonWaves
www.brightonwaves.co.uk

A monthly selection of local Brighton acts, offering a digestible preview of what you might be getting yourself into if you show up at the Pressure Point purely on the grounds that the band's name is We Live on Sputum and Gravy.

It's all linked by a charming young man who appears to be the bastard lovechild of Steve Lamacq and the Hairy Cornflake. I do apologise, I didn't mean to put the image of that conception into your head.

HOW TO FIND OUT WHO'S PLAYING

All the local magazines and websites, particularly www.myspace.com/brightonlivespace, will give you a rundown on who's playing and where. Some of the best places to pick up information are the record shops, which have posters for last-minute and low-key gigs. Rounder Records

and Resident should be your first ports of call for information on gigs, club nights and other music events, while Edgeworld Records is likely to have flyers for any lo-fi events that might otherwise be overlooked.

WHERE TO GET TICKETS

Dance 2 Records
129 Western Road (01273) 220023/329459
Tickets for everything related to dance, DJ and club culture, including big festivals and the likes of Cream and Ministry of Sound.

Dome Box Office
New Road (01273) 709709
For all the bigger events at the Corn Exchange, the Pavilion Theatre and the Dome itself.

Resident
(01273) 606312
Rounder Records
(01273) 325440
The places for tickets and general info on who's playing and when.

THE POP CELEBRITY
HALL OF FAME

It is a well-established fact that, apart from Fatboy Slim, everyone in Brighton is a musician of some sort. And with current interest in the music scene here at an all-time high (Brighton was Radio 1's 'Sound City' in 2003, and six local bands took part in a TV documentary series), it seems that the time is right to celebrate the town's euphonious achievements. Below is a helpful guide to the popstars of past and present who at one time or another have graced our city. I must admit, though, some of it may be based on hearsay and an overactive imagination.

Tampasm… rockchickshock syndrome

Splitting Images
celebrity lookalike agency

Leo Sayer Lookalike

Keith Thomas

Wonder if he gets a lot of work?

FAMOUS FOR 15 MINUTES

Kirk Brandon (Spear of Destiny, definitely wasn't Boy George's lover, oh no)
Frazier Chorus (Anyone remember Dream Kitchen?)
Genesis P. Orridge (Psychic TV frontman currently transforming himself into my granny through the wonders of plastic surgery and a nice grey bob)
Peter and the Test Tube Babies (Still going and still not very famous)
The Piranhas
Kevin Rowland (Dexy's legendary frontman with a distaste for music journalists)
Tampasm (Noisy all-girl band with attitude who appeared once on The Girlie Show then split)
These Animal Men (NME darlings who lived entirely off speed and hair dye)
David Van Day (star of vacuous Brighton magazines' vacuous photo spreads)

STILL THROWING TELLIES OUT OF WINDOWS

British Sea Power
Nick Cave
Norman Cook
The Electric Soft Parade
The Go! Team!
Simon Johns *(Stereolab/Imitation Electric Piano)*
The Levellers
Lo-Fidelity All-Stars
Gary Moore *(ex-Thin Lizzy guitarist turned noodly blues fart)*
The Ordinary Boys
Leo Sayer *(OK, Leo, we'll let you in just for this edition, after that freak number one)*
David Thomas *(Pere Ubu)*

Simon Johns controlling the famous "brown note"

WORLD DOMINATION IS JUST A T-SHIRT AWAY

Actress Hands
Jane Bartholomew
Bat For Lashes
Caramel Jack
Chungking
Clearlake
The Eighties Matchbox etc
Electrelane
Emiliana Torrini
Hardkandy
The Kooks
Metronomy
Oddfellows Casino
She Said!
The Tenderfoot
…and loads more.

The Brighton musician's
wheel of life

1. You answer an ad in the Guitar and Amp Shop and spend the evening with an unhinged alcoholic in his bedsit, listening to demo tapes of his old group.

2. After another year of this you decide to form your own band and bring some purity back to pop music.

3. You audition hundreds of guitarists until you find someone who owns an original 70s Telecaster. Even though he can't play it, you know a cool guitar when you see one and this is way more important.

4. You wait another three years for a bassist and a drummer to come along. When you finally get them it turns out that the bassist is a frustrated guitarist and the drummer is a psychopath who doesn't particularly like music but enjoys hitting things. They'll do for now.

5. At your first gig at the Freebutt the drummer punches the singer of another band, your guitarist fails to notice that he is playing the wrong set and then gets in a strop about it and you have a sneaking feeling that the bassist played slap-bass on one of the tracks. Your friends tell you that you sound a bit like the Stereophonics, which is ironic because you hate them.

6. You record a demo, have 40,000 made, spend a week arguing over the track listing, send one copy to Zane Lowe and put the rest under your bed, where they remain.

7. After six months, the bassist announces that although still committed to the band, he has formed his own band called Funkypanda, playing jazz-funk covers. You are alarmed to notice that he is starting to wear corduroy and grow a goatee.

8. Your demo returns from Zane Lowe with the message *"Sounds too much like the Stereophonics"*.

9. The drummer by now has taken to hitting the bass player rather than his drums and the only way to calm him down is with heavy and regular doses of ketamine.

10. You discover the existence of a Swedish synth-pop band with the same name as you.

11. The bassist announces that he is leaving to concentrate on his jazz-funk career, so you hide the drummer's stash of ketamine and unchain him.

12. You read in the paper that yet another Brighton band have just done a Lamacq session.

13. The drummer phones from prison to say that he can't make the next 400 rehearsals.

14. The guitarist comes round to your house, you smoke a joint together, reminisce about the good old days and moan about all the bands you know who have sold out. You jam through a couple of Turin Brakes numbers, then turn in.

15. A month later you turn on the telly and see the guitarist on *Stars in Their Eyes*. The words *"Tonight, Matthew, I'm going to be Jay Kay from Jamiroquai"* are like daggers through your heart.

16. You move into a bedsit, start drinking heavily and put an advert in the Guitar and Amp Shop.

17. The cycle is now complete.

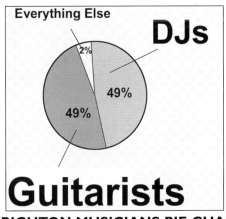

Everything Else

DJs

2%

49%

49%

Guitarists

BRIGHTON MUSICIANS PIE CHART

Local Heroes

This chapter pays homage to the handful of local artists who – rather than succumbing to the Brighton curse of endlessly knocking out screen prints of Al Pacino as *Scarface* – have bravely dragged their absinthe-raddled bodies out of (or in Dan Shelton's case into) the gutter to champion the unique, beautiful and bizarre.

Pearl Bates

www.pearlbates.com

Fantasy portraits of glamorous women seem to be the favoured subject for Pearl Bates, a Lewes-based artist with a penchant for ethereal yet stylish paintings. When asked why women had more of an allure for her than men, Pearl told me it was because *"women were more interesting and complex"*, but did allow an exception in my case. Part of the appeal of Pearl's work is the intensity of the characters she creates and the delicate narratives contained within her drawings and illustrations.

Read her piece on Lewes further on in this book and you'll be seduced, as I was, into seeing the place in a whole new light…

Greg Daville

www.site-to-be-destroyed.co.uk (latest exhibits)
*www.gallery-daville.co.uk (archive of complete
visual and written work)*

Beautiful and surreal, the images and
words of local artist Greg Daville touch
something deep in the subconscious,
where the monsters under the bed
still lurk. His website covers a whole
host of art past and present although,
for me, the Fourth Door Images are
the most stunning. In Greg's world,
strange creatures inhabit centre stage in
dreamlike landscapes, with motifs ranging
from fetishism to mythical buildings. If you
like unusual, striking images, pay this site
a visit. All artwork is modestly priced and
can be mail-ordered from gallery-daville.
co.uk.

To see his very latest work, visit *www.
site-to-be-destroyed.co.uk* which uses Flash
animation and photo-manipulated collage
to explore the theme of collapsing
buildings, with Greg's trademark haunting,
hypnotic imagery.

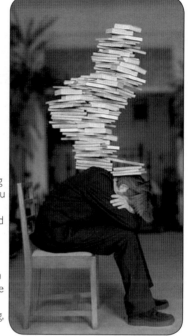

Chris Macdonald

93 Gloucester Road (01273) 601639
www.acmeart.biz

Chris Macdonald has spent the past
ten years in Brighton constructing
beautiful and strange sculptures out
of wood and found metal objects in
his studio on Gloucester Road. There
is something Daliesque about the way
he juxtaposes curious metal gadgets
(such as old camera parts or giant cogs)
with beautifully carved wooden items,
but the finished pieces themselves are
wholly original, the work of a man who
fell down Alice's rabbit hole and never
returned.

Chris's sculptures can be viewed and
purchased from his website or gallery at
the address above. If you want to visit
the gallery, it's best to phone before, or
he'll most likely be dancing around his
studio to Talking Heads or dreaming up
another work of art.

Neel

When not travelling round the world, Neel can be found loitering around the photo booth in St James's Street post office, dressed as a Prozac tablet, a Cluedo character or in his floral gimp outfit – this exceptional man has devoted his life to pushing the boundaries of photo-booth possibilities. Apart from getting a full-grown Dalmatian dog in the booth with him, Neel's most ambitious project to date has been arranging his own funeral; the invitation read *"everyone has to die one day... I'm just organised"*. Having made himself a coffin, Neel sent invitations to his 24 closest friends, asking each to come dressed as one of the many characters required at a funeral. Vicars, undertakers, grieving widows, the Sally Army, a choir and even an Elvis impersonator all happily turned up and, after a bit of dutiful mourning and a speech by the deceased, one by one they all filed into the photo booth for their picture, ending with Neel, dressed as the corpse. Nothing short of genius.

Paper Tiger

www.papertigercomix.co.uk

This UK-based comic anthology was, unsurprisingly, spawned in Brighton's fertile artistic breeding ground and is a cooperative venture designed to showcase up-and-coming self-published comic creators as well as more established alternative and underground comics people. Look out too for contributor Ben Naylor's very weird and wonderful *Adventures of Geoff Half Shark Half Octopus* in David's Comics in North Laine.

He usually goes for a stroll after lunch

Eve Poland

www.evepoland.com

Playful, humorous and erotic, Eve's art ranges from spooky-looking, mischievous cats to kinky ladies with whips (who seem to bear more than a passing resemblance to the lovely Eve herself). Not surprisingly for Brighton, the fabulous kinky ladies have attracted much attention; they've been exhibited in several galleries and sex shops and even the annual Erotica exhibition in London. Eve accepts commissions to paint whatever sordid fantasies you may have, though she draws the line at anything involving David Van Day.

Dan Shelton

www.theroleoftheartistinsociety.org

In 2003, inspired by the book *Flat Stanley* (about a boy who gets made very thin in an accident and posts himself to relatives in New York to save on the airfare), Dan had the bright idea of copyrighting himself as a piece of art. For this alone he won £10,000 prize money from local artist Fred (wife of *The Graduate* author Charles Webb). After a polite refusal from Tate Modern for offering himself as an exhibit, one wet February morning, Dan – wrapped in a specially made box – was transported by Securicor from his Brighton home to the pavement **just outside** the London gallery. Naturally, he made the front page of *The Times*.

Dan's next idea was for him and five other artists to roll between Tate Modern and Tate Britain. With the permission of three London Borough Councils and Police Constabularies, the six artists – dressed as French Surrealist painters – rolled the three miles of pavement between the two galleries. Though stopped at one point by an uninformed copper, who warned them that they *"constituted a potential terrorist threat"*, the roll was completed in three-and-a-half hours. Dan did confess, however, to feeling *"pretty sick afterwards"*. Look out for him performing with Voodoo Vaudeville.

Legends & Eccentrics

Brighton has always attracted more than its fair share of outlandish individuals, and below is a guide to some of the town's fruitiest and most lovable rogues, eccentrics and mavericks. Far from being branded loonies, these individuals are championed here for their style, courage, humour and lust for life. But does anyone remember the Bread Man, the guy who used to wander the streets of North Laine between six and seven in the morning with two French loaves strapped to his head like helicopter blades? Now he was a loony.

The Man who Waves at Buses

One of my early Brighton experiences was being tapped on the shoulder by a fellow passenger saying, *"there's a friend of yours trying to attract your attention"* at a bus stop on Western Road. Turning to the window I was confronted by a grinning stranger on the pavement, gesturing frantically, and no amount of shrugging and blank looks would dissuade him, even as the bus pulled away and his agitated form receded into the distance. It was the first of many wonderful encounters with The Man who Waves at Buses who, with all that waving everywhere from deepest Whitehawk to the arsehole end of Hove, must surely be the fittest man in Brighton. They ought to stick a giant picture of him waving on the side of the Brighton buses for the 'I'm on the bus' campaign – would he wave at himself, I wonder?

Fake Bush

Brighton's very own one-women tribute to Kate Bush is an affectionate and hugely entertaining parody of the great lady of pop, with performances that incorporate bubble machines, legkicks, cartwheels and of course "*zillions of costume changes*", which naturally include several fetching catsuits.

The alter-ego of the very lovely Ms Lucy Bundy, Fake Bush is not the only string to Lucy's bow as she also goes in for a spot of surreal balloon modelling, where she will make balloon models of anything the audience suggest, from Brighton landmarks to celebrities. It's all very silly, of course, but at the end of the day Fake Bush rules the roost. Look out for her cavorting around the Joogleberry Playhouse in a fetching salmon-pink catsuit, belting out *Wuthering Heights*. After three with your best screech: *it's me-a, Cathy-a, come home...*

Drako Zarhazar

Undoubtedly Brighton's greatest eccentric, Drako Zarhazar's life story reads like some improbable work of fiction: he has danced at the Moulin Rouge and the London Palladium, modelled for Salvador Dalí, starred in films by Andy Warhol and Derek Jarman and survived two serious road accidents and comas. Decorated with exotic tattoos and piercings, Drako is a character you simply couldn't mistake, even in Brighton; his forehead sports a tattooed triangle and his face is adorned with bright blue eyebrows, piercings and an impressive Dalíesque wax moustache. A visit to his flat is like stepping into the pages of a psychedelic porn mag: *all* the walls, the ceiling, cupboards and even the bathroom, are adorned with phallic images. From flaccid to fully erect, there are thousands of them everywhere, some stuck casually onto the wall, some hanging from the ceiling, others accompanied by humorous comments.

Ask him about his movie career and Drako is fairly nonchalant, preferring instead to describe his favourite moment as *"one night in Rome when someone filmed me putting a candle up someone's arse, which I lit and then, with a big whip, whipped out the flame"*.

DRAKO RECALLS MEETING DALÍ FOR THE FIRST TIME

"I remember being invited one day to a house on the outskirts of Paris. I walked down the stairs to a pool in the basement, and swimming naked in the pool were two beautiful girls. I remember coming and sitting on a big couch next to Salvador Dalí. He was just wearing a bathrobe and didn't say anything to me but kept watching these two naked girls swimming, when I suddenly noticed Dalí's hand moving up and down next to me. He was looking at these beautiful girls… and he was wanking. And I thought to myself, here I am on the outskirts of Paris, sat next to the famous Dalí, with him wanking over these beautiful girls. Isn't life incredible?"

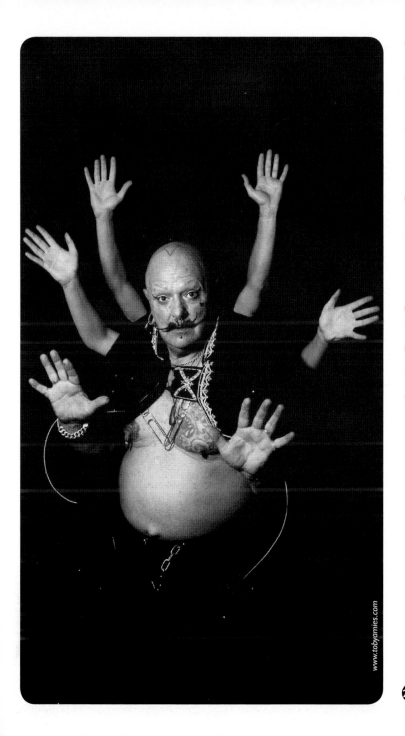

www.tobyamies.com

Roy Skelton

When Kemp Town resident Roy Skelton auditioned for a children's show called *Rainbow* in the early 70s, he didn't figure that it would keep him in gainful employment for sixteen years and turn him and his characters into cult heroes. But after providing the voice of Zippy and George for all these years that's exactly what happened, and Roy still receives sackloads of fan mail every month (most common questions: "*What is Zippy?*' and "*Is George gay?*")

On top of this, Roy provided the original voice for the Daleks for more than 30 years, tried to exterminate everyone from William Hartnell to Sylvester McCoy, and even played the parts of other universal miscreants such as Cybermen, Monoids, Krotons and David Van Day...

Though now in his seventies, Roy is still sprightly and youthful, with more than a hint of Zippy in his smooth round head and bullfrog voice, though whether his alter-ego is a placid camp hippo is another matter.

Sir Ralph Harvey

A well-dressed and genteel man, sporting the fading moustache of a brigadier, Ralph travels the world battling the likes of Vikings and Saxons with military re-enactment societies. He makes regular appearances around the country with his own outfit dressed as the cast of *Dad's Army* with himself, of course, as Captain Mainwaring.

More surprisingly, perhaps, Ralph is one of the country's leading authorities on the occult, heading his own local Wiccan coven, and is responsible for sorting out much of the poltergeist activity around the Shoreham area.

Also an actor, at the height of his fame Ralph played Hercule Poirot on Belgian television, where he became a household name, until the Agatha Christie estate stopped the TV company using the famous detective's name. From then on, even though he dressed the same and played the same role, Ralph had to be known as 'Inspector Sprout', but, somehow, it was never the same.

The Birdlady of St Peters

If you're wandering around town and notice a jabbering flock of several hundred seagulls, endlessly divebombing a shambling woman with gesticulating limbs, don't scamper in to help out – it's just the Birdlady of St Peters, fulfilling her endless quest to ensure the poor birdies don't go hungry. Often accompanied by a supermarket trolley to hold the score or so loaves of bread that are so necessary to keep our unique species of Brighton gull from becoming extinct (they can no longer digest raw fish, having been raised on a diet of doughnuts, candy floss and used nappies), the Birdlady does the dirty work that the council refuses to contemplate. Her favourite spot seems to be the grass around St Peters Church on Grand Parade but any green space near the seafront will do. Occasionally she fancies a change and you'll see her standing covered in pigeons, looking like a peculiarly ineffective scarecrow.

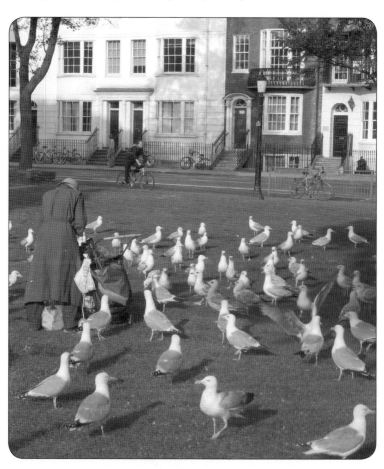

Letitcia

www.brightonbodyworship.com

Self-appointed sex goddess Letitcia has travelled the world, played every brothel from Singapore to Australia, seen the odd willy or two and lived to tell the tales. And very amusing they are too; you can even read them in her rather candid autobiography *Body Worship*. If the story of the guy who liked inserting other people's dried turds inside himself doesn't have you laughing uncontrollably (or put you right off your dinner), the chapter on men's hygiene will. As Letitcia explains:

"If a guy is a little grubby I'll give him a bedbath; men like the whole nursing thing. But I did have this one client, everything that could be wrong, he had it – dogbreath, the pungent aroma of twenty-year-old sweat…

Alarmingly, he produced a medical certificate from his doctor to allay my fears about this strange rash on his chest; I was more concerned that when he took off his underpants he appeared to have elephantiasis of the balls. They were the size of footballs. And as for his feet, well, let's not even go there! I sat him down and drew up a list of things he needed to attend to with regard to his body. It was the kindest thing I could have done."

You can often find Letitcia chilling out and having a cappuccino in Kemp Town before a busy day ahead. If you want to get to know her more 'intimately', try visiting her website. But guys, if you do give her a call, try and be more original with your opening questions. Apparently, *"can I get a suck without a condom?"* and *"what's the parking like?"* are still the most common.

Seb and Dunc

Brighton's most celebrated nerds, Duncan Games and Sebastian Briere-Edney are the proud publishers of *Colin Cuts*, the UK's premiere Colin Baker* fanzine, now approaching its 200th edition.

To Dunc and Seb, Colin Baker is the **only** important thing in the world; they eat, sleep and breathe Colin, and even encourage their readers to send Colin-related dreams in to the magazine.

A couple of years ago, inspired by finally meeting the great man, Seb and Dunc staged an exhibition of more than 200 different paintings, sketches and screen prints of their favourite Doctor for the Brighton Festival, simply called 207 Colins.

According to Seb, a typical day for the two of them involves *"getting up, making a brew, watching a bit of Colin for about three hours, petitioning the* Bring Back Dr Who *website, and continuing work on the next magazine. We also try and imagine what Colin would be eating that day. We'll consult our* Doctor Who *cookbook and sometimes invent recipes that we think Colin would like. We started eating a lot more puddings when we discovered he had a fondness for them."*

On the subject of girlfriends however, the pair are much more reticent and withdrawn.

"Women give you a wide berth when they find out what you're into," explained Dunc, 'but they don't know what they're missing. We can be sensitive. I cry sometimes. I mean, have you **seen** Dr Who and the Green Death?"

As Seb and Dunc would say, "Keep it Colin".

---

*For anyone unfamiliar with Doctor Who trivia, Colin Baker played the sixth incarnation of the Doctor, but was so unpopular with viewers that he became the first, and only, actor in this role to be sacked.

Michael "Atters" Attree

www.thechap.net/moustaches.html
www.ministryofmoustaches.0catch.com

This stylish and singular individual with a penchant for Edwardian boots, ruffles, cravats and three-piece suits can be found at local auctions, séances and Snoopers Paradise, where – as a sideline to his career as a satiric writer – he has an emporium selling Victorian ephemera, dinosaur bones and bygone monocles. It is, however, Michael's (or "Atters" as he is more widely known) fine moustache that has made him not only a hero round Brighton but also the youngest committee member of London's famous Handlebar Club, a place whose etiquette demands gentlemanly conduct, the wearing of a Club tie (it's drinks all round if you don't) and, as Atters cheekily put it, *"an ability to bore all outsiders with tales of the Empire and deceased comedians"*. A self-proclaimed "neo-hirsute hedonist", Atters is clearly proud of his lip foliage; he grooms it every day for 25 minutes and uses a snood (protective moustache net) to hold it at night. But mention the barbers and he gets twitchy: *"I won't let anyone near my smasher; one slip and you're a bloody surrealist!"* In fact, Atters has every right to be selective about who prunes his whiskers; he has been elected chairman of the 2007 World Beard and Moustache Championship and as a consequence is now grooming editor of *The Chap*. As Atters has successfully campaigned for Brighton to host this event, it's comforting to know that, despite all those scruffy beards, goatees and jazz dots out there, there is at least one man in our city who, as he succinctly puts it, *"has the balls to sport the facial topiary worthy of a gentleman!"*

CHEEKY PIN-UP
DREAM DATE
No. 1 Adorable Atters

CUT OUT AND KEEP

Brighton in Books & the Movies

BRIGHTON IN THE MOVIES

Brighton Rock
1947 Dir. John Boulting

Discover a Brighton of Bovril adverts and Brylcreem in this classic Graham Greene story set in the 30s, with plenty of fascinating scenes from the Old Lanes, Queens Road, Grand Hotel and the Palace Pier. In the story Richard Attenborough plays Pinkie Brown, an evil small-time gangster who tries to cover up a murder by marrying a young girl who could give evidence against him. While the ending is far better in the book (aren't they always?), this film is a genuinely chilling account of the gangster scene that once flourished in Brighton. If you're a Doctor Who fan keep your eyes peeled for a young William Hartnell.

Classic line from the film: *"People don't change; look at me. I'm like one of those sticks of rock. Bite all the way down and you still read Brighton."*

Me Without You
2001 Dir. Sandra Goldbacher

Following childhood friends Marina and Holly through their teenage years and beyond, this rather lacklustre tale of jealousy and heartache suffers a bit from *I Love the 70s/80s* syndrome, with *so* much emphasis on perfectly placed songs, band posters and kitsch furniture that the plot is almost inconsequential. The highlight comes midway through when the girls move to Brighton to study at Sussex University and – amid lectures on Barthes, Baudrillard and the other usual suspects – they both start a fling with tutor Kyle McLachlan, who plays the sleazy lecturer to a tee, complete with V-neck sweater, mane of hair, coke habit, and the classic chat-up line *"let's discuss this over tea at my place"*. From hereon in, however, the film gets increasingly tedious over the theme of Holly's unrequited love for Marina's brother Nad, and toward the end you may well be champing at the bit for it to finish.

Oh, What A Lovely War!
1969 Dir. Dickie Attenborough

Attenborough's first movie is an over-ambitious and heavy-handed affair, telling the story of the First World War through allegory, mild satire and *way* too much singing. The West Pier is the platform for events leading up to the war, and the film also includes many fine shots of the seafront, the Downs and Devil's Dyke.

Despite its flaws it's an interesting piece of British movie history, with some occasionally stunning moments. The scene in the trenches on Christmas day, when the German and English soldiers nervously meet in No Man's Land and share a drink, is genuinely moving. The film also boasts an incredible cast, ranging from thespian gods Laurence Olivier and John Mills, right the way down to the Fairy Liquid queen herself, Nanette Newman.

Quadrophenia
1979 Dir. Franc Roddam

Jimmy, a troubled young Mod, visits Brighton for a wild weekend but gets carried away, takes too many pills, loses his job and is so disillusioned with Sting's bad acting and solo career that he drives his scooter off Beachy Head. Or does he?

The shots of 70s Brighton (masquerading as 60s Brighton) are wonderful – it's all smoky cafes, Triumph Heralds and Wimpy bars. The fight scenes take place on the beach (where potatoes were substituted for stones!) and down East Street; if you want to find the famous alleyway where Jimmy and Steph cop off, go down East Street toward the sea. Near the end look for the shop LTS and above it is a sign for an alleyway

that reads 'to little East Street'. It's down there. This was once a graffitied Mod shrine, but with the next Mod revival not due for another ten years it doesn't attract as many visitors any more. Yes, the doorway is still there (now red), but it's locked so, no, you can't pop in and have a shag, though countless have tried…

Classic line from the film: *"I don't want to be like everyone else, that's why I'm a Mod see."*

The Brighton Movie Buff's Quiz

Well it's been in the book for three years now and still no-one's got it right so I'm upping the prize to **two** sticks of rock, a tub of lube and a night of carnal passion with Leo Sayer. Can't say fairer than that. But on with the quiz: who said the following line and what was the film?

"Give her a hat with an ostrich's feather in it and there's no girl in Brighton on a bank holiday could hold a candle to her."

Slade in Flame
1975 Dir. Richard Loncraine

The chirpy Brummie boys with huge lambchops star in this surprisingly sombre film, which charts the rise of fictional Midland pub band *Flame* from obscurity to Glam superstardom. Of course it all goes awry after one too many Babychams and ends with a brawl in the famous Grand Hotel. Look out for Tom Conti as the manager.

Villain
1971 Dir. Michael Tuchner

This 70s movie is a tough, bruising thriller with Richard Burton playing a vicious gay criminal. Though set in London the story does eventually move to Brighton when Burton decides to visit his dear old mother but the game is up when he gets caught by the fuzz on the West Pier.

Smokescreen
1964 Dir. Jim O'Connolly

Shot on location in Sussex and at the forgotten Brighton Film Studios, this low-key thriller stars Peter 'Genial Harry Grout' Vaughn as a dogged and niggardly insurance assessor on the trail of a suspected fraudulent claim. Peppered with British bit-part players who include Sam Kydd, Glyn Edwards and Deryck Guyler, this is a nifty B movie with some good shots of Brighton Station, the Grand Hotel and the West Pier.

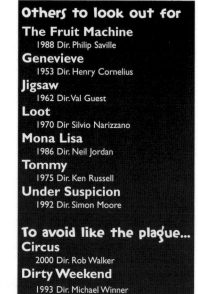

Others to look out for

The Fruit Machine
1988 Dir. Philip Saville

Genevieve
1953 Dir. Henry Cornelius

Jigsaw
1962 Dir. Val Guest

Loot
1970 Dir Silvio Narizzano

Mona Lisa
1986 Dir. Neil Jordan

Tommy
1975 Dir. Ken Russell

Under Suspicion
1992 Dir. Simon Moore

To avoid like the plague...

Circus
2000 Dir. Rob Walker

Dirty Weekend
1993 Dir. Michael Winner

PETER VAUGHAN · JOHN CARSON *in* SMOKESCREEN Cert U
YVONNE ROMAIN · GERALD FLOOD
Produced by: JOHN I. PHILLIPS   Written and Directed by: JIM O'CONNOLLY   Associate Producer: RONALD LILES

CARRY ON BRIGHTON

Carry On Girls
1973 Dir. Gerald Thomas

Where in Brighton?

It all takes place in the pretend seaside town of Fircombe (oooerrr!!) which is, of course, actually Brighton. The film features shots of the seafront, the West Pier and a fleeting glimpse of Regency Square. My favourite bit of the film is near the end, when the contest goes awry and Sid James – chased by a crowd of angry men – escapes down the West Pier in a go-kart. Look out for the outrageous gay stereotypes in the movie – there's the camp film director with the flowery shirt and mincing walk and June Whitfield's sidekick: a humourless, man-hating lesbian who dresses like Hitler. They just don't make comedy clichés like they used to.

The Plot:

Sid James is on the make as usual, this time as the buttock-slapping Councillor Fiddler, who organises a beauty competition only to be foiled by sour-faced women's-libber June Whitfield.

Trivia:

This was the first Carry On film that had to be broadcast after the BBC's 9pm watershed, as it was considered far too saucy!

Carry On at Your Convenience
1971 Dir. Gerald Thomas

The Plot:

Hailed as a Carry On masterpiece, this tale of industrial strife and romance at WC Boggs toilet factory meant that finally the lavatorial gags could really let rip (ahem). And, of course no Carry On movie would be complete without Brighton's own Patsy Rowland (as sex-crazy secretary Miss Withering) trying to get into Kenneth Williams' trousers. I just don't think you were his type, dear. Starring Kenneth Williams as WC Boggs and Sid James as… Sid. Well, why make life difficult?

Where in Brighton?

The gang take a bus trip down for their annual works outing and head for the rides on the Palace Pier.

Trivia:

Alternative title for the film was Carry On Ladies Please Be Seated.

Beatniks
Toby Litt

This is the tale of three modern-day hippies who move to Brighton to start a magazine called *Café Bohemia* but all end up in bed together instead. The book tries hard to be hip but fails and the descriptions of Brighton are woefully clichéd. Strangely enough, a Café Bohemia opened in Kemp Town just as the book was released.

Breakfast in Brighton
Nigel Richardson

Having almost made a legend out of one of the least likely pubs in Brighton (The Grosvenor) Nigel Richardson has, with this book, woven together a series of inconsequential but entertaining anecdotes about his relationship with the town. The book's McGuffin is a mysterious painting that Richardson is trying to find out more about, a conundrum that leads him to visit séances and spiritual churches, and meet art collectors, hammy old actors, fishermen and landladies. While the plot is rather scant it's a very personable and revealing insight into the darker, sleazier and posher corners of this city.

The Brighton Book

Released in conjunction with the Brighton festival in 2005 this is a cornucopia of short stories, recipes, poetry and cartoons by the likes of Jeannette Winterson, Louis de Bernières, Nigella Lawson and various local writers and illustrators all, supposedly, on the theme of Brighton. While there are some interesting and well-written pieces (and it's great to

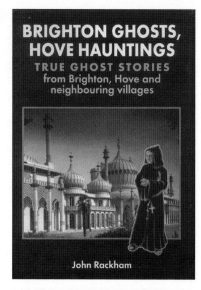

BRIGHTON GHOSTS, HOVE HAUNTINGS
TRUE GHOST STORIES
from Brighton, Hove and neighbouring villages

John Rackham

see anything by illustrator Woodrow Phoenix), the theme of the book seems to have gone astray somewhere down the line as there is plenty in here that has bugger all to do with the city.

According to Amazon, the "*perfect partner*" for this book is: *Weight: The Myth of Atlas and Heracles* – which is like twinning *Little Dorrit* with the Haynes Renault Clio manual.

Brighton Ghosts, Hove Hauntings (true ghost stories)
John Rackham

The result of five years' investigations and more than 400 interviews with people who claim to have had supernatural experiences in the local area, Rackham's book starts well – the introductory chapter *What are Ghosts?* shows his open-minded enthusiasm and inquisitive approach to the subject – and goes on to investigate supernatural sightings through the themes of location (Pavilion, churches, pubs, theatres) and subjects (smugglers, Ouija boards).

At over 300 pages it's more digestible as something to dip into now and again, rather than read from cover to cover.

Brighton Rock
Graham Greene
(See film guide)

Hangover Square
Patrick Hamilton
One man's pursuit of large quantities of alcohol and a rather unpleasant lady gold-digger in late 30s London and Brighton. Our hero is a social inadequate with a private income that allows him to be fleeced continually for whisky funds by his drinking buddies; not an easy character to sympathise with and a rather sombre read, but a salutary warning for Brightonians viewing hedonism as an end in itself.

Hamilton is one of our great minor novelists (no slur intended) but the tone of this classic book and his own struggle with alcoholism show what a childhood spent in Hove can do for you.

The Illustrated Mum
Jacqueline Wilson
Though the Ray Bradbury reference may be lost on the majority of its teenage readers, Jacqueline Wilson's widely acclaimed novel takes an insightful look into some of the problems surrounding an unconventional modern family and provides humour and compassion when dealing with 'difficult' issues such as a mother's manic depression.

Brighton was, of course, the natural choice of setting for Marigold (a single mum with a penchant for wacky clothes and tattoos) and her two daughters, Star and Dolphin.

The Neat and Nippy Guide to Brighton's History
Christopher Horlock
This concise and inexpensive little paperback covers Brighton's history at breakneck pace with Horlock taking a conventional, but playful approach to the town's chequered past and clearly relishing a good tale. Most of the highlights come in the first half of the book, when Horlock details the lives of Martha Gunn, Mrs Fitzherbert and the Prince Regent, and the ensuing *"drunkenness, gambling and hanky-panky"* that took place in the Pavilion. In fact the stories about Prinnie's wayward pals the Barrymore Brothers are hilarious, though afterwards even Horlock concedes, *"the rest of this guide is going to seem a bit dull after that lot!"*

A thoroughly digestible book that can be read from cover to cover in just a couple of hours. Recommended.

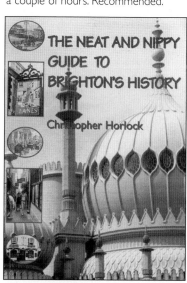

THE NEAT AND NIPPY GUIDE TO BRIGHTON'S HISTORY
Christopher Horlock

QueenSpark Books

(01273) 571710
www.queensparkbooks.org.uk
www.mybrightonandhove.org.uk

QueenSpark Books began life over 30 years ago as a local campaign to save the Royal Spa building in Queens Park from being turned into a casino by developers. The campaigners produced a regular newspaper, QueenSpark, which was sold at the princely sum of 1p (this was the 70s after all!). Then in 1974, Brightonian Albert Paul sent his life story *Poverty, Hard Work but Happiness* to the group and this became the first QueenSpark book, with Albert selling more than 1,000 copies door to door around Brighton. Since then, QueenSpark – set up as a voluntary non-profit making community publishing company – has produced more than 80 titles, including individual life stories by local people, community oral histories and the occasional poetry anthology. Gems include *Moulsecoomb Memories* and *Tales from the Fishing Community*.

The Snowman

Raymond Briggs

Christmas wouldn't be the same without this local children's tale, brought alive every year through the magic of television and the lilting tones of a Welsh eunuch. Next time it's on the telly look out for the flying scene and you'll see the Snowman and the boy sail over Brighton Pavilion and the Palace Pier as they head south to the errrr… North Pole.

The Vending Machine of Justice & As Good As It Gets

Simon Nolan

Simon Nolan seems to like writing comedies set around Brighton, as these two novels demonstrate. As

Good As It Gets is a trendy novel about a bunch of twenty-somethings who find five kilos of coke and decide that they could find a better use for it than the police, while *The Vending Machine of Justice* revolves around a bizarre case at Hove crown court and a few local zombies. While Nolan's books include some good descriptions of the pub and club culture in Brighton and have some genuinely funny moments, it's all fairly lightweight stuff and may disappoint those with a penchant for quality literature.

LITERARY EVENTS

In recent years it's Borders and City Books who seem to have taken up the mantle of organising book-readings and other literary events in Brighton. Look out for their monthly fliers in the shops for details of what's on. During the May Festival there's also a whole plethora of book readings and interviews from big names like Salman Rushdie and Hanif Kureshi, in different venues around the town.

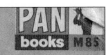

ANARCHISTS IN LOVE

Colin Spencer

A PUNGENT, EARTHY NOVEL
WITH A POWER TO SHOCK

'They are on the side of the
angels in their celebration
of love and in the anarchic
rejection of the stifling ties
of family and convention…
This is the strength of the
book' TIMES LITERARY SUPPLEMENT

Occult Brighton

With Brighton as the chosen resting place of Aleister Crowley, home to famous witch Doreen Valiente, birthplace of the notorious Temple of Psychic Youth and – until recently – host to the world's largest annual occult festival, it seems fairly clear that there's something a bit 'Sunnydale' about the place.

No less remarkable is the fact that the two greatest UK occultists, Dion Fortune and Aleister Crowley, have both written about Brighton in their novels. In Fortune's occult thriller The Demon Lover, the two heroes, Lucas and Veronica, have a "Brighton experience" as their "trip to the town makes them profoundly aware of their own karmic links and the magical task set before them".

It may come as no surprise to learn that Sussex was the last county to convert to Christianity. In 666 AD, no less!

BRIGHTON OCCULTISTS PAST AND PRESENT

Doreen Valiente

Described as the "Mother of Modern Witchcraft" this remarkable Kemp Town resident breathed life into rather fragmented rites and rituals contained in the Book of Shadows (the Bible of Gardnarian Wicca) using her poetic skills. Today, nearly every witch in every coven in the world repeats the sacred invocation Charge of the Goddess, penned by Doreen. She is credited with inspiring the current popular interest in witchcraft (though Buffy creator Joss Whedon might dispute this) and left several important works on the subject, including the carefully guarded Book of Shadows, whose contents are forbidden to non-witches!

CHARGE
OF THE
GODDESS

Genesis P.Orridge

This rather singular individual first made a name for himself back in the 70s through the group Throbbing Gristle and a series of rather explicit live-art performances known as the Coum Transmissions. Like all good subversives Orridge incurred the wrath of the establishment through these performances and one Tory MP even went so far as to describe him as a "*wrecker of civilisation*". But the worst was yet to come.

In the early 80s he moved to Brighton and set up the Temple of Psychic Youth (TOPY), a "*Cyberian Anti-Cult*", whose collective of like-minded searchers aimed to explore altered states through scarification, piercing, sado-masochism and sex magick. While this kind of thing is pretty much compulsory in Brighton nowadays, twenty years ago it was enough to cause a witch-hunt in the media. In 1991 a Channel Four documentary 'exposed' TOPY as a "*sick Satanic cult*" with witnesses speaking on camera of being drugged, raped and forced to eat babies in the basement of Orridge's house in Roundhill Crescent. The police raided the house and

Orridge – who was then in Thailand – was strongly advised not to return home unless he wanted his children taken away. Genesis settled in the US, where he still lives today, despite the fact that subsequent enquiries into the documentary showed it to be a malicious stitch-up by fundamentalist Christians (Orridge's house didn't even have a basement!).

What makes Genesis such a fascinating character still is his ability to constantly re-invent himself and – true to form – he is still courting controversy, having spent the past ten years exploring transexuality with his partner, Miss Jackie Superstar. The two have been breaking the boundaries of male and female polarity through plastic surgery, adopting each other's characteristics and dressing identically.

As Orridge was fundamental in making Brighton the tattoo and piercing capital of the UK, is he, one wonders, about to spearhead the dissolution of another great taboo with his latest venture? Can we soon expect to see hordes of transsexual clones alighting the train from Hassocks and Croydon every Friday night? I, for one, live in hope.

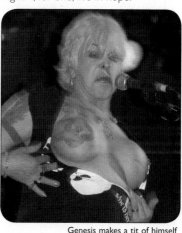

Genesis makes a tit of himself

Aleister Crowley

As the author of the *Book of the Law*, and dubbed "*the Wickedest Man In The World*", it's only natural that drug fiend and poet Crowley would have a connection with Brighton; and though he died in Hastings in 1947, he sensibly chose to be cremated at Woodvale Cemetery down the Lewes Road.

At his funeral, a selection of Crowley's work was read, as was the "*Hymn to Pan*", which thoroughly shocked the locals and prompted the council to hold an emergency meeting ensuring such a ceremony would never again take place in their town. Don't go looking for him though: he's all blown away by now.

OCCULT AWAYDAYS

Chanctonbury Ring
Five miles north of Worthing

This small Iron-Age hill fort, noted for its ring of beech trees (though most, sadly, were lost in the hurricane of 1987) is a beguiling place steeped in folklore. According to legend, if you walk or run seven times around the Ring at midnight, the devil will appear, offering a bowl of milk, soup or porridge (?!). If you accept these comestibles, he'll take your soul or offer you your heart's desire (which is obviously a bit of a gamble for anyone daft enough to risk it).

Long associated with witchcraft, Chanctonbury Ring was described by Crowley as a "*place of power*", while local witch Doreen Valiente revealed it to be the meeting place of an ancient coven. That the place has been used for occult practices is indisputable, as evidence of makeshift altars has been found there on several occasions, not to mention other known occult symbols and artefacts. Whether the Ring is a spot favoured by black or white witches is unknown but, as one Sussex archaeology and folklore website put it, "*Being Chanctonbury Ring, it is probably black*".

Chanctonbury Ring is also associated with sighting of UFOs and fairies; there have been countless reports over the years of strange coloured objects and dancing lights.

If you're planning a visit, it's best not to come alone. And certainly not at night.

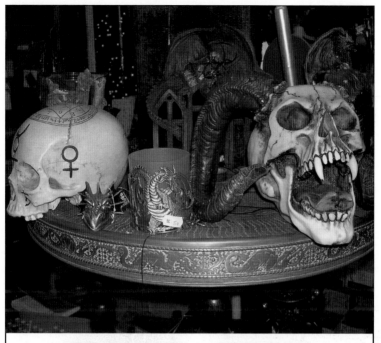

OCCULT SHOPS

Dragon's Gate
13 St James's Street (01273) 679992
Open Mon-Sat 10am-7pm

While the obvious "*hey, this looks like the shop from* Buffy" won't go down well with owner Jennifer Dragon, it's easy to understand why the shop elicits the lazy comparison. Packed to the hilt with charms, amulets, occult books, altar cloths, handmade wands, robes, Tarot packs (from Thoth to Bosch) and crystals, the place certainly looks the part, despite the pool table in the centre. But while Giles and co were pitched at disaffected teen goths, Dragon's Gate is – according to Jennifer – the real deal: a place for practising Wiccans and witches and those with a serious interest in occultism. Witness Jennifer enthroned behind the counter listening to *Beowulf* in the original Anglo-Saxon and you'll see what she means.

A good spot too for finding out more about occult events. And for those who dreamed of a Hogwarts for adults, be cheered! Jennifer is putting together an Academy of Magic some time in the future, although you won't be allowed to enrol unless you own a pointy hat.

The Gay Scene

Since the first gay herring fair in 1910 Brighton's gay scene has grown to become the largest and most celebrated in the country. Gay shenanigans had been going on **well** before then however – most of the Prince Regent's male friends were camp as Christmas and the Pavilion is a classic example of what can happen when you let a gay man loose on the decorating.

By Victorian times Brighton had become the destination of choice for the London homoset wanting to get away from prying eyes. Oscar Wilde met his lover Bosie in the Albion Hotel while Gladstone even had his own drag show. It is the town's theatrical tradition that really played the biggest role in creating the scene as we know it today; gay icons like Ivor Novello and Noel Coward lived here, lording it up and down with Laurence Olivier with whom, ironically enough, you can now ride up and down the seafront, should you catch the number 27 bus. And of course with the town already established as a fashionable pleasure capital (and with place names such as Dyke Close, The Queen's Arms and a Tidy Street) Brighton really was the obvious choice for the UK's gay headquarters. From the 60s onwards the gay community developed around Kemp Town, the Old Steine and St James's Street. You'll find most of the best bars, clubs and shops here as this is where the majority of Brighton's gay population still socialises, although truth is, they are now scattered all over the place: they're everywhere!

The original gay haunts in Kemp Town were developed for cruising but as it became so much easier to be 'out' in Brighton, the clubs and bars became less about a quick fumble in the loos and more about just hanging out, posing and socialising (though, believe me, plenty of naughtiness still goes on).

Statistics show that a staggering 23% of adult males in Brighton are gay, with the number still rising fast (which means if you're straight, single and still can't get a girlfriend, you might as well give up). As a consequence Brighton now has gay everything – gay shops, gay clubs, gay saunas, gay coffee bars, gay B&Bs, gay carnivals, gay plumbers, gay estate agents, gay comedians… and Simon Fanshawe. And with the advent of the civil partnership act, Brighton is poised to become the gay 'wedding' capital of the country, with his-and-his matching peach Audi TT wedding presents to match. So let's raise a toast and be queer and proud. As Emily Lloyd was so fond of saying in the Brighton-set Wish You Were Here, "Up Yer Bum!"

The Aquarium
6 Steine Street (01273) 605525
Authentic backstreet bar for the old-school crowd and home to the sharpest-tongued barman in town. Be warned, the Aquarium is *very* cruisy and populated by 'mature' gentlemen, many of whom prefer staring to speaking. A good place to get sucked off by a German tourist. If you pop in say hello to Mike; he's not German but he'll still suck you off.

The Queen's Arms
7 George Street (01273) 696873
Although it doesn't open until 3pm, once it does this traditional gay pub hosts more or less constant entertainment. From cabaret and quizzes to karaoke and piano playing, no matter *when* you arrive, something lively is always happening. It's also home to the world's saddest drag queen – mad, bad and dangerous to

know, she's like Arthur Mullard on crack. Increasingly popular with the girls at weekends, too (the pub, not Arthur).

The Queen's Head
3 Steine Street (01273) 602939
A fun place at weekends with quirky cabaret, good music and a young, mixed student-friendly crowd, this well-established hangout was recently refurbished. It now boasts a restaurant upstairs and a plasma screen the size of Wales, but I still miss the original Freddie Mercury pub sign.

The Bulldog
31 St James's Street (01273) 684097
www.bulldogbrighton.com
31-hour drinkathons, compulsory happy hours and promotions galore, the Bulldog is somewhere to just grin, drink and cruise: a place where nobody wants to know your name but everyone wants to shag you. Check out their mad game shows hosted by the skinniest drag queen in the city and marvel at the cheapness of the men. And while the lecherous old-school vibe seems to have been replaced of late with a growing, younger pre-club crowd, rest assured it's still a pub where you'll only leave alone if you *really* want to.

Brighton Tavern
99-100 Gloucester Road (01273) 680365
www.brightontavern.com
North Laine's own local gay bar has a nice friendly vibe that's more like a proper pub that just happens to be gay. Lethal free shots occasionally get handed round, and it's worth coming for their Sunday-evening music session, particularly if Rocking Billy is performing: he's a real live Teddy-boy DJ.

Amsterdam
11-12 Marine Parade
(01273) 688825
www.amsterdam.uk.com

This European style bar on the seafront attracts a large mixed crowd and when the sun's out the terrace is *the* place to be seen on the scene. When the Amsterdam first appeared it marked an important change, making Brighton's gay social scene more upfront and visible and not just about cruising. There's bare flesh galore here when the sun shines; the huge patio overlooking the sea is a prime spot for sitting in your thong with a mug of Horlicks and a Martini while shocking the Hassocks teenagers queuing up for Audio next door.

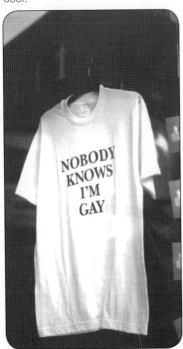

Brighton Rocks
6 Rock Place (01273) 601139
www.brighton-rocks.com

Stylish and decadent hide-out for the in-the-know crowd.
(See review in *Watering Holes*)

Charles Street
8-9 Marine Parade
(01273) 624091
www.charlesstreetbar.com

For fashionistas and uber-posers, Charles Street should be first port of call as it is *the* place for the trendy 20s/30s crowd and out-of-towners looking for action. A shedload of cash has been spent making it look like a vast *Star Trek* departure lounge, with a bar stretching to the edge of the galaxy, but if the décor here doesn't do it for you slip out onto the sundeck and you can bitch about the Aquarium Terrace eyesore opposite. Thursday night is for cheap drinks and even cheaper men. Steer yourself to the 'bridge', act à la Picard and watch the heaving gay mob swarm past.

Dr Brighton's
16 Kings Road (01273) 328765
(See *Watering Holes*)

Legends
31-32 Marine Parade
(01273) 624462
www.legendsbrighton.co.uk

It was all change for Legends as we were going to print. The New Europe Hotel and Schwartz Bar disappeared (no more bad backs and crawling home in his leather thong for my friend Carl Vincent), scheduled to be replaced in August 2006 with a complex bearing the name Legends which, they promise, will "*rival the best gay hotels, clubs and bars in Brighton*".

Haemorrhoid-support team training session

r-bar

7 Marine Parade (01273) 608133

Following endless reincarnations, r-bar (formerly a-bar, b-bar, c-bar, d-bar, e-bar, f-bar, g-bar, h-bar, i-bar, j-bar, k-bar, l-bar, m-bar, n-bar, o-bar, p-bar, and so on) has finally hit upon a willing formula and now everyone wants to be *taken up the r's.* New sofas, outrageous unisex urinals (well worth a gander) and improved music policy make visiting now a pleasure, as do the terrible drag acts – priceless entertainment to be had from the bad wigs alone. Upstairs is cosier and there's a bookable VIP lounge redolent of a gentleman's club, with leather-upholstered walls and a private hotline to the bar staff.

BARS THAT ARE NOT QUITE GAY BUT GAY-RUN AND HAPPY TO HELP OUT WHEN THE REST ARE BUSY

The Eagle, Gloucester Rd

The Hop Poles, Middle St

The Cricketers, Black Lion St

St James's Tavern, St James's St

Sidewinder, St George's Rd

Barley Mow, St George's Rd

(See *Watering Holes* for reviews)

CLUBS & CLUB NIGHTS

Club Revenge
32-43 Old Steine (01273) 606064

The biggest gay club on the south coast, open six nights a week with special events, drinks promotions, strippers and cheesy pop nights. It's a little on the expensive side but still ranks as one of the best in the UK. Sure, newcomers will find the inevitable cliques, but don't be put off: it really isn't difficult to meet new people here. With all those body beautifuls sweating it out on the upstairs dancefloor, you shouldn't find it hard to get caught up in the contagious party atmosphere.

Top tip: Be nice to the sexy barstaff – they're your best port of call for discovering the hottest parties.

The Club
8-9 Marine Parade (above Charles Street)
(01273) 624091

Formerly Envy (another example of Brighton clubs changing their names for the worse) the Club stands upon the hallowed ground that many moons ago was heavy metal Valhalla the Hungry Years. For years I joked about it being appropriated by the gay scene and then, suddenly, it was – bringing a whole new meaning to the phrase *"studs on your back"*. Popular with students and a younger crowd, the Club is a gay clubber's paradise, with visits from big-name London clubs and a cavernous space that makes cruising nice and easy.

Sunday Sundae
(resident at Audio at time of going to print)

Long-running weekly gay fest for fit boys and their trolly-dolly friends and fag hags.

Wild Fruit
www.wildfruit.co.uk

The big gay daddy of the scene, packed to the hilt with voyeurs and exhibitionists. Wild Fruit is one long night of feather boas, sequins, rubber hotpants and dancefloor anthems. Dress to impress and you'll be beating them off with a stick, or whatever comes to hand.

TV BARS

Harlequin
(formerly Ruby's, Marilyn's, Charlotte's, Tina's and Tony's Discount Toolshop)
43 Providence Place
(01273) 620630

Hidden behind Woolworths, off the London Road, this is *the* (if not the only) hangout for transvestites and transsexuals, though welcoming to all and sundry. During the week there's cabaret in the large glittery bar area upstairs which, unsurprisingly, can include some pretty wild drag acts and karaoke. Started by the king of camp, Danny La Rue, the whole place is a real flashback to the 80s but despite the tacky décor its owners work hard to keep the place vibrant and fun. Also home to Brighton's best fetish night, Vinylla.

Almost everyone in Brighton is gay these days

CRUISING AREAS

Almost the whole of Brighton is a cruising area, so take your pick: Queens Park, Preston Park, Dyke Road Park, Somerfield… just follow your nose and you can't go far wrong (unless you find yourself in Moulsecoomb, in which case – run!) If you want more concentrated trade, however, the following places might be of interest…

Duke's Mound

This small, sloping, dense shrubbery ten minutes' walk east of Brighton Pier is the oldest cruising ground in Sussex and comes complete with its own little eco-system and constant stream of lusty men. It affords enough privacy to those who require it, yet is risqué enough for naughty exhibitionists, while those splendid chaps from the Terrence Higgins Trust even come here at weekends to give out free condoms, tea, coffee and oranges at half time. While not commonly reported, there are occasional stories of people getting mugged after being picked up and taken to Duke's Mound, so take care. There have also been rumours for years of redevelopment at nearby Black Rock bringing an end to the naughty shenanigans, but nothing has happened yet. There *are* plans for a hotel, coffee shop, juice bar, sushi restaurant and Blobbyworld but seeing how long it took the council to build a bloody library, I wouldn't worry just yet.

Hove Lawns & Behind the King Alfred

A chilled-out seafront coffee bar, the Meeting Place can be a good spot for cruising during the day (though don't get your hopes up on a drizzly February afternoon), while at night the whole area from the Peace Statue to the King Alfred leisure centre can sometimes seem like one long glorious golden mile of talent. It is rather flat and exposed, compared with the bushes, but the beach is dark and can't be seen from the promenade. Alternatively, you can always pop round the back of the King Alfred for a quickie; try not to scare Nick Cave if he's out taking his pet bat for a flap.

Brighton Nudist Beach
Ten minutes east of Brighton Pier

If it's pervs, pebbles, flabby bottoms, curious bi-boys, randy gay men, a plethora of stiffies, lots of parading and a stray drunken hen party you're after, then get yourself down to the celebrated nudist beach. It's even conveniently close to the bushes should you happen to meet a likeable fellow. Straights are welcome in theory but in most cases will feel uncomfortable, especially if they get asked for a popper-fuelled hand shandy by a tattooed man with a heavily pierced penis and a parrot on his shoulder, as I was. And look out for Windmill Man.

SAUNAS

Used as social clubs in Brighton by the gay community, these saunas attract a wide age group and all come with rest room facilities.

Brighton Oasis
75-76 Grand Parade
(01273) 689966
Weekend pass Fri 12noon-Sunday
12midnight £20 Best to phone for other
prices as I wrote them down and then got
all confused by my notes

Not content with being the biggest, busiest and best in town, and keen not to be outdone by nearby neighbour the Pavilion, Brighton Oasis is decked out like the set of *Carry on Cleopatra* and comes replete with a whirlpool, maze, steam room, sunbed, qualified masseurs and battery-powered asps.

Amsterdam Sauna
11-12 Marine Parade
(01273) 688825

Part of the Amsterdam Hotel, this sauna is open to the public and has a steam room, shower and many dark rooms. As well as being open all night the Amsterdam holds women-only nights and a new trannie night, though I swear those hot sweaty tiles would be murder in high heels…

Sorry, I slipped on the soap!

Denmark Sauna
86 Denmark Villas, Hove (01273) 723733

A good-quality sauna popular with Hove residents. Expect the odd stray blue-rinse granny who's wandered in looking for a perm.

Bright 'N' Beautiful Sauna Club
9 St Margaret's Place
(01273) 328330

Tucked away at the foot of the tallest building in Sussex is the oldest sauna in Brighton, boasting a bubbling water feature and a semi-naked gladiator with a saucy glint in his eye. There's also a large steam room, huge relaxing TV lounge and nearby shops should you need to pop out for a jock strap or denture grip.

Pride: a recipe for excess

Early August www.brightonpride.co.uk

Take 110,000 highly-charged gay folk; dress them up in as many feathers, sequins, leather jock straps, masks, ribbons and glitter as you can; stir in every intoxicant known to man; pour on the sunshine; march them up and down the streets of Brighton and finish off in a huge park with dance tents, funfairs and more wildlife and antics in the undergrowth than a BBC nature programme and you're beginning to get an inkling of the utterly fabulous, depraved carnival that is Pride.

From just 103 people at the first angry, political Pride demonstration, this event has grown to become the event in the British gay calendar. The week-long arts celebration culminates in a huge carnival procession and parade with stunning floats, dancers, drag queens, classic cars and scantily-clad people of all types, enveloped by pumping music ranging from camp disco classics to present-day pop. The parade starts in Madeira Drive at 11am and then dances, shouts and camps it up all the way to Preston Park, stopping only for a sandwich and a glass of fizzy pop at the Woolworths café. And if you think the huge fireworks display marks the end of it, think again. It's followed by a weekend street party in St James's Street which, in the past few years, has just got bigger and wilder. Pride is simply fantastic, not to be missed!

SHOPS

Cardome
47A St James's Street (01273) 692916
Open Mon-Sat 10am-6pm

A wonderful cross between a local craft market, WH Smith's and a sex shop, Cardome lays claim to being Brighton's oldest established gay shop (close to twenty years in the business!) A good place to come for greeting cards (gay and straight), local hand-made art, jungle juice and T-shirts with slogans such as *"Some mornings I wake up miserable, other mornings I let him sleep"*. While the soft porn in the basement seems to have been replaced by saucy cards of late, friendly owner Mike will answer any discreet questions you may have about all aspects of the sex scene in Brighton (if he hasn't died of joss-stick poisoning, that is).

CloneZone
St James's Street (01273) 626442
Open Mon-Thurs 11am-7pm,
Fri-Sat 11am-9pm, Sun 12pm-6pm

Selling a range of toys, videos, fashion, cards and rubberwear, this is definitely a good place to get stocked up for a weekend of unashamed wickedness.

They also have a modest selection of music CDs from the likes of Kylie and a particularly wide range of magazines, including *Latin Inches* and *Euroboy*. If only there were a *Pale Northerner Monthly* I might earn some extra pocket money.

Prowler
112 St James's Street (01273) 683680
Open Mon-Sat 11am-7pm

Part of a small chain of gay lifestyle shops that include three in London and one (bizarrely) in Doncaster, Prowler proudly adds a little culture and sophistication to the formula. Catering as much for the girls as for the guys, the shop is perhaps best loved for its large selection of gay literature and 'How to' manuals as well as the cards, toys, mags, DVDs and AussieBum pants. If you're after something a little more saucy, you'll find it hidden away at the back of the shop. The manager explained, *"We want to be inviting to all. We even had a couple of nuns in the other day looking at cards. That's why it's important to us to keep the contents of the Blue Room separate from everything else. It doesn't have to be thrust into people's faces"*. Amen.

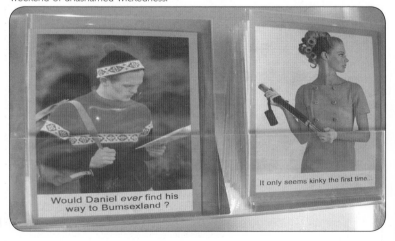

Would Daniel *ever* find his way to Bumsexland ?

It only seems kinky the first time...

UNDERSTANDING THE LINGO

The old gay dialect Polari was first developed back in the 1930s when homosexuality was still illegal (unless you were involved in theatre, where it was compulsory). This secret language enabled gay folk to get on with matters at hand without fear of persecution. It was later popularised by Julian and Sandy on the radio show Round The Horne and by the 1970s had evolved into such an esoteric and bizarre tongue that Oliver Postgate used it in The Clangers to send secret messages to many of his male lovers around the UK.

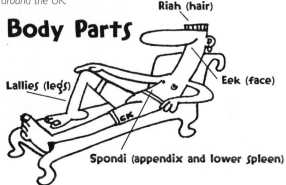

Body Parts

Riah (hair)

Eek (face)

Lallies (legs)

Spondi (appendix and lower spleen)

Bona polone/homi

Dictionary definition - Good looking woman/man
Eg. That bloke from the Cheeky Guide, what a bona homi!

Chicken

Dictionary definition - Waif-like young man
Eg. Check out the chicken in Somerfield.

Cruising

Dictionary definition - Sail to and fro for protection of shipping, making for no particular place or calling at a series of places.
Hmmm, that just doesn't seem to be what's going on in the bushes.

Trade

Dictionary definition - Sex/Your pick-up for the evening
Eg. Take your trade home and give him something to remember you by.

Varda/vada

Dictionary definition - To check out
Eg. Varda the legs on him/her/that lovely Regency sofa.

Others still in use

Kamp: Effeminate (Known As Male Prostitute)
Naff: Ugly/bad (Not Available For Fucking)
Omi-polone: Gay man
Lallies: Legs
Plate: Feet/to suck off
Scarper: To run off
Sharpy: Police
Troll: Walk about (looking for trade)

Example:
"Varda the naff lallies on the omi-polone! I've trolled for trade but it's scarpered 'cos of sharpy."
Translation: "Ey-up, looks like another bloody evening at 'ome, tugging me'sen off."

THE LESBIAN SCENE

For years the lesbian scene in Brighton seemed almost non-existent, which was strange considering the large number of gay women living here. And although, in principle, most of the gay bars welcomed lesbians, understandably few took up the offer – all that Kylie would put anyone off. Recently, however, a social scene for lesbians has been growing rapidly. There are now women-only saunas, lesbian speeddating nights and lesbian diving clubs (called Muffs… no, really!), not to mention the fabulous Marlborough pub, the Princess Victoria and the near-legendary Candy Bar.

The Candy Bar
33 St James's Street (01273) 622424
Mon-Sat 11am-11pm, Sun 12noon-10.30pm
www.thecandybar.co.uk

In its second incarnation on the main drag next to Café 22 and full to bursting with lovely ladies and their friends, the Candy Bar is a sassy venue with cosy snugs for canoodling and mirrors everywhere for checking your quiff's still intact. And its ever-changing nightly events mean there's always something new and fun to try out, whether it's killer pool, DJ nights hosted by the likes of Jimmy Somerville, drag-queen bingo or arm-wrestling competitions (Disarm a Dyke). The Candy Bar is even welcoming to men, provided they are accompanied by a gay girlfriend or two and don't mind a night of being dominated by females. But then, what man does?

The Marlborough
4 Princes Street (01273) 570028

Tucked away behind the Old Steine, Brighton's long-established lesbian pub attracts quite a young crowd of gay women, ranging from the civilised to the downright lairy. There are two bar areas: a lively one – usually occupied by feisty dykes monopolising the pool table – and a *slightly* quieter one next door which has nice big armchairs to sink into. Well-known for its little theatre upstairs, the Marlborough occasionally puts on plays, comedy nights and other events and is a good place to pick up gay magazines and information. It's also reputed to be one of Brighton's most haunted buildings – the ghost of Lucy Packham occasionally appears, gets her boobies out for the girls and then rolls them along the floor just for fun.

The Princess Victoria
22-23 Upper North Street (01273) 325491

Further up the hill and parallel to Western Road, this lesser-known gay-friendly bar is convivial, offers good pub grub and is popular with the ladies (though not exclusively). As soon as you walk in and see the full-sized, bare-breasted Princess Victoria figurehead with tequila-squirting rubber nipples, you know you'll be in safe hands.

SERIOUS STUFF

Safe Sex

Condoms are given free almost everywhere, from dispensers in bars and clubs (if you can't see any ask the barman) to 'glow boxes' on the cruising grounds and beaches. You've really no excuse not to use them. Syphilis, hepatitis and HIV infection rates continue to rise and the old *"it won't happen to me"* excuse is still as evident as folk trying to get an appointment at the clap clinic. Thankfully, most gay prostitutes in Brighton do enforce the condom rule. Just remember, sex is as safe as you're prepared to make it, so wrap up your peckers, guys.

For free advice contact the Terrence Higgins Trust (01273) 764200

Homophobia

Despite the fact that the gay community is a huge part of city life and most people in Brighton are totally cool and supportive of it, there *are* still plenty of attacks. Although it's sad to have to say it, be careful when you are out at night. Avoid snogging in the middle of West Street at 2am and you should be OK. The local police are both supportive and helpful if you have suffered homophobic or transphobic attack or assault. Get hold of one of the fantastic *True Vision* reporting packs and report any hassles, verbal or otherwise, that you may experience.

THE GAY WEB

The internet forms a bigger and bigger part of gay life these days, so keep up to date and in the know, see what you really did last night and look up a hot date before you even make it out the door. Good websites to check out include:

> *www.prideinbrightonandhove.com*
> *www.thtdirect.org*
> *www.safeinthecity.com*
> *www.gaybrighton.com*
> *www.gaydar.co.uk*
> *www.realbrighton.com*

Drink-a-pinta-spunk-a-day

GAY ORGANISATIONS AND SUPPORT GROUPS

Brighton & Hove HIV Project Bureau
(01273) 327474
By appointment only Tues/Thurs 9am-4pm,
Wed 9am-12.30pm

Employment, benefits, money and housing information.

Brighton & Hove Lesbian/ Gay Community Centre
113-117 Queens Road
(01273) 234005
Mon-Fri 10am-12noon
Drop in Thursdays 12noon-4pm, women only Fridays 12noon-4pm

Information centre and informal support on lesbian and gay issues.

Brighton Body Positive
(01273) 693266

Complementary therapies, information, support, and counselling for HIV/AIDS.

Brighton Women's Centre
Lettice House, 10 St George's Mews, off
Trafalgar Street (01273) 600526

Offering supportive help and information in a friendly atmosphere. Their services range from accommodation boards, photocopiers and computers to free pregnancy tests, crèche, counselling and legal advice.

Brighton Relate
(01273) 697997

Specialist advice for lesbian and gay relationships.

Community Safety Team
(01273) 294646

Help with issues around homo or transphobic harassment or assault.

Claude Nicol Centre
(01273) 664721

Testing and treatment for HIV (same day results Mon/Tues). Free and confidential service.

Street Outreach Service (SOS)
(01273) 625577

Mobile AIDS prevention unit, lots of advice, free condoms and lube.

Terrence Higgins Trust
(01273) 764200

Information about HIV and sexual health matters, free condoms etc.

Wilde Clinic
(01273) 664722

Gay and bisexual men's health clinic offering HIV testing, STI testing and treatment and hepatitis A & B vaccinations.

Ooh, you are Eiffel!

MY BRIGHTON & HOVE

Name: STELLA 'QUEEN OF BURLESQUE' STARR

The Dickensian little fish bar by the Fishing Museum There's something just perfect about the way the old guy who runs this place throws a freshly caught fish on the griddle; you eat your fish-in-a-roll outside – simple and delicious. As a quick fishy stop-off, there's none better!

The Racecourse If you really want to get a taste of the Graham Greene spiv side of things, come here. The building is tacky and municipal but this racecourse high on the hill, with its amazing panoramic views of Brighton, is quite something. The best thing to do (as I did as a kid) is stand by the fence as all the horses come galloping round – exhilarating!

Bali Brasserie in Hove The nearest we'll get (for now) to a Tiki bar in town. Marvellous kitsch bamboo décor and the entrance hall (the ground floor of a 60s block of flats) is worthy of the old Cunard cruise ships! If you want proper cocktails though, go to the very suave Valentino's bar next to the Theatre Royal.

MY BRIGHTON & HOVE

Name: MAIT 'PARDON MY FRENCH' FOULKES

Well, according to English fantasy French women only know about food, underwear and pink poodles. As I've never set foot in a dog parlour, and where I buy my underwear is my own business, let's talk about food…

The Saint My favourite restaurant. Gorgeous and inventive food with a French influence, pleasant service, relaxed atmosphere – and immaculate toilets. Good value for money.

Bodega D Tapa A tiny (really tiny – about two tables!) Spanish tapas bar which is truly authentic; the sherry and olive oil are produced by the owner's family in Andalucia.

The Real Patisserie, **Trafalgar Street** Alastair bakes the best bread and the finest French patisseries in Brighton. The chocolate-and-almond croissants, the macaroons and the pear-and-chocolate tart are to die for.

Sex, Fetish
& Body Modification

Brighton has long held the tradition of being the place for fat London bosses with hairy bums to bring their secretaries for more than just a telesales conference. And, being a fashionable resort and the perfect short break from the big smoke, it's easy to see why Brighton has earned a reputation for dirty weekends and countless indiscretions. Even the Prince Regent was at it, having secretly married Mrs Fitzherbert here. (The passageways connecting his Pavilion bedroom to her place were a means of ensuring their midnight rendezvous were kept secret.)

There are even rumours that Brighton has its own dogging scene up at Devil's Dyke, which – if you're unfamiliar with such antics – involves randy couples, cars and the odd voyeur (I'm sure you can piece the rest of the jigsaw together for yourself).

Brighton's saucy nature today comes more from the liberal nature of its citizens than anything else. It's a good place to live for anyone who wants to come out of the closet and feel relaxed with his or her sexuality. And as this town is home to everyone from fetishists to drag queens, you can feel secure here in the knowledge that, in your very neighbourhood, there'll always be someone kinkier than you.

Fetique

76 North Road (01273) 606080
Open Mon-Sat 11am-6pm, Sun 12noon-6pm
www.fetiqueuk.com

This friendly goth/fetish shop in the
heart of North Laine offers kinky
clothing and footwear for women of
all shapes and sizes (from 6-30). Stock
includes Flowers of Evil bustle skirts
(check out those goats' heads designs!),
leather kilts for men, metal collars,
boots, kinky ballet shoes and barbed
wire bracelets but their real speciality
is corsets. Whether you're after one
made of satin, rubber or even hard
leather they're bound to have it in, and
can accommodate any size or gender.

Nua

59A Ship Street (01273) 774001
www.nualifestyle.com

If manager Jeremy were ever to go on
Mastermind his chosen subject would
have to be dildos. Is there anything
this man doesn't know about them?
He can (and will) happily take you
on a guided tour of every single one

Fetique corset as modelled by a coy goth

here, which could take a while as the
place is stocked with dildos of every
shape, colour, size, material and flavour:
from rabbits to beautiful glass ones,
a large silicon range and ones that
can even be controlled remotely by
mobiles! Not only that, but you'll find
strap-on harnesses, a modest range of
quality collars, cuffs, bondage tape and
nipplewear; and the Shunga range of
edible scented body products, ranging
from delicious-smelling chocolate body
paint to egg-and-chips massage oil
(well, in my fantasies anyway).

Having fallen in love with the
flagship shop in Manchester, Jeremy
and partner Katherine set the place up
in late 2004 and their passion clearly
shows in the emphasis on quality, good
customer service, product knowledge,
care and a desire to keep the design
of the whole place subtle to avoid
offending anyone. In fact, the layout
of the shop is *so* discreet that people
have been known to wander in and
ask for a haircut or to "*look at the
jewellery*". Or perhaps I'm a bit out of
touch with modern euphemisms.

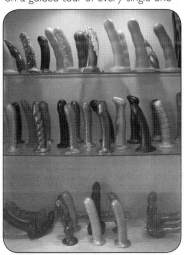
What *is* the collective noun for dildos anyway?

SEX, FETISH & BODY MODIFICATION

She Said

13 Ship Street Gardens (the twitten
between Ship Street and Middle Street)
(01273) 777822
Open Tues-Sat 11am-6pm,
Sun/Mon 12noon-5pm
www.shesaidboutique.com

The creation of Nic Ramsey, She Said
offers alluring and exotic lingerie,
superior quality toys, sexy knickers,
stockings, glamorous eveningwear and
a large range of corsets. Downstairs
there's more: a fine selection of dildos,
floggers (from horsehair whips to
bejewelled crops), strippers' poles,
restrainers, collars, nipple tassels and
even "*I Love Anal*" cards for granny's
birthday. It is the elegant touches,
though, that make She Said the
Marilyn Monroe to Ann Summers'
Jordan – the décor is beautiful and
stylish and the staff, too, dress to
impress.

A kinky and mischievous version
of the shop that Mr Benn used for
his psychedelic travels (though where
he'd have ended up dressed in exotic
underwear and a corset is anybody's
guess), with its sassy staff, sexy lingerie
and elegant layout, She Said must surely
lay claim to being one of the most
glamorous boutiques in England.

Ann Summers

75/76 North Street opposite the Clock
Tower (01273) 205744
Open Mon-Sat 9.30am-6pm, Sun 11am-5pm
www.annsummers.com

Banana dick lip, after-dinner nipples,
beginners' S&M kits, maids' outfits,
sexy lingerie, cheap rubber and PVC,
dildos, bondage tape and naughty
books. It's sex with a smile and the
perfect starting point if you're here for
a saucy weekend. Most of the clothes
are aimed at those dipping their toes
for the first time into the wonderful
world of sexy glamourwear; they're not
always great quality but then you won't
necessarily be wearing them out, will
you?

She Said lingerie, as modelled by Ladyboy of Bangor

accompanied), the basement offers a small selection of lesbian softcore videos and exclusive leather products such as harnesses. But it is Tickled's range of dildos and sex toys that are their real strength, particularly as they can be tried out discreetly (something not always possible in Ann Summers). But, I hasten to add, it's **not** a changing room down there so don't get stripped off naked as one customer did, they've got cameras and will have a good laugh watching you if you try. Instead, you can try the products out on your nose instead (which is apparently the closest test to how sensual a vibrator will feel on a lady's naughty bits).

Tickled also sell a range of silicon dildos, which are said to be long-lasting, durable and (according to Helen) *"can even be cleaned in the dishwasher"* as well as the latest remote-control-operated ones.

Worrying for men is the fact that their *"Brighton Babe"* T-shirt, satin sheets and dildos are still best sellers, which to me sounds like the ladies are having a fine time on their own these days. Boys, if you're not careful, you'll soon be relegated to simply washing the sheets and keeping the ladies in fresh supplies of batteries for the rabbit…

Tickled

15 Gardner Street (01273) 628725
Open Mon-Fri 11am-6pm,
Sat 10.30am-6pm, Sun 12noon-5pm
www.tickledonline.com

After witnessing an argument about why women couldn't buy dildos outside of male-oriented sex shops, estate agents Helen and Alison threw away their pinstripe suits and mobiles and set up Tickled. Exclusively aimed at women, this shop offers a range of sex toys, videos and novelty gifts, combined with friendly and discreet advice.

On the ground floor, the stock leans more towards the novelty and gift end of the sex market with good lovemaking guides, T-shirts, jewellery, handbags and cards, while downstairs things get more serious.

For ladies only (men must be

Flopsy waits to be lubed up

SEX, FETISH & BODY MODIFICATION

Taboo

2 Surrey Street (01273) 263565
Open Mon-Fri 9am-7pm, Sat 9am-8pm,
Sun 12noon-5pm, adults only
www.tabooshop.com

Leave the furry handcuffs at Ann Summers and enjoy a sex shop that sells the real McCoy, from quality whips, paddles, restrainers, anal toys, rubberwear, dildos, nipple clamps, fetish books, magazines, kinky shoes and boots to a whole room full of DVDs that vary from straight porn to girl-on-goat action.

While not as open as other sex shops in Brighton are permitted to be (presumably because of the nature of the stock) Taboo is welcoming, friendly and doesn't have that intimidating atmosphere you can find in some of Soho's sex shops (erm, allegedly). Also a good spot for finding out about local fetish nights, sex clubs and other kinky events. Well worth a visit.

Happy birthday Gran

Bad spider! Naughty spider!

FETISH EVENTS

Vinylla

Every three months (or so) at Harlequin,
off the London Road
www.vinylla.co.uk

Even for those (like myself) who like to visit TG up in the big smoke once in a while, Vinylla is a surprisingly good fetish night, aimed at those who want to *"dabble… get dressed up and dance without being too extreme"*. This softcore night has been running for many years in Brighton and remains ever-popular. Having outgrown the Hanbury Ballroom back in 2004 it is now more suitably housed in Harlequin's, which offers more room, two floors, a proper dancefloor and more darkness for discreet roleplay. While various fetish nights randomly spring up and fade away in this town, Vinylla remains the biggest and best.

Visit Brighton's best Sex Shop

Taboo

2 Surrey Street, Brighton BN1 3PA
T 01273 263 565 | www.tabooshop.com

Opening times: Mon - Fri 9.00–7.00pm
Sat 9.00–8.00pm | Sun 12.00–5.00pm
2 mins walk from Brighton Station

FOR THE LARGEST SELECTION OF
EROTIC CLOTHING, ADULT TOYS AND DVD'S

SEX, FETISH & BODY MODIFICATION

TATTOOS AND PIERCINGS

In the past ten years, Brighton has seen a real boom in tattoo parlours and body-piercing studios. The following studios are only a small selection of what's on offer but are recommended because they take the art of body modification seriously.

While tattooing is a widespread skill, bear in mind that design and style are very individual. If you are tempted, I'd recommend you make an appointment first with the artists below. Go in person to see if you feel comfortable with them and what you think of their work. All good tattooists should carry a portfolio.

*One last thing – if you're having something written, make sure your tattooist is clear on the spelling. One local tattoo parlour, which shall remain nameless, used to have a big sign outside that read: "Come inside, we have 1000's of **desings**". Enough said.*

Penetration

29 Sydney Street (01273) 623839
Open Mon-Sat 10am-6pm
"Vatican Approved since 1995"
Downstairs for tattooing,
by appointment only

Friendly and approachable, Penetration's resident piercers Danny and Nick extend such care to their 'patients' that, if you're a fainter, they'll mollify you with sweeties. For the more hardcore body-modification addict, they do PAs and ampallangs (for which you need a consultation to be… ahem… measured), surgical-steel implants and cosmetic dentistry. While he pierces your tongue, Nick will tell you all about when he got his willy pierced for the benefit of an Italian TV fashion programme (at which the Pope didn't bat an eyelid), while Danny politely asks that you *"please wash your privates"* before coming for a piercing down below. Prices start at around £15, lipring £17, ampallang £30.

In the basement, Mickey specialises in custom-designed tattoos, with a lot of influence drawn from Maori, Celtic, Haida and art nouveau traditions, while Dom covers custom, traditional and Japanese. They also do grey shading and cover-ups. In short, anything beautiful.

This does come off, right?

Into You Tattoo

4 Little East Street (01273) 710730
Open Tues-Sat 12noon-7pm
www.into-you.co.uk

When the most renowned tattoo
studio in the country opened here
in June 2005, it really nailed Brighton
as *the* tattooing centre of England.
Boasting the
    internationally famous Alex Binnie
and Paula Converse among its four
artists, Into You has an undisputed
reputation, particularly for large-scale
custom work. As well as tattoos, they
sell tattoo-related jewellery, books,
clothes and cool brands such as Sailor
Jerry and Lucky 13.

Of course, quality doesn't come
cheap – prices for tattoos start at
£40 for a simple letter or name while
hourly rates here are £60. But for
something as potentially life-changing
as a tattoo, why settle for anything
less than the best?

Punktured

35 Gardner Street (01273) 688144
Open Mon-Sat 10.30am-6pm,
Sun 12noon-5pm
www.punktured.co.uk

If you could get qualifications in piercing,
Punktured would be all grade As.
Bringing a friendly, open and caring
approach to a profession which still
has an image of domination by gloomy
monosyllabic hairy types, Julie and
the gang demonstrate their skill and
dedication through little touches such
as the giving of aftercare solution and
written instructions after all piercings,
and training their receptionists in first
aid in case anyone feels a bit wobbly
afterwards. Not adverse to a bit of
publicity, Punktured have been filmed
by Channel 4 and MTV, featured in
The Times and owner Julie even played
Bjork's body double in the *Pagan Poetry*
video! There are four resident piercers
here, two men and two women, all with

years and years of experience, offering scarification, ear scalpelling, sub-dermal beading, dermal punching and even ear-piercing (though their oddest request has to be from the woman who brought in her false nipple to be pierced). If you want your labia pierced by a grizzly old git high on ketamine try Crazy Dave's place in Kemp Town; if it's friendly professional treatment you're after, Punktured are top banana.

Temple Tatu

9 Boyces Street (01273) 208844
Open Tues-Fri 12noon-6pm, Sat 11am-6pm,
Sun 12noon-5pm www.templetatu.com

This impressive studio is located just off West Street. Although they do walk-ins, appointments are encouraged, to give people the chance to really examine their motives for getting a tattoo. The six resident artists have a deep knowledge and understanding of the history of tattooing and each design is unique. One artist, Adam, even specialises in traditional tattooing by hand.

Newcomers are made to feel at ease by discussing all the processes involved over a cup of tea. The reception room at Temple Tatu instills you with confidence in these guys' creative skills: from handmade sequin tiaras to Hindu tiles and stickers, this place has been decorated to welcome you and make you feel at home. I can't really tell you what they specialise in, as their portfolio is so varied (black, tribal, colour, cover-up etc) but they're quite particular about researching every design, so you can even find out what the tattoo you're about to get really means.

While here, look out for the kitsch alchemical shrine built by some mad-genius New Zealander with plastic dolls, driftwood, electric bulbs and old

soapboxes inside. You can activate it by inserting a coin and pressing your palms on the designated space. Lights flash, things whizz round, music plays and all sorts of odd things happen. If ever you get bored of it, guys, I promise I could give it a good home.

Wildcat

6 Gardner Street (01273) 606489
Open Mon-Sat 10am-6pm,
www.wildcat.co.uk

Not content with being the largest suppliers of body jewellery in the world, Wildcat stocks the very latest in genital stimulation, from the world's biggest steel dildo to butt plugs, glass vibrators, labia spreaders, ball crushers and even a urethral vibrator that stimulates the anal G-spot via the bladder (!).

Understandably, they keep this stuff downstairs out of the prying eyes of granny and granddad, who probably wouldn't understand (and if they did would most likely have a stroke).

Fans of Vince Ray will be pleased to know they've got a good selection of his art on crockery, T-shirts and bathroom tiles, while for the man/ woman who has everything, how about some fossilised Siberian woolly-mammoth-ivory body jewellery? Yes I know I make stuff up sometimes but trust me on this one.

Enjoy a good natter with the friendly staff in here, keep a look out for the shrunken heads above the mirror and the flyers for all fetish-related events around town but someone, please, try and get the buggers to turn off that bloody scary music and play some Herb Alpert instead.

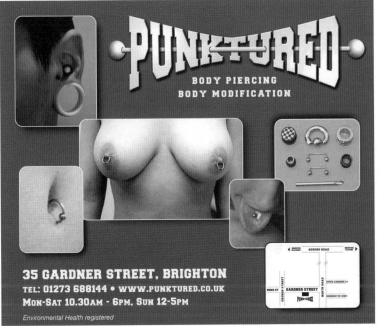

PUNKTURED

BODY PIERCING
BODY MODIFICATION

35 GARDNER STREET, BRIGHTON
TEL: 01273 688144 • WWW.PUNKTURED.CO.UK
MON-SAT 10.30AM - 6PM, SUN 12-5PM

Environmental Health registered

MALE STRIPSHOWS

The Adonis Cabaret Show

Babylon Lounge Kingsway, Hove
0870 7414092
Every Saturday throughout the year
7pm-10pm, club finishes 2am
Admission £35 (for two-hour show, one
free cocktail, buffet dinner, and a free photo
with the boys)
www.adoniscabaret.co.uk

With enough screaming to kill a
cat, hordes of lairy women and
Chippendale-style performers, the
Adonis Cabaret is packaged very
much for the hen parties and gangs of
girls who descend on Brighton every
weekend: it's a no-holds-barred male
stripshow, designed to get the ladies
wet with excitement and ready for a
full night out in Brighton.

Hosted by drag queen Davina,
the show's highlights include the boys
in the shower, some silliness with a
giant piano keyboard, the boys dressed
as firemen and the boys dressed…
well, in nothing at all. As well as the
cabaret, the night includes a free drink,
buffet, raffle and tickets to another club
of your choice for the night (though
you can also stay on if you choose as,
afterwards, it turns into a nightclub
spinning tunes from the 80s and 90s).

For those who enjoy suave,
sophisticated, crooner-style
entertainment, it's best to keep away.
But for those after a raunchy night out
with the girls, as our reviewers Michelle
and Sarah put it:
*"They promise the FULL MONTY and
that is exactly what you get. The show is
on for two hours, and worth every penny.
The music is brilliant and we danced till
the end. We loved it."*

Top tips: If you're a wine-drinker it
pays to buy by the bottle. Arrive early
for the best seats and don't forget your
camera!

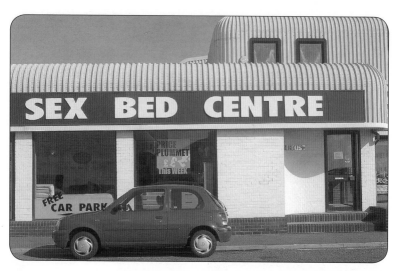

LAPDANCING CLUBS

The Pussycat Club
The Basement, 176 Church Road, Hove
(01273) 735574/709100
Open Mon-Thurs 7pm-2am,
Fri-Sat 7pm-4am
Admission from £5-£25, £10 for each
lapdance, £20 VIP lapdance
www.pussycat-club.co.uk

Top Totty
75 Grand Parade (01273 689503)
Admission £15
www.toptottyclub.co.uk

Men, if your idea of a good night out
is having a girl rubbing her voluptuous
breasts in front of you, then you may
want to pay one of these places a visit.
Attracting stag nights, rugby teams and
visiting businessmen by the coachload,
the clubs offer a chance to enjoy
lapdances, poledancers and a range of
overpriced drinks. If you don't know
the law, strictly no physical contact is
allowed between customer and dancer
but popping to the loo afterwards
to give yourself a hand shandy **is**
permitted.

Shy voyeurs, be warned – it's
quite small in there and not the sort
of place you can hide yourself away.
A.. erm… friend had to go down
once to chat to the owner about the
review but auditions were going on
all afternoon, so he ended up as the
judge. When one of the women said
she'd been quite nervous in front of
him, he unwittingly blurted out – *"It
was just as hard for me".*

Brighton welcomes all forms of forbidden love

PROSTITUTION

You'll find a variety of cards and phone numbers in the phone boxes around the Old Steine and Western Road areas. £40 for 30 minutes is a typical price but if you shop around you might get a student discount. Typically, new laws have been pushed through to stamp out the card system here, which has pushed prostitution back onto the street a bit more. There are also numerous brothels around town but we couldn't possibly tell you where they are, sorry. Here, instead, are a couple of saunas where you can have a nice massage.

reward-card system: save enough points and you can have a free two-girl Swedish massage or a digital watch.

Top To Toe
Lower Market Street 0870 740 9442
Open 10am-10pm, basic cost £30

Another five-star establishment boasting a sauna, a jacuzzi, uniforms and videos. An international range of lovely ladies await to tickle your fancy with a sensuous massage.

SAUNAS

Ambassador's Sauna & Massage (as featured on Radio 4's *The News Quiz*)*
Portland Road, Hove 0870 7409439
Open 12noon-10pm, basic cost £20

This highly rated five-star sauna with jacuzzi offers a full range of services, including more unusual massages and photographic portfolios of all the members of staff in various costumes (such as Tarzan's Jane and Miss Santa). Private parties can be catered for and in summer there's even an outdoor massage facility.

Like Sainsbury's, they have a

Jeremy Hardy read out the review!

BRIGHTON SEX TOURS

BY SEX GODDESS LETITCIA

Inspired by a news article about Thomas Cook's red-light tours in Amsterdam (no really, it's in their 2006 brochure), I am a self-appointed Brighton & Hove sex tour guide. In conjunction with the open-top tour buses, I will be the fearless leader guiding you into temptation. All aboard! You may jump on and off as many times as you like, though this may not be the case with the luscious ladies… so be warned. Perhaps you may wish to grab a complimentary handful of rubbers from the Terrence Higgins Trust in Ship Street beforehand?

Down the side streets of Western Road there are, of course, more parlours than you can shake a stick at, though you will need a Russian and Ukrainian translation manual and don't forget to ask for proof of age. Highlights include the bottom of Preston Street where you'll find thinking man's crumpet 'Debbie', who is bilingually proficient in English **and** Italian. For gentlemen who prefer the ladies to be in charge, at Holland Road you can sample the delights of 'Spankyouverymuch'. It's worth knowing that there's a chemist next door for Germolene or arnica if she's over-zealous.

Climb aboard once more and you can visit the minxes of Marine Parade (myself included). Continue on to Marina Village and, frankly, if you knock on any door there will be a hooker behind it.

On your journey back, if there are gentlemen… ahem… 'light in the loafers' you can disembark at Duke's Mound. Stroll nonchalantly down the path and the most you will have to pay is the price of a packet of fags. Even condoms are thoughtfully provided here by the local Outreach project.

Feeling thoroughly besmirched, stagger back along Marine Parade and there's just one last stop. That's right, the Claude Nicol Centre at the Royal Sussex on Eastern Road. Er, clap clinic, to those itching to know.

Letitcia with an 'old friend'

Swallows

Massage and Escort service

SEX, FETISH & BODY MODIFICATION

Mind Body Spirit

From Yoga and Tai Chi classes to Buddhist centres and homeopaths, Brighton has the lot, and in abundance. Look in the corner of every park and you'll find someone practicing Qi Gong, meditating, doing yoga or (more typically for Brighton) reading about it. If you're curious about what day courses are on offer, or need somewhere to meditate or practise headstands, your best starting point is to pick up a copy of Wave magazine from the shops and cafés in the Lanes.

Since living in Brighton I have developed many new interests, and probably wouldn't have discovered things like Ayurveda without being in the town where anything goes and where so many different lifestyles co-exist. Sure, there's the usual mystical crap, places where your cat can have its aura cleansed, but if people believe in it, what's the harm? I love the fact that Brighton people are, on the whole, tolerant and open-minded. After all, why shouldn't you enjoy meditating and chanting as well as, say, clubbing, carpentry and fisting?

SHOPPING

Neal's Yard

2A Kensington Gardens (01273) 601464
Open Mon-Sat 9.30am-5.30pm,
Sun 11am-4pm
www.nealsyardremedies.com

A franchise of one of London's original herbal emporiums, this place has become Brighton's de facto alternative doctor's surgery. With a veritable armoury of (mainly organic) herbs, oils, tinctures, vitamins and homeopathic remedies, Neal's Yard also has at its disposal some very clued-up staff (all naturopaths, homeopaths and herbalists) who can help you make informed choices about what you might need. Self-help books are also on hand, as are all the obligatory pampering products should you be suffering from nothing more than a prolonged bout of self-indulgent whinnying. The most usual complaints they deal with are still colds and hayfever but once some guy came in for herbal hormone replacements for his dog. Typical Brighton.

Winfalcon Healing Centre

28/29 Ship Street (01273) 728997
Open Mon-Sat 10(ish)am-5.30pm,
Sun 12noon-4pm

Brighton's no-holds-barred New Age shop, Winfalcon stocks every crystal, stone and karmaceutical known throughout the cosmos. Upstairs, it runs workshops in things like *Psychic Development* and *Know Your Inner Butterfly*, and offers the opportunity to have your aura photographed, so bring a comb. Here is the place to score stuff even the most green-eared hippies might think twice about – unicorn posters, books called *Full Esteem Ahead* and stickers saying, "*It's A Druid Thing*". But, for a shop of this nature, it seems all the more bizarre (and unintentionally funny) that the bloke who runs it is one of the most miserable buggers I've ever had the misfortune to come across. Now here's a guy in need of a taste of his own medicine...

A warm welcome awaits you at Winfalcon

Bell, Book & Candle

46 Sydney Street (01273) 818101
Open Mon-Sat 10am-6pm, Sun 11am-5pm
www.bell-book-candle.co.uk

A fetching log-cabinesque interior houses the anticipated selection of cards, books, candles and models of your favourite deity. This recent addition to the North Laine trinket collective pushes the spiritual envelope a little further than most though, with Hindu figurines made from River Ganges mud for the more discerning shrine, and plenty of Jewish accessories such as Kiddush cups, Torah scrolls and gefilte fishfingers.

Spiritual Matter

21A Prince Albert Street (01273) 206593
Open Mon-Sat 11am-5pm, Sun 2pm-5pm
www.spiritualmatter.co.uk

In the heart of the old Lanes this mini-temple, run by celibate Krishna monk Dharani, sells books and gifts on a Hindu theme. There's a good range of Vedic literature, statuettes of old favourites Ganesh and Buddha, music, clothing, Hare Krishna-related material and, according to Dharani, the best incense in town. Probably the widest selection of cow postcards in Western Europe.

Messianic condensation therapy bags: the latest must-have treatment in Brighton

THERAPY AND BODYWORK CENTRES

Bodhi Garden Dharma Centre
7A Ship Street Gardens 07796 331167
www.bodhigarden.org

Tucked away in a skylit and quiet ex-art gallery in Brighton's oldest lane is this sacred space, dedicated to Buddhist meditation and study. Described as a "*non-denominational Dharma centre*" and operating as an umbrella space for numerous Buddhist groups (Theravadin, Tibetan, Zen, Gaia House etc), the Bodhi Garden organises drop-in evening meditations, talks, quality courses and weekend day retreats for Brighton's burgeoning Dharma bum scene. There is also an extensive library. As a charitable concern, it walks the Buddha's walk by not charging for teachings – almost everything is by donation. Monthly programme details are available at the centre.

The Buddhist Centre
14 Tichborne Street (01273) 772090
Weekdays open 12.30-3pm for visitors

This group is part of The Friends of the Western Buddhist Order and their centre is situated just off the beaten track in North Laine. It has two stunning meditation and yoga rooms and a library where you can drop in to study or borrow books and tapes for a nominal fee.

The Order members wear strange little white collars, are very friendly (try asking "*how will I know when I've reached enlightenment?*" and marvel at their patient response) and make a decent cup of tea.

Look out for more unusual stuff going on here too, like theatre and lectures. I went to a great talk during the May Festival one year where a Buddhist theatre director talked about the genius of Tommy Cooper and Frankie Howerd. Sunday school was never like this.

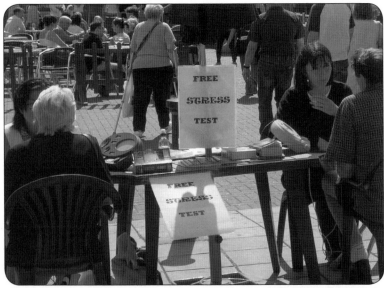

Simulate a day at work on your day off courtesy of Brighton Scientology nutjobs

Brighton Natural Health Centre

27 Regent Street (01273) 600010
www.bnhc.co.uk

A registered charity, this place has now been going for a staggering 25 years, so they should know what they're about. There's a range of movement classes covering the various yoga disciplines and dance types, Pilates and Feldenkrais, and two classrooms, one of which has a mirrored wall for those who need to check their leotard isn't sagging. Something of a rarity in Brighton, changing cubicles are also provided, which saves snagging your foundation garments on the cistern handle.

The Clinic Upstairs

Above Hocus Pocus, 38 Gardner Street
(01273) 572204/572101
£15 weekdays, £20 weekends
www.hocuspocus.co.uk

Follow the shop's spiralling incense upstairs to discover this little-known world of shift-working tarot readers and two cosy therapy rooms regularly used for massage, reiki, spiritual healing, psychotherapy and NLP. But the real gem here is the floatation tank (the

only one in Brighton), offering that unique opportunity to switch off your mind, relax and float, gravity-free. Ideal, in fact, for accelerated learning (play a language tape and you'll be fluent in no time), hypnosis (available upon request), creative thinking, meditation and planning the perfect bank job. Please don't start playing with yourself though: you'll get the water all messy.

Dolphin House Clinic

14 New Road (01273) 324790

This started as an acupuncture clinic 20 years ago and has since blossomed into two multi-skilled clinics housed under one roof – one a charity-based children's clinic (the first of its kind in Europe), the other an adults' natural health clinic offering osteopathy, homeopathy, acupuncture, psychotherapy, nutrition, medical herbalism and totally legal full-body massage. Being next to the Theatre Royal means there is the added interest of possibly bumping into a celebrity actor who either twisted an ankle treading the boards the night before or who simply can't find the other sort of massage parlour.

Evolution Arts and Natural Health Centre

2 Sillwood Terrace (off Western Road)
(01273) 204204

One of Brighton's longest-running centres for all things arty and alternative, Evolution offers everything under one roof – aikido, didgeridoo playing, pottery, anger transformation, African drumming, stained-glass making, flamenco guitar courses, nutrition workshops, bear-baiting etc. Look for their brochures around town, but be warned the courses here can be a tad expensive.

Natural Bodies

28/29 Bond Street (between branches of
Velvet) (01273) 711414
www.naturalbodies.org.uk

Set up by Gary Carter (known to make the ladies swoon), this is definitely one of Brighton s more capable yoga centres, which runs around 20 sessions a week, from beginner level to the very advanced. Classes are mostly drop-in, cost around £5 and run throughout the day, with workshops at weekends. Follow the screams and you'll find them on the first floor. All the teachers are friendly, clean and sober and come from the Vanda Scaravelli (an expert Italian yogini) school, which emphasises gentle movement and breath work to undo tension and reinvigorate the body. Tying yourself in muscle-bending knots and shouting Look at me! is definitely not what is encouraged in here. I can thoroughly recommend these classes as I've been coming (sporadically) for about five years now, and my mum doesn't tell me off for slouching any more. Be warned: they *never* answer the phone,

so get a programme and find out when to come.

North Laine Holistic Therapies

1 Kemp Street (off Gloucester Road)
07821 760669

Tiny five-person co-op with commensurately lower prices than are often found around town, it's a cosy single treatment room concern (though they're looking for more) offering reflexology, reiki, hopi ear candles, and massage flavours from aromatherapy, reiki, Thai, and Swedish, through to the full English with a fried slice. They also make their own body-care products such as moisturisers and lip balm from wholly natural ingredients, so if you can't be bothered to walk all the way to Boots or tend to fret about your skin's absorption of heavy metals, this is the place to come.

Subbuteo girl

the children's clinic

Dolphin House 14 New Road
Brighton & Hove East Sussex BN1 1UF

T 01273 324790 F 01273 729491
E info@thechildrensclinic.co.uk

Planet Janet
86 Church Road, Hove (01273) 738389
www.planet-janet.com

This co-operatively-run project in Hove comprises a healthy options-type café (worth a visit just to sample their tahini salad dressing) and Osho-orientated shop on the ground floor, plus five consulting rooms and a group room divided between upstairs and the basement. Depending on who is renting which, you will generally find an entertaining cocktail of Chinese kick-boxing, oneness meditations, chakra dancing classes, tai chi and astrological counselling. Each room is named after a planet, apart from the colonic hydrotherapy room, which is appropriately called The Moon Room. Some drop-in yoga/meditation classes also take place. See website for details.

Samurai
69 North Road (01273) 570940
www.shinjindojo.co.uk

Housing a shop at street level where you can pick up those stray weapons from your shopping list like swords, staffs, whip chains and nunchaku, this underground martial arts centre focuses on jujutsu and the art of the Ninja. Done up to resemble a traditional Japanese dojo, it's hard to injure yourself in this place because

the entire floor is sprung and padded; disappointingly they've never had any serious sword wounds occur, although they claim mysteriously, "*we do have the means to deal with it*". I looked around for the iodine bath but it was evidently well hidden. You can sign up for a free taster class if you've never been before, and if you fancy turning your adorable five-year-old into a trained killer they also run mini-Ninja classes.

The Treatment Rooms
21 New Road (01273) 818444
www.thetreatmentrooms.co.uk

While there is no denying their expertise, there's an element of the geisha about this gorgeously decorated salon, where you feel the only ugly people allowed on the premises are the customers. Massages, body wraps and facials are the main items on the menu here, and for premium prices you get premium pampering: fresh robe and fluffy slippers, your feet gently washed, candle-lit rooms, soothing music, a post-treatment relaxation area with Moroccan recliners, and a glass of herbal tea. You'll walk out of here feeling as light as your wallet, but delighted to be alive.

Unit 4

20-26 Roundhill Street
www.aiyp.co.uk
peteblackaby@aol.com

Perched serenely on the summit of Roundhill, above The Level, is this centre of yogic excellence. Started up by Brighton's legendary yoga guru and Kinks fanatic Pete Blackaby, it is almost entirely devoted to yoga of the Scaravelli style, with classes for all levels guided by Pete, his protégés and other excellent yoga teachers. More specialist stuff, such as yoga for pregnancy, teacher-training courses, Feldenkrais treatment and one-to-one classes is also available. The centre houses two treatment rooms as well, one for bodywork, the other for acupuncture. There is no phone so drop by to find out more or use the web/email details listed above.

WHERE TO FIND OUT MORE

The Brighton Natural Health Centre Alternative Practitioners Directory

www.bnhc.co.uk

This is a comprehensive list of local practitioners who do everything from acupuncture to rebirthing. You can pick it up free from the Centre (see *Therapy and Bodywork*) or access it online at their website.

Wave

(01273) 818160
www.thelatest.co.uk/wave

This is a glossy, coffee-table publication devoted to holistic/spiritual/health matters which, being in tune with bodily cycles, comes out every lunar month. Recurring themes include relationships, the latest must-have products, personal-development workshops, the latest must-have products, new therapies, environmental news and the latest must-have products. Every issue includes a paid-for directory of local courses, groups, workshops and therapists.

A CAUTIONARY MESSAGE FOR YOGA VIRGINS

While Brighton has some truly excellent yoga teachers in its midst (including the legendary Peter Blackaby), there are a small minority of practitioners in this town who, quite frankly, are clueless and still seem to be operating on that ludicrous 80s principle of 'no pain, no gain'. Should you find yourself at a beginners' yoga class where the teacher launches straight into difficult and demanding poses (and without even bothering to check if anyone in the group is pregnant or suffers from high blood pressure or back problems) you are well within your rights to advocate that he/she be tarred, feathered and torn apart by wild dogs for their negligence. And don't be afraid to ask how your teacher was trained. Most training of any repute lasts a minimum of two years, while you'd expect a teacher to have done at least six years of yoga practice themselves before even considering taking a class. Finally, if you're interested in giving yoga a try, but feel confused by all the different styles out there (Hatha, Astanga, Iyengar, Jenga, Menga, Mango etc), the drop-in classes at Natural Bodies make a perfect starting point.

Kids' Brighton

Brighton haS aLways bin a grate place for kidZ. With scaRy rides oN the peer, sPeshul theerter and sinnyma events, paddling poos and the seefront, there's always plenti of mischEEEf for uz to get up to (OK, so we downt hav a beech sootaBle for Bukets and spaides but at leest me dad can be spard the time—onnered fate of being Berried up to is nek in sand). And wen its chucKing it down in the middel of Orgust, their is ~~inumberabable~~ ~~enoomerrible~~ lots of famly—fiendly cafays, bars and restyrants were uz Ankel—bitters our free to run a rownd, scream and be sick. Fact is, nearlee evrythin in BrIghton apart from the nitelife is kidz—frendly. But then, tHeres alwayz the Event...

WEIRD & WONDERFUL THINGS TO DO

Junior Dukes

Kids' cinema at the Duke of York's,
Preston Circus (01273) 602503
*www.picturehouses.co.uk/site/cinemas/Brighton/
local.htm*

With its own hardcore cult following of diminutive movie buffs, Junior Dukes is, if nothing else, the cheapest babysitting facility in town. As well as showing new and old children's movies every Saturday, its organisers host a raffle for the kids, hand out sweets and, if it's someone's birthday, let him/her press the button to 'start' the film (OK, it's a con, but it makes them happy).

At the end of the movie there's even time for the children to draw pictures inspired by the film. According to one girl who works there, *"some are quite disturbing: recently, one kid drew a microwave that turned 'packets' into 'proper food like McDonalds'"*. Have a look behind the bar next time you're there – that's where they stick the best ones. Highly recommended.

Drusillas Park

Alfriston (01323) 874100
Adults £12-13, kids about £11-12

About 30 minutes' drive from Brighton, and not cheap, Drusillas is nonetheless a great place to keep the kids happy for a day as they feed the squirrel monkeys, otters and penguins, nag you to let them adopt an animal (don't worry, you won't have to bring it home with you), ride the Safari Train at breakneck speeds of up to 3 mph and squirm at all the creepy-crawlies. My favourite bit is the meerkat compound where you get to go through these tunnels underneath and pop up in the middle… meerkat style!
Recommended.

Kids' Komedia

Gardner Street (01273) 647100
Adults £6, children and concessions £5
www.komedia.co.uk/kids.php

Running most Sundays during term times, Komedia present the best in children's national and international touring theatre for three- to seven-year olds. The venue opens one hour before the show for drawing, cappuccinos and sticky treats.

Middle Farm

A27 between Lewes and Eastbourne
(01323) 811411
www.middlefarm.com

Great tearooms, a food shop, animals to fondle, cows to milk and the marvellous English Cider Centre where, after sampling a few brews, you'll be on your back belting out a few old Wurzels tunes.

Coombes Farm Tours

Church Farm, Coombes, near Lancing
(01273) 452028 £5/4
www.coombes.co.uk

A real working farm with tractor and trailer rides. Come between March and April and the kids can even see lambs popping out of their mummies' bottoms. Yum.

Typical Brighton Dad

Pottery

There are many places in Brighton that offer pottery workshops which are great fun if you've got kids (or even if you haven't). Why not put your baby's handprints onto a mug or let them paint a mug or a vase? I spent a terrific afternoon with my nephew at Painting Pottery Café last year and he made me a plate with a picture of me on it playing the guitar, which was really sweet. (But between you and me, the picture was rubbish. *No-one* has hands that big...)

Paint Pots
39 Trafalgar Street (01273) 696682
Painting Pottery Café
31 North Road (01273) 628952
Hands-On Pottery
Saltdean (01273) 300198
The Pottery House Café
175/177 Portland Road (01273) 773697

Toddler Gym Sessions
Portslade Sports Centre, Chalky Road,
Portslade (01273) 411100
Under-fives' supervised play-area with trampolines, bouncy castles and gym equipment. And, no, you can't have a go, it's strictly for the kids.

Museum Trips
(01273) 292818
Brighton & Hove Council runs lots of activities at the museums and libraries throughout the year, especially in school holidays. For full details call the number above and check museum reviews in *Weird and Wonderful Things to Do*, which I've just realised is confusing as this section is also called *Weird and Wonderful Things to Do*. I was trying to be clever by doing a mini-version of the book within this chapter but it's all backfired. Bugger.

You're not really supposed to let them inhale
too much pottery paint

Cupcake (0-14yrs)
98 St George's Road, Kemp Town
(01273) 624134
www.cupcake-kids.co.uk

This beautiful shop in the heart of Kemp Town village offers an unusual and unique collection of gifts for children (age range "*2lbs to fourteen years*") with a French country-farmhouse flavour to many of the clothes and toys. There are lots of groovy things like Breton shirts, patchwork quilts, nostalgic wooden toys, retro fabrics, Victorian playthings, mushroom lamps and pirate lunchboxes. And the staff here are very obliging: they'll even sport their range of ridiculous animal balaclavas if you ask nicely.

Daisy Daisy (0-8yrs)
33 North Road (01273) 689108
www.daisydaisy.me.uk

Specialising in top-quality wooden toys, ranging from mobiles to their best-selling dolls houses and castles. Also stocks nursery goods and home accessories such as height charts, books, mirrors and clocks. Kids love this place as its owner Hilary is more than happy for them to come and play with everything on display (though she might draw the line if they start chewing on a train set).

Purple Heart
22 Gardner Street, North Laine
(01273) 696935
www.purple-heart.com

Fairtrade and traditional toys, baby shoes, toiletries and hand-painted wellies. The array of bright colours in here is like an explosion in a paint factory, so wear sunglasses if you're visiting with a hangover.

Wigwam/Wigwam Baby
267a/93 Preston Drove
(01273) 505504/554056
www.wigwamstore.com

While their Baby shop specialises in nursery goods and developmental toys, their (elder) sister sells clothes, wooden toys and a fruity selection of slogan T-shirts including *Enjoy Milk*, *Future DJ* and *Made in Brighton*. Sadly there isn't one bearing the legend *Daddy Left Me Before I Was Even Born*.

Typical Brighton Mum

Er, can I give it back now please?

RESTAURANTS

While the following places don't offer naff plastic toys and Klassic Kids Menuz (ie. dogburger and chips), they do have quality food, are welcoming to families and don't mind the odd bit of yelling and dribbling (from the kids, that is).

Bardsley's (fish and chips)
22-23a Baker Street (01273) 681256

Donatello's (warm stuff)
3 Brighton Place (01273) 775477

Dorset Street Bar (cafe/bar)
28 North Road (01273) 605423

Dig in the Ribs (TexMex)
47 Preston Street (01273) 325275

Food for Friends (veggie)
18 Prince Albert Street (01273) 202310

Lee Cottage (Chinese)
6b Queens Road (01273) 327643

Piccolo's (Italian)
56 Ship Street (01273) 203701

Café Paradiso (continental)
Hotel Seattle, Marina (01273) 679799

282
Woodies Diner (egg 'n' chips)
366 Kingsway, Hove (01273) 726777

PUBS

The places below will generally provide a warm welcome and some scoff until early evening, giving the nippers free rein of the garden or family room. Harumph, in my day we were locked in the car with a packet of cheese-and-onion crisps and told not to play with the handbrake.

Battle of Trafalgar
Guildford Road (01273) 327997

The George
Trafalgar Street, (01273) 681055

Hove Place
First Avenue, Hove (01273) 738266

Lion and Lobster
Sillwood Street (01273) 327299

The Ancient Mariner
Poet's Corner, Hove (01273) 748595

Open House
Springfield Road (01273) 880102

Pub With No Name
Southover Street (01273) 601419

Aaaaah, look, he's rolling his first fag

INDOOR PLAY AREAS

Funplex
The Hyde Business Park, Auckland Drive,
Bevendean (01273) 690888
www.funplex.co.uk

Westows Play and Football
School Road, Hove (01273) 711944
www.westows.com

PARKS/ OUTDOOR PLAY AREAS

Blakers Park
Southdown Road

A quiet park with good play
equipment, sandpit, tennis courts and a
recently refurbished café that's open all
year round.

Hove Park
Old Shoreham Road, Hove

One of the two parks worth a visit
in Hove. It's a large, open area loved
by squirrels and offering bowls, a
playground, static climbing rock, a
miniature railway and café. Keep an
eye out for the wallabies and old ladies
that breed prodigiously in this part of
town.

The King's Road Play Area
Brighton seafront, near the West Pier

Brilliant play area, right on the seafront,
with lots of fun equipment. Always
rammed in summer with thousands
of trendy Brighton parents sitting
around and sharing muesli recipes.
Refreshments and loos are nearby.

(For all other Brighton parks see *Here,
There and Everywhere*)

WEBSITES

*These two have loads of useful info and,
seeing as your sprogs are probably more
adept with a browser than you, it makes
sense to get them to do the hard slog of
looking things up.*

www.abcmag.co.uk
www.brighton-hove.gov.uk

BRIGHTON & HOVE COUNCIL SERVICES

Childcare/crèches
Children's Information Service
(01273) 293545

For information on all types of
local registered childcare provision,
nurseries, holiday and after-school
clubs, call the number above. Every
summer they also organise outdoor
events for families all over the city. Ring
for a free brochure.

Another victim of Brighton's notorious
winged canines

What's On

DIARY OF EVENTS

Isn't it only right that the town that likes to party should be host to the biggest arts festival in England? Not only that but throughout the year Brighton plays host to food, film and comedy festivals; car rallies, bike rides, Pride, Burning of the Clocks, Children's Parade, and a firework display every two weeks or so. And with numerous political party conferences, where else could you combine a lovely seafront environment with the pleasures of egg-throwing?

The Fair at the Level
End of April, into May

Two weeks of flashing lights and projectile vomiting, signifying that the festival has begun and summer is just around the corner.

Brighton Science Festival
Last week of February
www.brightonscience.com

For five days every February the streets of Brighton become a sea of corduroy as thousands of bald-headed and bearded men and women descend upon the town. When not wandering round the Lanes talking to themselves they can be found lecturing and doing live experiments at various city venues. This festival, the brainchild of author Richard Robinson, has scientists teaming up with local schools, colleges and museums for open days. You can also catch them letting their hair down at local debating nights Café Scientifique and Catalyst Club, where lively late-night lectures inevitably turn into a load of drunken egg-heads in lab coats doing the Can Can. See website for details.

Arts Festival

May
www.brightonfestival.org.uk
www.brightonfringefestival.co.uk

In May Brighton goes bananas. For three weeks the whole town is packed with comedians, novelists, opera singers, dancers, circus acts, street performers, musicians and thousands of blokes on stilts trying to juggle. This is the largest arts and entertainment festival in England and brings performers from as far afield as Peru, China and New Zealand, and audiences from as far afield as Hollingbury. If you want to see the town at its most vibrant and colourful, this is the time to visit.

Along with the book-readings, plays, concerts and comedy in a plethora of venues around town, one event not to be missed is Streets of Brighton: for one weekend (weather permitting) the roads are packed with strange cabaret acts, bizarre costumes, troubadours, minstrels, and some fiddle player on a trapeze wire displaying his disregard for melody, technique or tuning.

Alongside the main festival runs the Brighton Fringe Festival, offering more homespun and contemporary performances from DJs, bands, comedians and theatre groups in numerous smaller venues, theatres and pubs in town. An important part of the Fringe are the Open Houses, where artists all over Brighton open their homes for several weekends and everyone finally gets a chance to nosey around other people's houses, clock a few ideas for what to do with their kitchen and pretend to look at the art.

One stunning addition to the festival in recent years has been the Spiegeltent, which has become something of a focal point for the whole event. As well as hosting some fantastic burlesque cabaret, gigs, comedy and dance, this beautiful original 1930s German cabaret tent with its mirrored wooden interior becomes **the** late-night festival club after 10.30pm and a place for mingling with performers, organisers, audiences and other assorted riff-raff.

During Brighton Festival you can expect everything from guided tours of the gay scene to special club nights, experimental theatre, street parties and parades. Look out also for the Dieppe Market, the Mackerel Fair and the Blessing of the Nets, which usually takes place on the third weekend of the festival. Over 700 events, two festivals rolled into one, and an inevitable free fireworks party or two. Unmissable.

London to Brighton Bike Ride

Middle of June

With the environmentally unfriendly and mean-spirited idiots who run our railways having banned bicycles on trains between London and Brighton back in 2005, I'm wondering how the poor buggers who cycle the 50-odd miles down here for the annual bike race are going to get home now. Guess they'll have to change it to the "London to Brighton and back to London Bike Ride" from now on.

Pride

August (See *Gay* chapter)

Food And Drink Festival

September

Established for a few years now, this month-long event, organised by a collective of Brighton's restaurant owners, offers special cookery courses in the kitchens of some of our finest restaurants. You'll find weekend food stalls in the city centre and special events including wine tasting and banquets at the Pavilion, all culminating in a huge food fight at One Paston Place.

Annual John Lidbetter All-Weather Prize International Open Stone Skimming Competition

Sunday afternoon, mid to end September
(Check press for exact date and time)

Simple, silly, free to all and utterly pointless, this fabulous competition was dreamed up and organised by man-about-town John Lidbetter. The rules are simple – each contestant is given three stones for three skims, has to choose a skimming name (FatBoy Skim?) and tries their best. Whoever scores the highest is the winner. The prizes include a bottle of champers for Best Style and a cup for the outright winner, which is kept on display in the Lion and Lobster pub. Of course, with Brighton being woefully fruitless for flat stones I'd recommend starting your searches now for those three perfect bouncers, and I'll see you in September for the skim-off. Recommended.

Brighton Live stalwarts Clearlake

Comedy Festival

Beginning of October
www.brightoncomedyfestival.com

Every October, all the big names in comedy descend upon Brighton and can be seen over an intense few weeks at the Brighton Dome and Corn Exchange. Ticket prices can be a little intimidating (often over £15 for just an hour's stand-up) but as long as you avoid the Chuckle Brothers you're pretty much guaranteed a laugh.

Brighton Live

October
www.brightonlive.net

One week, 100 gigs; over 250 Brighton bands and all for free. Is Brighton good to you or what?

Lewes Fireworks

5 November

Still upset about a bunch of Protestant martyrs who were burned here centuries ago by the wicked Catholics, the people of Lewes remember the occasion by hosting the biggest and most phenomenal bonfire-night celebration in the UK.

Along with the procession of carnival style floats, you'll get the chance to see the townsfolk dressed up in Freddie Kruger jumpers, marching down the streets holding flaming crosses and throwing bangers around. Around 8pm, the crowds head off to bonfires in different corners of the town where, some years, loonies dressed as cardinals stand on scaffolding and encourage the audience to hurl abuse (and fireworks) at them. A few effigies of the Pope, political figures and crappy celebs are then ceremoniously blown up for good measure, followed by huge firework displays.

The whole event has a very dark, anarchic pagan feel to it; there are definite hints of the *Wicker Man* in there too. It's only a short train ride from Brighton but I recommend getting there no later than 6pm if you want a good view of it all. Best not to take any pets or wear highly flammable clothing. Highly recommended.

Veteran Car Rally
First Sunday in November

Not being a car nut I find it hard to join in the excitement of the enthusiasts who congregate down at Madeira Drive, share notes on the pros and cons of tungsten-drive camshafts and then disappear back to their stately mansions.

But, as one of my friends put it, *"surely the sight of a lot of lovely old cars putt-putting away stirs the little boy in you?"*

Brighton Film Festival
Late November
www.cine-city.co.uk

Cinecity, the Brighton Film Festival, is the city's annual celebration of celluloid. Established in 2003, it takes place each year at the end of November and presents a packed programme highlighting the best cinema from around the world. The festival's home is everyone's favourite, the Duke of York's, but Cinecity screens in all the city's cinemas and in a range of unusual locations – whether it's projections onto the Pavilion or in the police cells of the old police station.

Past events with a Brighton flavour include Hove resident Nick Cave selecting his favourite Berlin-set films, and a 25th anniversary screening of cult classic *Quadrophenia,* with the cast and crew given a Vespa escort to the Grand.

Interestingly, according to statistics, each Brightonian puts on an average of 4lbs after Cinecity (from all that sitting around and overdoing it on the popcorn, hotdogs and Duke of York's cake).

Burning of the Clocks
Winter Solstice (22 December)

While most seaside towns go into hibernation for the winter, Brighton celebrates the shortest day with this fantastic pagan procession along the seafront, culminating in a fireworks display. Expect hundreds of strange and beautiful designs around the theme of time, and lots and lots of candles. The whole event evokes that perfect, dark wintery spirit, mixed with the excitement of knowing that Christmas is just around the corner. One of my favourite events in the Brighton calendar. Highly recommended.

Christmas Day Swim
11am Christmas Day

(see Brighton Swimming Club in *The Sea* chapter)

Poseidon's Day
28 December

Once a year, 23 Brighton councillors gather on the nudist beach to offer blessings and sacrifices to this venerable sea-god. Hosted by Simon Fanshawe, the dancing, nudity and orgies normally go on until the small hours, weather permitting.

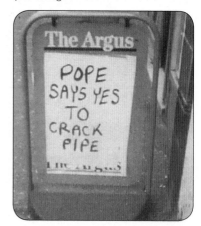

LOCAL PRESS

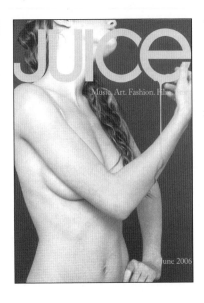

In this town people will sell their own grandmothers just to get good wall space in a café for their poster. The problem in Brighton is not so much finding information, as how to avoid spending the weekend sifting through thousands of flyers, posters and magazines trying to find a club that plays Rush. In the last year alone the number of magazines in Brighton seems to have quadrupled. Some even have adverts for luxury yachts and overpriced designer clothes. Aaargggghhhhh!! Why is everyone in the bloody media hellbent on trying to turn Brighton into something that it's not? Here's a small selection of the highs and lows…

The Blue Guide
Free monthly mag with a slant on the sex scene and carrying enough ads for brothels and prozzies to keep the most ardent stag party content. Not to be confused with… er... The Blue Guide, a free monthly mag which specialises in highbrow cultural events for Sussex.

Insight City News
Don't get me started on this one. It's a travesty considering what this magazine used to be like. Now it's flaccid, dry, self-indulgent, unintentionally hilarious and looks like it was designed by children. Classic example of what happens when you let self-serving businessmen take control. It doesn't even make good loo paper or burn well. And before you ask, yes, it's full of pictures of David Van Day flashing his mullet at the camera.

Latest Homes/Latest 7
Free weekly full of pictures of houses you can't afford mixed with gossip, news, TV listings, local stuff and the odd bit of comedy.

The Source
Digestible monthly glossy aimed more at the student market, with detailed listings and the odd good feature.

The Anus
Cheeky Edition

Brighton's thousand-year-old daily rag features everything from local news (usually about Falmer Stadium) to those classic Nazi rants in the letters page from Angry of Hangleton. And, while indispensable for those wishing to keep up with local issues, every now and again The Argus likes to surprise its readers in a Richard-Madeley-does Ali-G sort of way, with bizarre and funny stories. Highlights from the past ten years include:

OVER AND SPROUT

A Beano-style tale about a policeman who slipped on a sprout while chasing a flasher outside the fruit and veg market. "The detective, who enjoys flying, came crashing to the ground like a sack of spuds... he said he was in a lot of pain but the accident has not put him off sprouts."

LIMPETS MUCHING AWAY AT COASTLINE

I can only deduce that this was a four-in-the-morning job after the full effects of the hash cakes had kicked in.

GIRL FINDS CHRIS EUBANK IN MOULD STAIN

Many years back The Argus did this now-legendary feature about a model who discovered Eubank's apparition on a mould stain on her living-room wall. Freddie Starr, eat your heart out!

I FOUND JESUS IN MY PANCAKE

Following on from the success of mouldy Chris came this similar theme. "The 29 year old couldn't believe his eyes when the outline of a beard, nose, eyes and hair appeared among the burn marks in the batter... 'I suppose if it is a sign, there's no reason why it shouldn't be on a pancake,' he exclaimed." (But how did he know it was Jesus and not any old beardy bloke?)

JESUS SPOTTED IN CLOUD FORMATION

And lo, our lord descended from heaven, but only as far as the altocumulus layer.

I FOUND A SCORPION IN MY SUITCASE...

CREATURE COMFORT: Gemma Cox with the case in which the scorpion stayed for two days in her bedroom

I found a scorpion in my suitcase

HOLIDAYMAKER Gemma
ught an unusual
n her
owaway
its tail,
ator,

She had dumped her
suitcase on her floor after
a two-week break on the
Greek island with friends.
She then went to sit down
near the unpacked case to
watch the England v Brazil
World Cup match.

ma, 19, from Ironstone
said: "I caught a
of the corner
ing ran
d 30cm

OHNID: The scorpion scuttled away and hid

...And even –

JULIE BURCHILL FOUND IN TRIFLE

Though this later proved to be a typing error and should have read – "Julie Burchill fond of trifle."

Highlights from the A-boards:

The Argus

**CITY TOO
EXPENSIVE
TO LIVE**

The Argus

**TRAFFIC
WARDEN
ATTACKS
ROCKET**

The Argus

**SUSSEX
PORN RING
QUEEN
ARRESTED**

WEBSITES

For daily listings:
www.brighton.co.uk
www.whatsonbrighton.co.uk
www.visitbrighton.com
www.brightonsource.co.uk

www.brightonfriends.co.uk
Friends Reunited for Brighton. Free to register and simple to navigate. Not sure how many people use it though.

www.brightonlife.com
User reviews of pubs, clubs, restaurants and hotels, and a peculiar forum where you can get to know some extremely rude and occasionally clever people.

www.thisisbrighton.co.uk
Associated with *The Argus* newspaper, this website includes local news with classifieds, sports, leisure and up-to-date information on local events.

www.myspace.com/ brightonlivespace
Probably the most comprehensive live-music listings for the town, written by people who actually seem to go to most of them, with gig reviews and a ridiculously enthusiastic weekly digest about what's on the way.

www.mybrightonandhove.org.uk
This community website contains quirky and little-known aspects of local history, together with people's memories and photographs. Regularly updated by volunteers, the site publishes local knowledge and answers enquiries about Brighton & Hove past and present. The group is affiliated to QueenSpark Books and supports its aims of giving local people a voice.

www.hedweb.com/brighton
Fifty bizarre Brighton deaths catalogued by local writer and broadcaster Dick Witts, ranging from poisoned chocolates to the trunk murders and the tale behind the death in the Green Dragon pub (now the Office). While the presentation is a bit dull, the tales themselves merit a read for anyone with a love of Brighton and a sense of the macabre.

www.pimple.tv
Though nothing to do with Brighton, this hilarious website was put together by local maverick filmmaker Tom Hickmore and comedy writer Paul Sinclair, and features more than 50 short films (no longer than ten seconds each), ranging from 50s sex-education spoofs to the sperm-drinking lady and Brighton's own Stella Starr doing a spot of nipple-tassel swinging. Marvellous.

Pimple TV invites you in for a nice cup of tea

WHAT'S ON

Places to Sleep

Brighton has hundreds of places to sleep, from hotels, B&Bs, guesthouses, hostels and hotels to that old Mod favourite – under the pier in a sleeping bag. And since the arrival of such places as Hotel Du Vin, the Pelirocco and Blanch House, some visitors can even expect to find their room decorated by their favourite bands, themed as some Moroccan harem and kitted out with DVD players, PlayStations and even the odd porn film. With the growth of all these new stylish places, however, the price of a good room in town has increased considerably. So, in our efforts to bring you a flavour of what's out there, we've tried to cover a range from the priciest to the cheapest, the friendliest to the rudest, and the simplest to the most outrageous.

DEAD POSH

Currently under extensive renovation, a lot of the rooms are now looking more modern than the Grand, so if patterned carpets aren't your thing, you and your Platinum card might feel more comfortable here. There is a small, heated swimming pool (if you don't want to get greased up for swimming in the channel), three restaurants and a tacky nightclub. *Rooms £80-180 without meals, suites £220-280*

The Grand
Kings Road, Brighton seafront
(01273) 224300
www.devereonline.co.uk

The most famous hotel in Brighton and, at £1,500 a night for the Presidential suite, far and away the most expensive. This **may** seem a bit steep, but it's worth bearing in mind that Ronald Reagan and JF Kennedy have flossed their teeth *in this very room*. The over-the-top grandeur of this white palace is matched by its facilities, which include pool, health spa, hair salon and a full-sized, indoor dry-ski slope, which was said to be a favourite of Ronnie's.

Dress code: Armani, Nicole Farhi etc. No jeans unless you're royalty.
Singles £80-150, doubles £135-250, without meals. Add £50 if you want a sea view (or save your cash and walk the 9.4 feet to the door and look from there).

The Hilton Brighton Metropole
Kings Road, Brighton seafront
(01273) 775432
www.hilton.com

Another swish affair situated right on the seafront between the two piers and, again, catering for the more affluent ladies and gentlemen.

Drakes

43-44 Marine Parade (01273) 696934
www.drakesofbrighton.com

If you fancy a hot bath with one of the best sea views in Brighton then Drakes is the place for you as the majority of the rooms in this sexy and sumptuously designed twenty-room hotel actually come with a freestanding bath in the bedroom, right in front of the window (if you're on the right floor you can wave your loofah at top-deck bus passengers). The pampered feel extends to wet rooms with gigantic showerheads and underfloor heating, electrically driven curtains that hide wardrobe and desk space, recycled bamboo-board floors, hot and cold aircon, broadband internet and big flatscreens and DVD players everywhere. The hotel even has its own DVD library to pick from, though they're currently restocking the naughty films as the staff kept pinching them. Downstairs there's a groovy private bar that never closes, serving their own custom-designed cocktails, and a second incarnation of the fabulous Gingerman restaurant. Given the latter's popularity with locals it might be an idea to prebook your dinner here to avoid disappointment. Despite the glorious luxury and breathtaking rooms, Drakes believe their defining style is service: they'll prepare your room any old way you like, so it can be ready on your arrival with a hot bath drawn, *Carry on Columbus* playing on the DVD, balloons, champagne or even a special 'love hamper' from She Said erotic boutique. You don't even have to leave the room to get a haircut. Anything is possible apparently, *"as long as it's legal"*.
Singles £95-125, doubles £245-295

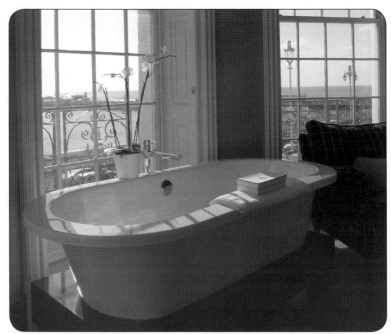

QUITE POSH WITH A HINT OF BOHEMIAN

Amherst
(01273) 670131
www.amhersthotel.co.uk

Amherst pride themselves on making their guests feel special and, judging by the vast number of glowing independent reviews I read of this place on the internet, they seem to do just that. All the rooms are tasteful and modern while little touches like offering breakfast in bed, free snacks, herbal teas and broadband data points in every room show that lots of thought has gone into the place. And being located very close to the seafront (they prefer to keep their address secret to avoid walk-in trade), several of the rooms here have terrific sea views. What more could you ask for? A foot massage while you tuck into your bacon? If you ask nicely they'll probably do that for you too.
£120-150 per night at weekends

Brighton Pavilions Hotel
7 Charlotte Street (01273) 621750
www.brightonpavilions.com

Vehemently non-smoking (try it anywhere except the patio and you'll be out on your ear) and possibly the cleanest hotel I've ever seen. All the rooms are themed and beautifully decorated along the lines of Titanic staterooms or Roman villas, while the Safari room even has a mosquito net for those who prefer their protection not to come out of a foil sachet. They've spent £250,000 here and it shows. A rather large American lady did recently snap a toilet seat in half but don't worry, they've replaced it.
Singles start at £45, doubles £90-100, £100-144 for a four poster

Hotel Du Vin
Ship Street, Brighton (01273) 718588
www.hotelduvin.com

Stunning design, beautiful rooms, friendly staff… the Hotel Du Vin just oozes style. The rooms are named after famous wine houses and include dual-pedestal baths where you and your lover can get up to all sorts of adventures. There are 37 bedrooms in total and a fabulous carved staircase; if you come to visit, keep your eyes peeled for the gargoyles. The restaurant and the adjoining bar come highly recommended (see other reviews) but do try and avoid getting a table near Julie Burchill (she loves this place) or you'll be subjected to her jabbering nonsense all night. During the summer try to book well in advance, as there seems to be about a three-month waiting list for some of the suites.
Doubles from £120, all rooms en-suite.

The Oriental Hotel
9 Oriental Place (01273) 205050
www.orientalhotel.co.uk

Though describing itself as 'shabby chic', it's fairer to say that the Oriental is modern, tastefully decorated and complemented by special touches, such as the aromatherapy burners, fresh flowers and artwork that adorn each room. You'll need to choose carefully here as the quality of rooms can vary wildly from spacious, elegant doubles to some thin, poky singles with poor views but, to be fair, that's reflected by the varying prices. There is so much more to celebrate at the Oriental than to criticise, not least the beautiful mosaic-tiled bar and breakfast area and Kipper, the friendly Staffordshire Bull Terrier. And their eco-friendly approach means the breakfast is organic and *everything* is recycled. So watch out if you suffer the same fate as poor Mr Leeman from *Fawlty Towers* (he died) or you might find yourself out on the compost heap…

Doubles £60-100 midweek, £80-125 weekends, singles £35-40

Oriental Hotel's resident salty seadog Kipper

Blanch House
17 Atlingworth Street (01273) 603504
www.blanchhouse.co.uk

Located just off the seafront in deepest Kemp Town, Blanch House probably just pips it for being the best of the new breed of fashionable themed Brighton hotels as despite its ultra-trendy décor it doesn't suffer the Nathan Barley factor, ie. *so* hip you want to punch it. All twelve of the rooms in Blanch House are imaginative, interesting and spotless, from the deluxe White Room with its huge Jacuzzi to Boogie Nights, with its 70s chocolate-brown and orange colour scheme to the smaller Alice Room with silver-embossed wallpaper, chandelier and queensize bed (popular with girls who want to feel like a princess for the night). Each room also comes complete with CD player, TV, chocolates and other special treats that I promised not to mention. Look out for Amanda's collection of snowstorm globes and make the most of the fantastic bar that serves specialist cocktails. In fact, not only can you eat, sleep, drink and party here but you can even get married. The story goes that owners Chris and Amanda were so disappointed at what was on offer in

Brighton that they had their restaurant licensed and got married 'on the job', so to speak. And they all lived happily ever after.

Rooms £100-250, breakfast included
Special midweek rates available

Hotel Pelirocco

10 Regency Square (01273) 327055
www.pelirocco.co.uk

Located just off the seafront in Regency Square, the Pelirocco is Brighton's answer to the famous Chelsea Hotel in New York. Here artistic heroes, record labels, clubs and trendy boutiques have transformed each space into an individual pocket of creativity. And with such fabulous, flamboyant and unique rooms as Bettie's Boudoir, Modrophenia, Pussy

and Cissy Mo's Magic Garden it is easy to see why the Pelirocco created such a media phenomenon when it first opened. Ever evolving, it seems that with each visit they have something new on offer. The latest rooms include an extravagant 40s Diana Dors-themed room complete with chaise longue and a furry jewel-encrusted telephone, while downstairs the Durex Play Room has an eight-foot circular bed, wall-mounted plasma screen, stunning bathroom and even a pole for a spot of late-night cavorting! The Pelirocco even offers a Durex Menu from which visitors might purchase body massagers, vibrators and condoms or rent *Debbie does Dallas* for the night.

Of course, some might find all this hedonism a bit OTT. As with Brighton's ever-changing tastes in trendy themed bars and nightclubs, the time may come when the fashionistas will be clamouring for simplicity and elegance with their bacon and eggs, rather than decadence and post-modernism. But, for now, Pelirocco is the very latest in Brighton chic and for all you hip young gunslingers looking for a bed and lap-dancing pole for the night, it's **the** place to be.

Singles £50-65, doubles £95-125, Durex Play Room £190-240
All rooms include Sony PlayStations

Hotel Neo
19 Oriental Place
(01273) 711104
www.neohotel.com

It only occurred to me as I sat down to write this review that the inspiration behind this hotel's décor probably came from the address. And maybe owner Steph is a little short-sighted, thought it was Oriental **Palace** she was moving into and decided to take up the challenge to turn her new hotel into somewhere to rival the Pavilion. Not that Neo is all dragon motifs and koi carp; the Eastern theme is largely confined to the bedrooms, which are lavishly decorated with oriental wallpaper and artwork and come with complimentary kimonos while the king-sized chiropractor-endorsed beds and red velvet elicit thoughts of boudoir seduction.

Elsewhere the hotel is decorated with objets d'art, huge chandeliers, ornate mirrors and a giant stag's head by the entrance that adds a touch of eccentricity. And Steph clearly has a love of all things black: it's a colour that prevails throughout, from the bathroom tiles to the carpets (which, yes, they hoover every day!) adding a surprisingly sumptuous feel to the place.

In fact, Hotel Neo can't put a foot wrong as far as I'm concerned; even the little cocktail bar – serving toffee-apple martinis – and their breakfast menus are something out of the ordinary.

Stylish without being gimmicky, Neo is a rarity in Brighton: a perfect mix of glamour, eccentricity **and** elegance. Highly recommended.
Doubles £105-150

NICE & EASY DOES IT

Avalon
7 Upper Rock Gardens (01273) 692344
www.avalonbrighton.co.uk

How many other hotels do you know that make their own breakfast jam and volunteer to change the type of lightbulb if you don't like it? Tom and Brian have kept up the excellent standards here and the quality of the rooms is sterling; there are CD players in most and DVDs in some, and even a four-poster bed. And if Fido has a tendency to wee on your favourite armchair when you leave him at home they'll even put him up for the night too. They do target the gay community, but everyone is welcome.
Singles start at £25, doubles from £60

Brighton House
52 Regency Square (01273) 323282
www.brightonhousehotel.co.uk

Newlyweds Christine and Lucho, who took over Brighton House in September 2004, have dispensed with the traditional English fry-up on grounds of health and taste and gone for an all-organic breakfast buffet which, together with stylish décor, use of environmentally-friendly cleaning products, wi-fi internet and a no-smoking policy has made this B&B a major success.

Hotel Neo gets a visit from the Moose Inspector

They have even been awarded four AA red diamonds, which is the equivalent of making it to the Gold Run on *Blockbusters*. Oh god, now I really am showing my age.
Rooms start at £35 for a single, £55 for a double

Cavalaire House
34 Upper Rock Gardens (01273) 696899
www.cavalaire.co.uk
Run by Derek and Garry (with a little help from Buffy the Airdale Terrier), this friendly B&B on Upper Rock Gardens has ten colourful and bright rooms, all with internet access and fancy soaps, and one with a rather swanky four-poster bed. They do a cracking breakfast using free-range and organic produce wherever possible, also catering for veggies and even offering strawberries and fresh fruit salad in summer. When Jimmy Somerville came to stay he wrote in the guest book, *"serviced and ready to go"*! Quote *"luvvies"* for a special deal.
Double £60-99, triple £99-135

George IV Hotel
54 Regency Square (01273) 321196
www.georgeivhotel.co.uk
A tasteful period-setting B&B that manages to avoid being chintzy and has some well-priced rooms. The one to bag is Room One, with its balcony offering an unspoiled view of the sea and dilapidated birdcage that is the West Pier. And while the views of the rooms round the back aren't exactly awe-inspiring, the ladies might get a thrill watching guys work out in the gym opposite. As well as offering continental breakfast in bed, George IV's USP has to be the old jukebox in reception, a present for owner Steve's 40th birthday. **Huge** brownie points

for there being a *Cheeky Guide* in every room when I came to review!
Standard double £60-80, sea view £80-100, Room One £90-120

The Lanes Hotel
70 Marine Parade (01273) 674231
A traditional and slightly old-fashioned seaside B&B in majestic red brick and flint – for those who prefer the B&Bs of 70s *Carry On* films to trendy hotel boutiques with themed rooms and free dildos. The Lanes' notorious waterbed may have gone (*"too many accidents"*) but they've still got the four-poster beds and some good seafront views. And, thanks to their soundproofed basement, they're very welcoming to hen parties and don't mind if the girls go wild with glitter, balloons and angel-wing – although they do ask that they remember to get dressed for breakfast! Watch out for the ghost on the fourth floor though and don't forget to thank Jamie for your breakfast.
Doubles £60-140

New Steine Hotel
12a New Steine (01273) 681546
www.newsteinehotel.com
Owned by the ever-smiley Herve (*"I like people"*), the New Steine had a refurb last year and is now looking cool and modern. Rooms are attractive and clean with fancy toiletries and complimentary mineral water. The bistro downstairs offers fine French food cooked by a fervent French chef, and there's a natty mural of a Gallic street scene so you can amuse yourself during meals playing 'spot the oignon'. Herve also snapped up Gulliver's Hotel a few doors down, which has been fitted out in similar style.
En-suite singles £28-38, doubles £49-79

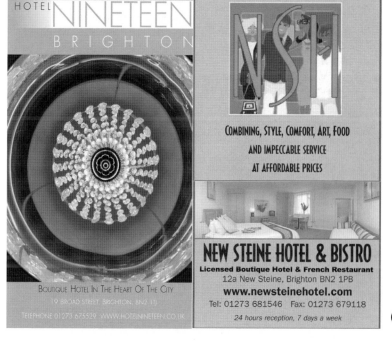

THE LAST CHICKEN IN THE SHOP

Abbey Hotel
Norfolk Terrace (01273) 778771

Not to be confused with the Abbey Lodge in Kemp Town, the Abbey Hotel is probably the cheapest weekly rental hotel in Brighton. The cheap, self-catering rooms are on the first three floors and on the whole are cramped and pretty hairy. If they're really all you can afford I'd rather you came and slept on my floor. A couple of years ago some American guy totally pissed off the manageress by plonking a pair of shoes on the counter and saying, in an arrogant voice, *"Have these cleaned by the morning"*. She's still angry about it so, if you're afflicted with a transatlantic accent, tell them you're Canadian.
£29.50 for a single, doubles start at £53

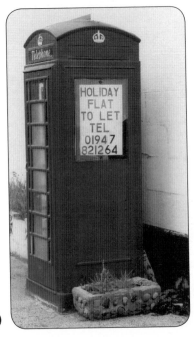

Cecil House Hotel
126 Kings Road, Brighton (01273) 325942
www.cecilhotel.co.uk

Rubbing cheeks with the Metropole seems to have inspired a buffing-up of the rooms here, which are simple but pleasing. The rest of the hotel may still be slightly rickety, but for these prices the sea view is a steal and, unusually for a Brighton hotel, they do allow single-night bookings at weekends if you're booking more than one room.
Singles £25-45, doubles £50-70

B&B AND GUESTHOUSE STRIPS

If you don't have any luck with the ones listed, or fancy going it alone, you will find countless B&Bs and guesthouses in the places below. In the most traditional B&B areas, like Madeira Place, prices change daily and sometimes in accordance with what they think you'll pay, so be terribly polite and dress down for the occasion and you'll get a better offer.

Madeira Place, Lower Rock Gardens and New Steine
Close to the seafront but lacking a proper sea view. Fairly cheap, plentiful and near just about everything.

Grand Parade
Right in the town centre, ten minutes' walk from the sea and close to North Laine.

Regency Square and Bedford Square
These squares are found just past the West Pier and rooms overlook the sea (unless of course you get one at the back with a view of the gasworks).

For a wide range of Brighton hotels with independent reviews from satisfied and dissatisfied customers, try *www.activehotels.com*. For cheaper or mid-price B&Bs/hotels, here are a few others that don't smell of cat wee:

Aegean Hotel
5 New Steine (01273) 686547
Ainsley House
28 New Steine (01273) 605310
Alvia Hotel
36 Upper Rock Gardens (01273) 682939
Ambassador Hotel
22 New Steine (01273) 676869
Colson House Hotel
17 Upper Rock Gardens (01273) 694922
Funchal
17 Madeira Place (01273) 603975
Leona House
74 Middle Street (01273) 327309
Maison Mascara
33 Montpelier Road (01273) 385959
Quality Hotel
West Street (01273) 220033
Royal Pavilion Townhouse Hotel
12a Regency Square (01273) 722123
Square
4 New Steine (01273) 691777

Baggies Backpackers
33 Oriental Place (01273) 733740

Run by the very lovely Jem and Val, Baggies stands head and shoulders above the crowd, thanks to being run by people who genuinely care about their hostel and the people who come through their door. Everything here has been carefully thought out, from the free loo roll, laundry powder, tea and coffee to the two separate hangouts: a TV room with over 1,000 videos to choose from and a TV-free chillout/dance room with enough guitars, CDs, ashtrays and tealights to keep the most experienced backpacker happy. All rooms have built-in basins and are always clean and fresh. And while Jem and Val work hard to keep things shipshape, before you ask, no, it doesn't feel like having mum and dad around to cramp your style; quite the opposite. *"We want to make the party work too!"* is their motto, and that's precisely what they do best, making sure everyone is happy, safe, supported and, above all else, having fun. Recommended. *Dorm rooms £12-13 all year round.*

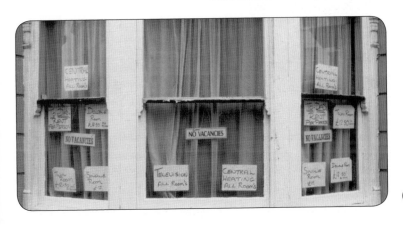

Grapevine/North Laine
Grapevine
75-76 Middle Street (01273) 777717
www.brightonbackpackers.com

What used to be Brighton Backpackers on Middle Street had, according to its manager, become *"a right shithole"* and he wasn't wrong. The good news is that it was all change here at time of going to print, with The Grapevine in North Laine becoming the hostel and the hostel in Middle Street becoming a new budget hotel with more rooms round the corner on the seafront. If you've visited before this might all seem a little confusing but probably worth the headache if it means a fresh start and a lick of paint.
Hostel £13-15 per night
Grapevine budget hotel Middle Street £20-40 per night

St Christopher's
10-12 Grand Junction, opposite Brighton Pier (01273) 202035
www.st-christophers.co.uk

Arguably the best value for money off-season (£10 a night!) St Christopher's is clean, well run, offers some great sea views, some nice high ceilings (no banging your head getting into bed), very charming staff and a full continental breakfast. The lack of any form of communal space (except the soulless TV-filled bar downstairs) is, however, the place's major downfall. If you're seeking a party atmosphere you'll be far better off elsewhere but if it's a roof, a comfy bed and a filling breakfast you're after, this just might be the best value in town.

Top tip: Steer clear of their Junction Nightclub unless you're in a stag or hen party and don't know any better.
Dorm £10-25, hotel room £20-45

Walkabout Hostel
78-81 West Street (01273) 770232
www.walkabout.eu.com

With Brighton Backpackers (Grapevine) promising a major refurbishment in April 2006, the path has been left clear for Walkabout to take on the mantle of *"a right shithole"*. Lowlights include the squalor, the location (sandwiched between two of Brighton's most vile nightclubs on West Street), the ridiculous levels of noise at weekends, the bar and the communal TV room that feels more like a Care in the Community waiting room. Highlights include er… erm… er…
£14 per night, £70 per week

CAMPING

Sheep Cote Valley
Behind the Marina off Wilson Avenue (01273) 626546

Non-member peak charges — caravan from £20ish-35 a night with electric hook-up, two people in a tent (with car parking) starts at £15ish per night.

MY BRIGHTON & HOVE

Name: DAVE 'GILDED PALACE OF SIN' MORRISON

The view east at the junction of Guildford Road and Buckingham Road Showing a layered view of the buzzing station taxi rank, all the way down Trafalgar Street and St Peter's Church beyond. Inexplicably yet consistently spine-tingling, especially at dusk on a wet night.

The Hanbury Ballroom Practically a second home, my favourite-ever venue in nineteen years of living here, even edging out The Lift and the old Concorde. Run and staffed by people who just live and breathe music, it's always a genuine pleasure to be there as a promoter or a punter. Could do with a new PA, mind.

The pet cemetery in the garden next to Preston Manor A truly peaceful and by-and-large unknown spot in a scruffy, drab garden, but a place of magic for me. Long-forgotten carved stone tributes to beloved animal companions lean against the mossy walls, promoting a longing to discover their tails… er… tales.

MY BRIGHTON & HOVE

Name: CAROLE 'RADIO 4'S LADIES OF LETTERS' HAYMAN

The sunsets The winter ones, when it's bitingly clear and cold, are splendid with livid reds, pinks and purples.

The seagulls Well my own two pet ones, anyway. They're very loyal – it can't be just the takeaways I chuck 'em, as my partner insists – and nest every year on the roof below to bring up their chicks. I've been granny to at least twenty fluffy bundles since I moved here.

Hot yoga A Brighton craze and I've caught it. Didn't know I had that much sweat in my body – flows like melted lard – well, no, best butter. Joints feel youthfully supple afterwards and skin glows.

Outside Brighton

Beachy Head

Notorious suicide spot as featured in the closing scenes of *Quadrophenia* and several *Monty Python* sketches. It can get pretty windy up there so be careful near the edge but keep your eyes peeled for the red-and-white striped lighthouse and the spooky old burned-out car halfway down the cliffs, I think it's still there. It takes about 45 minutes to reach Beachy Head from Brighton and, while there's not much else around, it's worth the visit for the spectacular views and having your head blown off. There's also a pub nearby if you get thirsty, though the plethora of Samaritans adverts **might** have a sobering effect on your spirits.

(Leave Brighton and continue heading east along the coast to Eastbourne)

Devil's Dyke

So the story goes that the devil started to dig a deep chasm to let the sea in to drown all the pious villagers of the Weald but an old lady – on hearing the sound of the devil's mechanical digger – lit a candle in her window, held it in front of a colander and tricked him into believing it was sunrise. The devil scarpered but his unfinished business – a 300ft valley in the heart of the Downs – remains. Now I know there are several flaws in this local myth (like what kind of idiot mistakes a colander and candle for the sunrise, and why didn't the devil just come back the following night anyway?), but we'll let it pass as it's a good yarn.

A visit to the Dyke is heartily recommended; this striking geographical feature offers plenty of opportunity for long walks, terrific views across the Downs and a shortcut down the steep hill to the Shepherd and Dog in Fulkin for steak-and-ale pie, chips, a few pints and a heart attack as you attempt the journey back. The Dyke is a rather lovely fifteen-minute drive out of Brighton and in summer you can even catch an open-top bus there from the city centre. Expect crowds at the weekend and doggers in the carpark at night.

(Take Dyke Road out of Brighton, cross the motorway and follow signs)

Ditchling

A quintessential English village with a few famous inhabitants, good pubs and a cake shop with the best treacle tart in the world. Past the strange little museum and village pond as the road bends to the left there's a very agreeable walk offering excellent views of the Downs. Go up the hill, take a picnic, enjoy the view and expect to share your field with a few friendly cows.

(Take Dyke Road out of Brighton, join the motorway going east, take the left turning for the Beacon and follow signs)

Eastbourne

To many Brightonians, Eastbourne is the world's largest open-plan hospice, proffering more hearing-aid shops than cafes, a neat line in poodle parlours and hosting a population of the walking dead. And while this isn't too far from the truth (OK – it is the truth), this sedentary coastal town still has enough tricks up its sleeve to merit a visit, even if you *are* under 60. For as well as the very pretty area known as the Old Town (for obvious reasons), Eastbourne has a surprisingly attractive seafront. Lacking the naff commercialism of Brighton's seafront, Eastbourne's is – rather refreshingly – adorned with lush greenery. In summer the promenade teems with palm trees, flower beds, bushes and trees, brass bands are in full swing and old couples in cardies and blazers stroll along arm in arm. Add to this the facts that the beach is infinitely cleaner than Brighton's, the pebbles are smaller and the pier and seafront aren't rammed with drunk Londoners and hen parties, and the prospect of spending a lazy day here sloping around, lounging on the beach and swimming can be very appealing.

Of course let's not get too carried away, Eastbourne's town centre could rival that of Doncaster's for blandness, but when the grime and chaos of Brighton get too much for you, a day out here *can* feel like a nice long soak in the bath. Just don't stay too long – you might end up all wrinkly.

(Take the eastern coastal road out of Brighton, or the A27 for a quicker inland route, and you'll be there in 45 minutes)

Stanmer Park

Head out of Brighton towards Sussex University and you'll find this large park. There's ample room here for big footie games, frisbee throwing and a chance to take some long rambles in the woods. There's also an organic farm, a small church and a great teashop, (though it's unfortunately located next to a stableful of cows, so if you sit outside be ready for some fruity odours and flies dive-bombing your baked potato). This is the closest place to Brighton where you can forget the crowds, especially if you take the walk past the village and continue up the hill. Look out for the tree trunk carved into animals behind Stanmer House and extra Brownie points if you get to see the Earth Ship, a startling demonstration of how much cash **you** could stop giving Seeboard and Southern Water if you built your house like this.

(10 minutes' drive from Brighton, on the A27 towards Lewes)

Lewes

Generally speaking, this is a cosy little town, ideal for taking one's parents for an afternoon stroll round the castle and a nose through some old bookshops. It is most notorious, however, for being host to the largest fireworks event in the UK (see diary of events). Below the surface, the town has more than its share of occultists, witches and eccentrics, but whether you get any feel of this from an afternoon visit is another matter.

The best pub here, without a doubt, is the Lewes Arms, a wonderful little place tucked away down one of the many side streets. Host to a number of bizarre games, including 'Toads' and an annual Pea Throwing Competition (the rules of which are very amusing), it's probably your best port of call for a real taste of Lewes and a chance to meet some of the town's fruitier characters.

(15 minutes' drive from Brighton, east along the A27)

Welcome fool, you have come of your own free will..........to

PEARL BATES' GUIDE TO LEWES

Church Twitten
Flanked by fabulous, buckling flint walls, which are inset with mysterious, Hobbit-sized wooden doors.

May's General Store
Cliffe High Street

A true Aladdin's Cave stocking everything from organic almond croissants to vintage clothing and alternative remedies.

The Long Room
Cliffe High Street

The hub of elegant evening activity, while during the daytime you can lounge about in the stylish brown leather armchairs and gobble expensive olives.

Catlin's Tobacconists
High Street

Help yourself to Turkish Delight, fill a paper bag with old fashioned humbugs, buy twenty B&H for the missus and share a bit of gossip with Mr Caitlin, in this delightful shop that's been in existence since 1915.

The Grange Gardens
Southover Road

Here you will find gorgeous, well-manicured rose gardens, as well as beautiful and expansive lawns.

The Old Needlemakers
Market Street

An arts-and-crafts mall in an old brick factory. whose basement holds The Box Room – a treasure chest packed with curios from times past.

Bill's Café
Cliffe High Street

Birthplace of the legendary café/deli.

The Flea Market
Market Street

Located in an old church, and stuffed with all manner of charming oddities.

The Garden Room
Station Street

Pick your way through the crowd of ceramic hares and other trinkets that festoon the place, and plonk yourself at one of the slightly uncomfortable tables for a characterful cuppa.

Useful Info

TOURIST INFORMATION

10 Bartholomew Square

09067 112255 (but watch out: at 50p per minute, it seems a bit of a rip-off!)
Open Mon-Fri 9am-5pm, Sat 10am-5pm,
Sun 10am-4pm

By a strange twist of fate most of the staff here are ex-circus performers. Ask them about their days in the big top and they'll be happy to share a few stories. If it's information you're after they can also sort out on-the-day bookings for B&Bs and hotels, as well as for National Express coaches and day trips. You'll also find all the customary gubbins about local tours, museums and places to visit.

TOILETS

The public versions, though thin on the ground (owing to the majority having been turned into cafes and florists), are surprisingly clean and

some 'family-friendly' ones now feature the occasional nursing chair and stool, ideal for putting your feet up after a bracing stroll down the seafront. I can personally recommend the toilet in Pavilion Gardens; last time I was in there three gentlemen were simultaneously shaving; I await reports on whether this also occurs in the Ladies. Brighton toilet attendants are notoriously, well, attentive, and will personally sanitise you for a small charge.

You'll find a small selection of public loos down on the seafront, whilst if you're caught short on the High Street or close to the Palace Pier I suggest you shit in the following…

Burger King

63-65 North Street
The Terraces, Madeira Drive

McDonald's

Churchill Square
157-162 Western Road

DRUGS

Add Action
(01273) 321000

Because drug use is widespread in Brighton, the clubs are very strict with their policies. You will see countless clubs whose advertising features PVC-clad models smoking huge reefers for a club night called *Dope-tastic!* or something. The reality is that all they really want to do is sell you expensive gassy lager. One whiff of grass and you'll be chucked out. If you want to purchase legal highs check out the Guarana Bar. If you want to purchase illegal highs ask around for the bloke who plays table-tennis.

HOSPITALS

Brighton General
Elm Grove, Brighton (01273) 696011

Royal Sussex County
Eastern Road, Brighton (01273) 696955

Nuffield (Hove)
55 New Church Road, Hove
(01273) 779471

Police warning: if you see this man…run

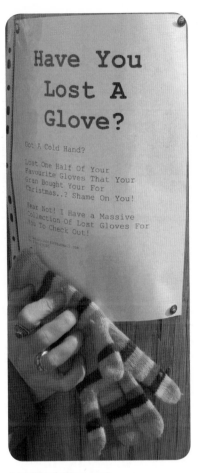

Nuffield (Sussex)
Warren Road, Woodingdean (01273) 624488

Southlands
Upper Shoreham Road, Shoreham
(01273) 455622

OTHERS

Police
For Brighton, Hove and more or less everywhere in East Sussex.
0845 6070999

Samaritans
(01273) 772277

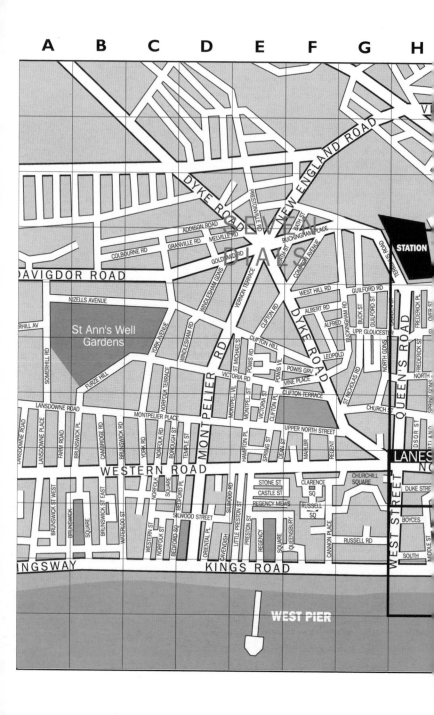

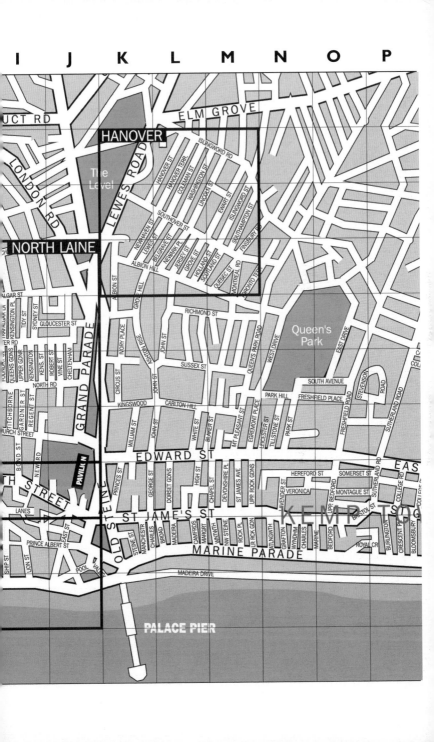